07807

The Nonconformist Conscience

By the same author:
Patterns in History (Leicester: Inter Varsity Press, 1979)

The Nonconformist Conscience

Chapel and politics, 1870–1914

D. W. BEBBINGTON
Lecturer in History, University of Stirling

London
GEORGE ALLEN & UNWIN
Boston   Sydney

George Allen & Unwin (Publishers) Ltd,
40 Museum Street, London WC1A 1LU, UK

George Allen & Unwin (Publishers) Ltd,
Park Lane, Hemel Hempstead, Herts HP2 4TE, UK

Allen & Unwin Inc.,
9 Winchester Terrace, Winchester, Mass 01890, USA

George Allen & Unwin Australia Pty Ltd,
8 Napier Street, North Sydney, NSW 2060, Australia

First published in 1982

British Library Cataloguing in Publication Data

Bebbington, D. W.
    The Nonconformist conscience.
1. Dissenters, religious—Great Britain—History
2. Religion and politics
3. Great Britain—Politics and government—1837–1901
4. Great Britain—Politics and government—1901–1936
I. Title
322'.1'0941   BX5203.2
ISBN 0–04–942173–5

Library of Congress Cataloging in Publication Data

Bebbington, David.
    The nonconformist conscience.
Includes index.
1. Great Britain—Politics and government—1837–1901.
2. Great Britain—Politics and government—1901–1936.
3. Great Britain—Church history—19th century.
4. Great Britain—Church history—20th century.
5. Dissenters, Religious—Great Britain—History—19th century.
6. Dissenters, Religious—Great Britain—History—20th century.
7. Christianity and politics—History—19th century.
8. Christianity and politics—History—20th century.
I. Title.
DA560.B37 1982   320.941   81–12910
ISBN 0–04–942173–5   AACR2

Set in 10 on 11 point Times by Photobooks (Bristol) Ltd,
and printed and bound in Great Britain by
William Clowes (Beccles) Limited, Beccles and London

Contents

Preface

Nonconformists, the chapel-goers of England and Wales, have regularly played some part in political life. Since the origins of religious Dissent in the late sixteenth century, there have been two periods when their corporate political influence has been particularly high. One, in the middle years of the seventeenth century when Cromwell rose to power, was comparatively brief, but the other, in the late Victorian and Edwardian years, was longer. This book offers an analysis of their political attitudes and activities during the second period. It was a time, in the wake of the Reform Act of 1867, when the British parliamentary system had become sufficiently open to encourage pressure by organised groups of electors like chapel-goers. Yet it was before the Franchise Act of 1918 that widened the electorate to include the rank and file of unskilled workers who remained largely untouched by organised religion. Between these two constitutional milestones, Nonconformists were particularly well placed to make their mark in politics. Party leaders listened carefully to their views and Nonconformists themselves were eager to exert the maximum leverage on the fulcrum of power. Growing numbers, they confidently believed, entitled them to a share in deciding how the nation should be run. Politics was a significant concern of the chapels.

The interaction of religion and politics is a fascinating theme as the idealistic aspirations of the one are in constant tension with the practical constraints of the other. Nonconformists tried to stamp their own standards of behaviour on public life, but encountered a barrage of criticism for allowing their political views to be shaped by self-interest or the interest of party. That is how the phrase the 'Nonconformist conscience' came into common currency in 1890. The Liberal Party, supported by most Nonconformists, was in alliance with the Irish Nationalists when the Irish leader, Parnell, was revealed to be an adulterer. Nonconformists insisted that Parnell must resign his position, and set in train a course of events that brought about his political eclipse. The 'Nonconformist conscience' had spoken out, critics asserted, only because it was realised that the Liberals would lose votes at the next election if Parnell did not go. The phrase was used to suggest that Nonconformist moralising on political themes was no more than hypocrisy. Leaders of the chapels, however, soon became proud of the phrase. It turned into a symbol of their belief that Christians had a responsibility to make known their views on national issues. Friend and foe were united in seeing the phrase as an apt characterisation of the distinctive Nonconformist style that aimed for political goals with all the fervour of religious conviction. Nonconformists turned humdrum pressure-group politics into vociferous crusades. This book attempts to dissect the Nonconformist conscience and so to lay bare the dynamics of the campaigns generated by the chapels.

The subjects that roused agitations among Nonconformists are treated in turn. There were issues on which they took the initiative, like the quest for religious equality and the battles to secure public control of the nation's schools, and others on which they were stirred into action by conditions they disapproved of, whether social problems in Britain or cruelties abroad. The emphasis throughout is on the corporate activities of Nonconformists, and so the organisation that did most to mobilise the rank and file, the Free Church Council, is examined in depth. Because the focus is on the political issues that concerned Nonconformists *en masse*, the theological views of their leaders, and even their versions of the social gospel, do not loom large. Of central importance, however, are the Evangelical roots of the popular religious attitudes that had grown up in the chapels, and these are necessarily given considerable attention. Nonconformists had become deeply entrenched in the Liberal Party by the opening of the period, and so another of the recurring themes is their relation to the Liberal leadership. But a few were not Liberals. Opposition to the Liberal Home Rule policy was sufficiently strong to create a Nonconformist Unionist Association that repays scrutiny. By the end of the period there were also individuals who supported the infant Labour Party, and their existence had a significant impact on the corporate political stance of the chapels. Nonconformity and the origins of Labour, however, is a topic that I hope to develop elsewhere. Here the main subject is the attitudes of Nonconformists who were very much a section of the Liberal Party.

The sources for this study include manuscript material, biographies, daily newspapers and monthly journals, but it rests chiefly on the Nonconformist weekly press. The *Christian World* published ample news of all the Nonconformist denominations and gave sufficient space to political events to cater for those who did not take a daily newspaper. It covers the whole period, and the *British Weekly*, a rival published from 1886 onwards, usefully supplements it. A bibliography has not been included since references to these and other sources are collected at the end of the book.

It is a pleasure to acknowledge the help given by many people in the preparation of this book. Warm thanks go to the following, who read its draft at various stages, in whole or in part: Dr J. C. G. Binfield, Prof. R. H. Campbell, Dr P. F. Clarke, the Rev. Prof. R. F. G. Holmes, Dr M. C. W. Hunter, Dr I. G. C. Hutchison, Mrs D. H. Lacey, Dr K. J. McCracken, Dr K. O. Morgan, the late Rev. Dr E. A. Payne, the Rev. Prof. E. G. Rupp, Dr B. Stanley, Dr N. Summerton, Dr G. Sutherland and Prof. W. R. Ward. Their critical comments have been invaluable. In addition I should like to record that I am most grateful to those who gave help and guidance during work on the PhD dissertation covering the years 1886 to 1902 that lies behind this book. Their names are listed in the copy of the dissertation deposited in Cambridge University Library. I am also glad to thank all those at the University of Stirling who have expertly typed the text, especially Miss M. E. A. Hendry, Miss A. M. Henderson and Mrs E. Skinner. Most of all I want to thank my wife Eileen, to whom, with love, the book is dedicated.

D. W. BEBBINGTON

1 Nonconformists and their Politics

If we make politics a part of our religion, as I claim we should, then in the conduct of our national policy, moral principles must be supreme. (George White to the Baptist Union Assembly, April 1903)[1]

In the last years of the nineteenth century and the early years of the twentieth, Nonconformists were in confident mood. Their position in the life of the nation seemed to be improving steadily. Their form of religion, a warm and homely brand of Protestantism, was attracting a regular flow of converts. Outbursts of religious enthusiasm swelled their numbers, especially during the Welsh revival of 1904–5. 'Clearly', observed their chief newspaper, the *Christian World*, in 1906, 'if figures have any value at all, the future rests with the Free Churches.'[2] Famous preachers like C. H. Spurgeon and Joseph Parker could hold vast congregations, while missionaries sent by the chapels were bringing the Christian gospel and British civilisation to an ever-increasing number of the heathen. Many Nonconformists were rising socially. A whole race of successful industrialists, such as the millionaire hosiery manufacturer Samuel Morley, had been bred in the chapels. Nonconformists could also point out in their ranks men of culture and refinement like R. F. Horton, a Congregational minister who had been the first non-Anglican fellow of an Oxford college. They were outgrowing, they felt, Matthew Arnold's charge of Philistinism. In many localities chapel-going was as socially acceptable as church-going. In such areas Nonconformists could occupy the highest public office. Municipal service led on naturally to broader political activities. In this period Nonconformists prided themselves on the influence they exerted in public affairs. 'Nonconformity', declared Guinness Rogers, a leading Congregationalist, in 1884, '. . . has not been so powerful a force in the nation since the days of the Long Parliament.'[3] Corporate political pressure seemed legitimate and laudable, a way of encouraging Christian standards in all departments of life. It was part of a psychology of optimism that dominated the chapels in the late Victorian and Edwardian years.

The optimism was grounded in the growing strength of Nonconformity. Numbers had increased throughout the nineteenth century and by 1900 there were in England and Wales 1,763,000 members in the main Nonconformist denominations. This figure compares with one for the same year of 2,043,000 Easter Day communicants in the Church of England. The disparity had become a relatively small one in the late nineteenth century. Nonconformists at the time sometimes contended, with a measure of justice, that after due adjustments their figures were higher. The statistic for the Church of England (the only measure of support available) refers to communicants on the day of highest attendance in the year. It would include many whose religious attachment was little more than nominal. The Nonconformist figure, on the other hand, refers to members. To join a Nonconformist church was, at least in theory, a step implying commitment of a high order. Many attended chapel regularly without becoming members, and the Nonconformist community was certainly far larger than the membership at this date. It is true that the Church of England was growing more rapidly than Nonconformity. Nevertheless active Nonconformists must have outnumbered active Anglicans at the turn of the century. This was the comparison most frequently made at the time. Another, however, was more significant. Relative to population Nonconformist membership was in decline. Broadly speaking the proportion of Nonconformists in the population increased in the first half of the nineteenth century, levelled out in the third quarter and began to fall in the final quarter. This was a prelude to the absolute decline in Nonconformist membership that has been so striking a mark of the twentieth century. The peak, of over 2 million, was recorded in 1906. Thereafter the fall has been almost continuous, and even before 1914 it was provoking serious heart-searching. But up to 1906 people were seldom aware of the ominous decline relative to population. What they knew about was the absolute growth shown in the annual denominational returns. The Nonconformist conscience was generated at a time of apparent strength.[4]

Nonconformists were to be found all over England and Wales. The best guide to nineteenth-century ecclesiastical geography is the Religious Census of 1851, the only official investigation of national religious statistics ever made. It shows that Nonconformist attendances exceeded Anglican attendances in twenty out of the twenty-nine towns designated the chief manufacturing districts. Nonconformists, and especially the Wesleyans, had done well in the centres of industrialisation. But even in the county where they provided the lowest number of sittings relative to the Church of England – Herefordshire – their proportion was 28 per cent. Nowhere was Nonconformity negligible.[5] Nor was the pattern simply that Nonconformists were strong in the cities but weak in the countryside. Rather the pattern was one in which Nonconformity had filled the gaps left by the Church of England. It was characteristically to be found where the influence of squire and parson was weak during the demographic explosion of the early nineteenth century: in parishes where landownership was divided rather than concentrated in the hands of one man; in settlements on parish boundaries; in market towns, especially decaying ones; in new industrial villages; in large parishes; and in places where squires or parsons were absentee.[6] These factors were more commonly at work in the north and west, and so Nonconformity was stronger there than in the south and east. Where whole areas were affected by these factors Nonconformists could dominate the religious culture, as did Wesleyanism among the tin-miners of Cornwall and Primitive Methodism among the pit-men of Durham. The extreme case was Wales, where national resentment against the Church of England helped Nonconformity to become the religion of the people. The distribution pattern had not altered drastically by the turn of the century. The chief change was a consequence of the growth of the suburbs. The effect, especially at a time of agricultural depression, was to accentuate the flow of rural workers to the towns. Nevertheless in 1902 still less than half the Primitive Methodists (47 per cent) lived in towns with a population of more than 10,000. On this definition, 59 per cent of Wesleyans, 66 per cent of Congregationalists and 67 per cent of Baptists were urban.[7] Nonconformity was well positioned to play a part in municipal life and yet was sure to be conditioned by the rural background of so many of its members. It was a nationwide movement.

Yet it was divided denominationally. The Methodists sprang from the Evangelical Revival of the eighteenth century. Wesleyan Methodists, who formed the largest Nonconformist body, were the direct heirs of John Wesley, governed by the Conference of preachers that had met each year since his time. The Primitive Methodists had split off from the Wesleyans in the first decade of the nineteenth century because they wished to use revival techniques which the Wesleyan Conference judged extravagant but which they supposed to be the mark of the earliest, or 'primitive', Methodists. The Methodist New Connexion, the United Methodist Free Churches and the Bible Christians, who all prided themselves on giving more responsibility than did the Wesleyans to laymen and the localities, joined together in 1907 to form the United Methodist Church. In 1932 the Wesleyans, the Primitives and the United Methodists were to combine as the Methodist Church. Only the tiny Wesleyan Reform Union, based on Sheffield, was to remain independent. Each Methodist denomination had its own distinctive constitutional arrangements and (perhaps more important) family traditions. The Wesleyans, tightly controlled by Conference and closer to the Church of England, were particularly inclined to stand apart – and even to repudiate being Nonconformists. But all Methodists shared the heritage of John Wesley's passion for saving souls and Charles Wesley's hymns. Methodists, as an observer noted of the Wesleyans in 1902, were characteristically 'more filled with religious enthusiasm than are the

Congregationalists, more emotional than the Baptists, and [take] a more joyous view of life than either'.[8]

Most of the other denominations were older than Methodism. They had separated from the Church of England in the seventeenth century to form what was sometimes called by the nineteenth 'the Old Dissent'. The Congregationalists were the most numerous of these bodies. They were the left wing of the orthodox Puritans, still sometimes called Independents in the late nineteenth century, those who believed that each congregation possessed the right and duty to order its own affairs. The Baptists were very similar, holding identical views on church government, but differed in arguing that only conscious Christian believers, and not infants, should be baptised. Both denominations had been swept along by the Evangelical Revival and their message was substantially the same as that of the Methodists. By the late nineteenth century there was some tendency for Congregationalism to move further towards 'Christian humanitarianism', while the Baptists were more insistent on doctrinal definition. Other Evangelical bodies were the Calvinistic Methodists, the largest Nonconformist body in Wales, who, despite their title, were organised on Presbyterian lines; and the Presbyterian Church of England, which catered primarily for Scottish migrants and had its strength in the north-east of England. Not all Nonconformists, however, were Evangelical. A section of the Old Dissent, the Unitarians, had resisted the tide stemming from the eighteenth-century revival. Descended from seventeenth-century Presbyterians, they had embraced the most advanced ideas, first of the Enlightenment and then of romanticism, and so, aloof from popular religion, they had shrunk numerically during the nineteenth century. The Quakers retained features of their pre-Evangelical mystical faith, but had assimilated much of the Evangelical ethos. Always distinct and tightly knit, they were on the fringe of Nonconformity. Unitarians and Quakers apart, Nonconformist fragmentation was transcended by a powerful bond of unity. Despite all their differences, the leading denominations were overwhelmingly Evangelical in theology and tone.

Social divisions had some correspondence to denominational divisions. The Unitarians and Quakers, largely because of their distance from popular religion, normally possessed a higher proportion of professionals and employers than other denominations. At Quaker weddings in Inner London between 1885 and 1913, for instance, more husbands were employers or managers than were manual workers of any kind.[9] Congregationalism drew on all sections of the middle classes from manufacturers to clerks, but seldom attracted working people. Conversely, Primitive Methodism consisted primarily of the working classes, with a sprinkling of clerks and shopkeepers, farmers and schoolteachers. The other Evangelical Nonconformist denominations were ranged in between. Baptists often reached lower social groups than the Congregationalists: in London north of the Thames, for example, nearly all the Baptist churches seemed in 1902 to be preponderantly working-class.[10] The Wesleyans included a number of wealthy businessmen, but were also strong among shopkeepers and could appeal effectively in the countryside to agricultural labourers. Denominations, however, were not socially monolithic. The opinion-forming Baptist chapels were hardly distinguishable from their Congregational counterparts.[11] The most important social division was between individual congregations rather than between denominations. Nonconformists, far more than Anglicans with their residual parish loyalties, tended to sort themselves by class. This process was accentuated by the growth of towns: the urban Nonconformist had a wider choice of places of worship than his country cousin. Hence within the same denomination, if not within the same chapel, there would be people of a very different social type. Nonconformity was not simply a front organisation for the middle classes.

Yet Nonconformist membership was not drawn from all social groups. There was hardly a footing in the upper classes. In 1869 there were three Unitarian peers, and after 1906, when the Congregational cigarette manufacturer W. H. Wills was ennobled, there was a steady trickle of Nonconformist elevations to the peerage.[12] The Earl of Tankerville who succeeded to the title in 1899 had become a Baptist by conviction four years earlier.[13] But this representation in the House of Lords was trifling (a fact with significant political implications). Dissenting gentry were nearly as rare, although successful Nonconformist manufacturers and even lawyers were beginning to acquire country seats. The vacuum at the other end of the social range was more disturbing. The poor were absent from the chapels. In the poorest neighbourhoods church attendance was lowest. In Bethnal Green at the turn of the twentieth century, for instance, only 6.8 per cent of the adult population attended chapel (and only 13.3 per cent went to any place of worship).[14] The lower working classes were hardly touched. To attend a place of worship, let alone to join it formally, implied a form of respectability which many unskilled workers shunned. Perhaps even more important, it entailed a commitment to financial contributions that many of the poor, especially those without an assured income, could not afford.[15] Consequently working-class Nonconformists tended to be drawn from the élite of skilled workers and their families. Such people, together with the lower middle classes of shopkeepers and clerks, formed the backbone of Nonconformity. The chapels were most attractive to those on the borderline between the classes. If their vision was sometimes restricted, their conviction normally went deep.

Chapel was commonly the only focus of social life for these people beyond home and work. Friendship, recreation, rites of passage, social insurance – all and more could be found in the life of the local Nonconformist community. Sunday services formed only a tiny part of the chapel round. On Sunday there was also Sunday School twice a day, perhaps with a prayer meeting and an after-meeting as well. During the week there might be (as there were at a Nottingham Baptist chapel in 1893) a fellowship class on Monday, a choir practice on Tuesday, a Young Men's Christian Band on Wednesday (with a fortnightly women's sewing circle), and a prayer meeting on Thursday. Christian Endeavour (devotional meetings for young people) and a Band of Hope (temperance meetings for children) were added shortly afterwards. By 1914 the Friday evening slot had been filled by a Men's Sick and Benefit Club where there were draughts and billiards, and at which men contributed 1s a month to cushioning their families from distress if they should fall ill. There was also an annual cycle of events: a summer Sunday School treat, harvest festival, Christmas entertainments, a Sunday School Union procession at Easter and, the chief event of the year, the Sunday School anniversary – a day of visiting preachers, money-raising, new clothes and excitement. Marriages, funerals, bazaars, evangelistic missions and special musical events would punctuate the year and often entail elaborate preparations. Cricket, football, bowls, tennis, hockey, rambling and cycling were all sponsored.[16] Men could find in all this a satisfying alternative range of activities to those promoted by the public house or working men's club, often the only other social centres available. Women seeking entertainment frequently had no option but chapel life. Hence Nonconformity could influence a far wider constituency than its membership. But among the core, those who planned and organised the events, a strong sense of solidarity arose. The chapel community gave meaning to their lives. Chapel values could not fail to shape their politics.

Ministers were in an ambiguous position in the chapels, at once leaders and paid agents. They were expected to invigorate the life of their congregations by stirring sermons and by participation in their activities. They could earn extra respect by prominence in local voluntary organisations such as charities and hospitals. And they commanded increasing esteem by their educational standards. Between 1870 and 1901 the proportion of Baptist ministers without formal education fell from a half to 18 per cent. By 1901 8 per cent of the Baptist ministry and 16 per cent of the Congregational ministry had been connected with a university.[17] Yet Nonconformist ministers relied on their congregations for employment, lacking the security that the incumbent clergy of the Church of England derived from the freehold ownership of their livings. Methodist ministers were shielded by the central authority of Conference, although an upset in one ministry might harm future prospects. Congregational and Baptist ministers were most exposed, not least because unemployment was a real threat: in 1901 8 per cent of Congregational ministers were without churches.[18] Consequently there were restrictions on pulpit freedom. Deacons, the lay office-bearers, might rebuke a minister. Or the congregation might melt away and so diminish chapel income that the minister could no longer be paid. Alleged doctrinal vagaries could be the reason for such events. But so could political preaching. A deputation from a London congregation at the turn of the century told their pastor, 'We share your views, but politics are not what we come to hear from the pulpit . . .'[19] When some ministers began to incline to socialism, they had to tread even more carefully. Only the very advanced introduced politics into their sermons. There were also limits on what ministers could say outside the pulpit. Normally, no doubt, they needed no constraint to reflect the views of their constituency. But congregational influence helped ensure that when ministers took the lead in social and political affairs they did act as faithful spokesmen of the chapels.

The opinion formers were not so much the ministry in general, as an élite, both ministerial and lay. These respected figures were strategically concentrated in well-to-do congregations in city centres or superior suburbs. By the end of the century most occupied Gothic structures. One such building was Bowdon Downs Congregational Church, on the southern extremities of Manchester. Set amidst secluded villas, it was cruciform, with stained glass, a tastefully played organ and a communion table of cedar from Lebanon and olive from the Mount of Olives. Its minister from 1876 to 1904 was Alexander Mackennal, intellectual and urbane, who read his sermons and took his holidays in Italy. Among the congregation were William Armitage, a prosperous cotton-spinner and benefactor of Nonconformist causes; Arthur Haworth, who ran an immensely successful yarn agency, entered Parliament in 1906 and achieved junior office in 1912; and Frank Crossley, a gas-engine manufacturer who eventually left Bowdon, demolished some Ancoats slums and moved there to run a holiness mission for the workers.[20] These were men who could realise their visions as well as their ambitions. A Wesleyan equivalent was the handsome Gothic church at Chislehurst, Kent, opened in 1870 to serve the growing number of successful Londoners who wished to live in the country but within reach of the city. Its first six ministers (Methodism moved them on every three years) included three who became president of Conference. Its members included T. P. Bunting, Sir Clarence Smith, and James and William Vanner, all household names in Methodism. In 1881 its two society stewards (the chief office-bearers) were Robert Perks, subsequently the leading Nonconformist Liberal in the Commons and eventually a baronet, and G. H. Chubb, of the lock and safe company, the promoter of the Nonconformist Unionist Association and eventually a peer.[21] Such men were widely accepted as the representative men of Nonconformity. They quite naturally played a prominent part in public life as well as in their denominations.

The politics of Nonconformity were overwhelmingly Liberal up to the

First World War and even beyond. Before the Home Rule issue arose, few individual Nonconformists were not Liberals. Even in the increasingly Conservative Lancashire, the chief Congregational church in central Manchester, Cavendish Street Chapel, had a solidly Liberal diaconate in 1880.[22] When, at the Congregational Union assembly of 1886, Joseph Parker declared that 'Toryism is wickedness', the main Nonconformist newspaper received several letters agreeing that a Conservative in a Congregational church was a contradiction in terms.[23] There was usually an obvious explanation for the allegiance of the rare Conservative Nonconformists. A Wellingborough Baptist brewer, for instance, transferred to the Conservatives during the 1880s on account of temperance pressure in Liberalism.[24] Only among Wesleyans, were Conservatives to be found in any numbers. They were commonly employers like G. H. Chubb and Joseph Mitchell, a Barnsley colliery-owner, or else senior ministers of Wesleyan officialdom such as W. L. Watkinson – or both, as in the case of Walford Green.[25] Yet all fourteen Wesleyan MPs between 1868 and 1886 were Liberals.[26] Partisanship among the Old Dissenters, though not among Methodists, permitted the chapels to be used for Liberal rallies. By the 1885 general election a bishop was complaining that Congregational churches had become a huge political organisation.[27] And in that year the Shropshire Baptist Association approved Gladstone's address and urged on the members of its congregations 'the obligation to conscientiously exercise their right of voting at the approaching Elections in support of measures of progress, freedom and peace'.[28] Liberalism appeared to be the natural vehicle for Nonconformist political opinion.

Why was Liberalism so attractive? First, it was because the Liberals had inherited the Whig advocacy of the principles of civil and religious liberty. Only from the Liberals could Nonconformists expect redress for their disabilities. Following the Reform Act of 1832 Dissenters had formulated a list of their major grievances. They wanted civil registration of births to replace the baptismal registers kept by the clergy; they objected to the fact that the only legal marriages were ones performed in parish churches according to the Book of Common Prayer; they wanted relief from the church rates that they had to pay for the upkeep of parish churches; they resented their exclusion from the ancient English universities; and they disliked the compulsion to use the service of the Church of England at burials in parish graveyards. The Whig government dealt with the first two grievances in 1836. The third, the most sharply felt, was redressed on Gladstone's initiative in 1868. The fourth was largely remedied by the Liberal government in 1871, the last on Gladstone's return to power in 1880. Members of the Old Dissent called repeatedly for these reforms. Methodists did not, as their authorities (especially among the Wesleyans) insisted that such worldly political issues were a diversion from the work of the gospel. Yet the Wesleyans shared a resentment against the social discrimination symbolised by their disabilities. They found church rates particularly objectionable. The strong feeling aroused against the penalties they suffered as non-members of the Church of England ensured that Wesleyan voters as early as the 1840s were overwhelmingly Liberal.[29] Nonconformists of all shades were drawn to Liberalism by their hope that it would abolish their practical grievances.

Some Nonconformists pressed further their case against the privileges of the Church of England. Edward Miall roused many of the Congregationalists and Baptists of the 1840s through his newspaper, *The Nonconformist*, to attack the root from which their grievances sprang. The state, he argued, should accord no special position to one church. Disestablishment became the cry. Miall elaborated a whole political theory, voluntaryism, on the basis that religion should always be supported by voluntary giving and not by state aid. The Liberation Society, one of the strongest of mid-nineteenth-century pressure groups, was set up to bring about disestablishment. In its early years it would pay no attention to lesser Dissenting objectives and single-mindedly opposed Whigs as much as Tories if they failed to endorse the voluntary principle. It actively dissuaded Nonconformists from supporting the Whig Party. After 1853, however, experience of practical politics led to a change of approach. It now drew all the grievances of Nonconformists to the attention of Parliament and tried to woo advanced Liberal candidates to its views. Its local committees and lecturers probably helped the return of a number of Liberals at the 1857 election and its Welsh campaign in the 1860s certainly contributed largely to the sweeping Liberal gains of 1868 in Wales. The distant goal of disestablishment might be achieved if the Liberals could be persuaded. Irish disestablishment in 1869 seemed to vindicate this strategy, even if party leaders offered little encouragement to expect further instalments. Liberationism increasingly had the same effect as the Dissenting disabilities: it tied Nonconformists to the Liberal Party.

Another reason for the allegiance of Nonconformists to the party was their concurrence in its principles of general policy, or at least the principles of its more advanced wing. Their resentment of ecclesiastical privilege was of a piece with radical criticisms of the 'feudal' establishment. Their conviction that churches should be free from state interference chimed in with the views of free-traders. Nonconformists were common in organisations like the Anti-Corn Law League that anticipated the policies of late nineteenth-century Liberalism. Peace, retrenchment and reform were the essentials of the party programme. At the 1880 general election the best-known Nonconformist preacher of the day, C. H. Spurgeon, issued an address to the electors of Southwark urging support for the Liberal candidates. His four main points were expressed as questions: 'Are we to go on slaughtering and invading in order to obtain a scientific frontier and feeble neighbours? . . . Shall all great

questions of reform and progress be utterly neglected for years? . . .
Shall the struggle for religious equality be protracted and embittered?
. . . Shall our National Debt be increased?'[30] Spurgeon added the distinctive Nonconformist aim of religious equality, but otherwise his points
were peace, reform and retrenchment. Nonconformist agreement with
Liberalism extended to the underlying social philosophy. It was generally
believed that the laws of political economy were the foundation of
social harmony. Hard work would lead to prosperity and that would
benefit the community. Charles Williams, Baptist minister at Accrington,
castigated both sides in industrial disputes for failing to perceive that
their interests coincided.[31] Again the Norwich mustard manufacturer,
J. J. Colman, by 1874 a Congregationalist, declared that 'all differences
of opinion between Employer and Employed might, if they both had a
determination to do what was right, be amicably settled'.[32] Trade union
leaders like the Methodist MP Henry Broadhurst had an identical belief
in a moral imperative to class collaboration. Nonconformists endorsed
the values of which the Liberal Party was the political expression.

Their loyalty to the party was confirmed by their faith in its leader.
There was among Nonconformists what a correspondent of *The Times*
called in 1890 a 'fascination, amounting to fetishism, of the great name
and personality of Mr Gladstone'.[33] This was rather odd, because
Gladstone was himself a rather stiff Churchman who held that Nonconformists were schismatics. Yet as early as 1853, long before he became
the advocate of policies they approved, he had earned the respect of
Dissenters for his conscientiousness. From the 1860s, when he took up,
in turn, parliamentary reform, the abolition of compulsory church rates
and Irish disestablishment, respect ripened into veneration. He established personal contact with the leaders of moderate Dissent outside the
Liberation Society and by 1877 he was prepared to speak at a conference
on 'Pew and Pulpit' organised by the Congregationalist Joseph Parker
at the City Temple. There was wariness, especially but not exclusively
among the more traditional of Nonconformists, that Gladstone har-
boured Roman Catholic sympathies. His Irish University Bill of 1873,
for instance, appeared to have been drafted with Jesuit-like ingenuity to
ensure Catholic dominance within a few years. Suspicions of crypto-
popery, however, largely disappeared when in 1874 Gladstone issued his
best-selling pamphlet *The Vatican Decrees* denouncing the temporal
power of the pope. The way was open for the unreserved admiration that
reached a new pitch when in the later 1870s Gladstone became the
standing critic of Disraeli's jingoistic foreign policy.[34] The politics of
G. W. McCree, a London Baptist minister, according to his son, were
summed up in the three words, 'William Ewart Gladstone'.[35] The
devotion of Nonconformists to the leader was a further factor ensuring
that they formed what Gladstone himself called 'the backbone of British
Liberalism'.[36]

Nevertheless, between 1870 and 1874, there was a 'Nonconformist revolt' against the Liberal leadership. The cause was disagreement over education policy, a subject which will be discussed in Chapter 7. Nonconformists believed that the principles of religious equality were being flouted by a government they had done much to elect and became its vociferous critics. At the 1874 general election the apathy of Nonconformity contributed to the Liberal defeat. But in the wake of the revolt Nonconformists became more firmly integrated in the party than before. After 1874 there was no more constant theme in the output of Guinness Rogers, the chief Nonconformist political commentator, than that the chapels were loyal to Liberalism. The Conservative victory at the general election had shown the futility of weakening the Liberal Party. Nonconformists generally agreed with Rogers that, if they were to secure further benefits from the party, they must put more effort into it. During the 1870s they moved nearer its centre. Nonconformist notables were having an increasing say in constituency politics. They were being elected to the school boards set up under the 1870 Education Act, and they were obvious potential Liberal candidates for town councils and Parliament. Men such as William Woodall, first chairman of the Burslem School Board from 1871 to 1880 and Liberal MP for Stoke from 1880, came to the fore through their work in administering elementary education.[37] At a national level the largely Nonconformist pressure group, the National Education League, was transformed by Joseph Chamberlain, himself a Unitarian, into the National Liberal Federation. The constituency group in touch with this 'caucus' was commonly led, as at Leeds, Sheffield and Nottingham, by Nonconformists. They were gaining the ascendancy, at least in the Liberals' traditional urban strongholds. Nonconformity was more closely bound up with Liberalism than ever before.

It was at this stage of Nonconformist relations with the Liberal Party that the Nonconformist conscience emerged. The phenomenon had appeared before the tag was applied to it in 1890, but it had not existed long. It is tempting to apply the phrase to Nonconformist public attitudes of the mid-nineteenth century because they had been marked by a moral and perhaps moralising tone, but that would be anachronistic. The distinctive features of the conscience gradually gathered momentum only during the 1870s and 1880s. Those features were three: a conviction that there is no strict boundary between religion and politics; an insistence that politicians should be men of the highest character; and a belief that the state should promote the moral welfare of its citizens. All were new in the late Victorian period. Previously Nonconformists had assumed a contrast between Christian work and worldly activity, with politics decidedly on the worldly side of the divide, legitimate but risky. They had, of course, hoped that politicians would be men of personal integrity, but had not supposed that this could be treated as a qualification for office. And they had argued that because the state was likely to harm its citizens by decreasing their self-reliance, it should confine itself to a narrow sphere of interference in their lives. All these attitudes were characteristic of people who felt politics to be an alien world. That was beginning to change. In 1868, 14 per cent of Liberal MPs were Nonconformists; in 1874, 19 per cent; in 1880 24 per cent.[38] They were outsiders less and less as time went on. Accordingly, Nonconformist leaders began to claim that politics were within their orbit. Political life must be brought to the bar of their moral judgement.

The first of the characteristic attitudes of the conscience period, that religion and politics should not be kept apart, was embodied in Silvester Horne. Simultaneously minister in pastoral charge and MP, Horne regarded the double yoke as the proper fulfilment of his principles. His Congregationalism he interpreted as a commitment to democratic rule, and so was overjoyed to be elected as a champion of the people against the peers at the election of January 1910. He was no priest, he argued, and so not separate from the world. His task was not to follow John the Baptist into the wilderness, but Christ into society. There was no distinction between the sacred and the secular. 'We believe politics may be as truly sacred a task as theology; and that how best to safeguard youth against cruelty, manhood against temptation, and human life against poverty and disease is as Christian a study as to expound the doctrine of election, the ecclesiastical use of incense, or the legitimacy of the chasuble.'[39] These were advanced views that would not be shared by many in the chapels. Political life, like novel reading, was still treated as a dangerous snare in some quarters. But Horne was not alone. Browning Hall, a Congregational settlement in south London, promoted candidates for the local council since it regarded 'everything as religious which is not irreligious'.[40] And John Clifford, by the 1890s the leading Baptist minister, was prepared to call for a more moral foreign policy at rallies held on Sundays.[41] The sabbath could be put to political use. Religion and politics should go hand in hand.

The second conviction of these years, that power should be entrusted only to men of sterling personal qualities, was grounded in the belief that politics is primarily a matter of taking moral decisions. Principle must be the politician's lodestar at all times, and he must have an unblemished character. This was the attitude underlying the outcry against Parnell. His private life had been unworthy and so he was not fit for public life. Two men were held up as examples to be followed. Gladstone had demonstrated that it was possible to sustain a high moral tone in the hurly-burly of the political world. His reputation outlived him. Clifford declared at the Baptist Union autumn assembly in 1900, two years after Gladstone's death, that the late Prime Minister was still for them the pattern statesman, and was received with 'an outburst of the most enthusiastic cheering'.[42] The second example was Cromwell. He had wielded power with a deep religious awareness. In the phrase of Lord Rosebery that Nonconformists repeatedly used in these years, Cromwell was a 'practical mystic'. And he had been one of them, a Congregationalist. A biography of Cromwell published in 1897 for the 'Young Free Churchmen of England' announced that he was the man of the hour for them to imitate. Cromwell's faults were forgotten or glossed over, and he was depicted as a successful Nonconformist politician.[43] A manly character, upright and decisive, was seen as the panacea for the problems of politics.

The third new feature of Nonconformist politics in these years, the more favourable estimate of state action for moral purposes, constituted the most drastic change of mind. Legislation, it was believed, could improve the character of the nation. Earlier in the nineteenth century Nonconformists had normally contended that coercion could induce only an appearance of moral behaviour, and so was worse than useless. The gospel alone could make people lead truly upright lives. A sermon preached in 1887 by Hugh Price Hughes, the Wesleyan leader of progressive Nonconformist thought, was intended to meet this objection that 'you cannot make men moral by Act of Parliament'. The law, according to Hughes, could certainly make them immoral, and he instanced the state of legislation on the liquor traffic. The statute book registered the moral progress of the nation, for it reflected public opinion. But that did not mean that there must be no legislation in advance of public opinion. On the contrary, it was imperative to guide opinion. Law, in Hughes's view, was educational as well as coercive, for people learned better ways from Parliament. In this way, prize fighting, for instance, had been successfully eliminated earlier in the century. There remained much scope for transforming the criminal law.[44] Hughes's attitude came to be widely shared by Nonconformists. Sympathy for *laissez-faire* was steadily superseded by a wish to legislate against particular social evils. Voluntary effort must continue, but the state should play a far greater role in society. This growing belief, representing as it did a break with traditional Liberal axioms, was to have important repercussions.

Why did the Nonconformist conscience displaying these traits appear? Contemporaries often pointed to the existence of social evils such as drunkenness and prostitution and found in them a sufficient explanation. People prompted by the compassion of Christ could not ignore the human need around them. Religion had to call on men of integrity and the state to take action. Such an explanation, however, is not adequate. The problems of society were seldom new. Mass gambling did, admittedly, first become a craze in the 1880s, at the time when the conscience was gathering strength.[45] But other targets of Nonconformist criticism were notoriously of long standing. Prostitution, if York is typical of the rest of the country, may well have passed its nineteenth-century peak in the early 1860s.[46] The growth of the conscience cannot be accounted for by the novelty or increasing gravity of social problems. What changed was not the problems so much as Nonconformist awareness of them. As H. M. Bompas, a Baptist lawyer who was an acute analyst of Nonconformist life, wrote in 1892 of the previous few years, 'a deeper sense of the misery and sin of portions of the population, especially in the great towns, has taken hold of the leaders of Nonconformist thought'.[47] The reasons for this 'deeper sense' need to be identified. Furthermore, the existence of the social evils does not explain why Nonconformists turned to the state for a remedy. For years they had been grappling with the problems by voluntary effort and their politics had remained unaffected. The pressure for legislation on issues such as urban overcrowding still calls for explanation. Human need in itself throws little light on why there developed a new phase in Nonconformist public life.

More recently the Nonconformist conscience has been interpreted as a consequence of the broadening of the intellectual horizons of the chapels or as a quest for increased political power to match rising social aspirations.[48] It is certainly true that Nonconformity was emerging from sectarian attitudes into the mainstream of national life during these years and was therefore deepening its interest in the world around. Yet it would be wrong to suggest that Nonconformity was lured into deserting its Evangelical tradition for the sake of new ideas or new social status in the years before the First World War. The politics of the chapels were primarily determined by the Evangelicalism that still gave them their reason for existence, their message, their energy. Conversions from sin were their aim. Since political activity could not achieve the salvation of the sinner, it had been dismissed as a waste of time for the ordinary Christian at the peak of the Evangelical Revival around the turn of the nineteenth century. Politics might be a special calling for a Wilberforce, but quietism was the normal stance of the whole Evangelical world between the 1790s and the 1820s. In the 1830s, however, there emerged in the anti-slavery movement the prototype of mass Evangelical political activity. On both sides of the Atlantic orators stirred the religious public to indignation at the existence of slavery. Their technique, as one of the most skilful English agitators explained, was to argue that slavery was 'criminal before God'.[49] Once slavery was identified as sinful, it could not be tolerated by Christians. It became their duty to press for its abolition. Anti-slavery sentiment put down deep roots among Evangelicals of Church and chapel alike. And the shrill style of agitation ushered in by the movement was to be an abiding feature of political life. Mass upsurges of Evangelicals took place on a wide range of other issues. Anti-Catholic movements convulsed national life, especially in 1845 and 1851, and were grafted on to Conservative politics. There were campaigns against the toleration of idolatry in British India and against desecration of the sabbath by railway companies at home. Much of the Dissenting participation in the Anti-Corn Law movement was of the same type. Church-based protest movements were as common in America, and have remained so. A German observer has noted that a characteristic feature of church life in Anglo-Saxon countries has been 'the organized struggle of the Church against some particular worldly evil, the "campaign", or, taking up again the crusading idea of the middle ages, the "crusade"'.[50] On both sides of the Atlantic there has been a tradition of popular Evangelical political pressure.

The Nonconformist conscience consisted of a series of crusades along these lines. In each field that concerned Nonconformists, their political activities in the late Victorian and Edwardian period approximated to the style of Evangelical agitations against particular wrongs. This was true of their campaigns for higher moral standards in society, but it also became increasingly true of their efforts in their own interests (as over education) and of their contribution to apparently secular issues (like Home Rule). Every question they took up was moralised. Conversely, causes lost their mass appeal when their connection with wrong ceased to be obvious: this was true, for example, of industrial conciliation. Political campaigns, like evangelism, had to be directed against sin. Nonconformist identification of wrongs to be fought sometimes appears capricious, but in reality it was not so. An Evangelical biblicism dictated their targets. They condemned only what fell into one of two categories: either disobedience to biblical ethics or what directly opposed the spread of the gospel. Under the first heading came immorality of any kind, but especially sexual immorality and drunkenness. These seemed self-evidently wicked. Under the second came obstacles to the gospel ranging from erroneous religious practices, especially the apparent idolatry of Rome, to conditions that inhibited church-going, such as urban over-crowding. 'We ought to be first in the field against all wrong', declared George White, a Norwich shoe manufacturer, in his presidential address to the Baptist Union in 1903, 'and especially against those social conditions which hinder the work of evangelisation amongst the masses.'[51] There was a consistency about the objects of Nonconformist denunciation. But there was far less consistency about the timing of their campaigns. A particular wrong would be condemned intensively for a few months, but interest would gradually subside and a fresh evil take its place. The target was usually dictated by events reported in the press. Thus an outburst of anti-gambling feeling would follow a well-publicised Derby win by Lord Rosebery or a protest would be mounted against atrocities in the Middle East when news of them filtered through from Turkey. Indignation depended on information. The conscience developed in response to wrongs defined by Evangelical criteria and revealed by public events.

The moral crusades that made up the Nonconformist conscience shared common features of policy. First, because they were designed to remove wrongs, their aims were negative. They offered condemnations of the existing state of affairs rather than proposals of anything new. The point was well made by Arthur Guttery, the leading campaign speaker in the Primitive Methodist ministry of the Edwardian years: 'It was not his business, he said, to propose schemes of redress or to suggest legislative measures. That was the duty of Statesmen and of Cabinets. It was his business to . . . denounce abuses and wrongs and shams and inequalities . . . '[52] Very often campaigns in this tradition, like the anti-slavery and anti-corn laws movements, had been explicit 'anti'. It was so in the years of the conscience: there were the anti-Contagious Diseases Acts and the anti-gambling movements. Protest was their purpose. A second feature of their characteristic policy was a call for action to be urgent, often immediate. The Wesleyan minister who first used the phrase 'the Nonconformist conscience' demanded Parnell's 'immediate retirement from Parliamentary life'.[53] The urgency was the consequence, not of political calculation, but of the moral imperative that dictated policy. If anything was wrong, it must be eliminated quickly. It also followed, thirdly, that compromise was impossible. How could there be compromise with wickedness? This intransigence is well known from the position of the largely Nonconformist-supported United Kingdom Alliance that nothing less than total abolition of the liquor traffic was acceptable. A principle was firmly maintained if it would lead to the abolition of a social evil. The same strict adherence to a formula marked each of the Nonconformist campaigns. Fourthly, speakers would commonly add a sanction to their policy demand. They did not shrink from announcing that persistence in wrongdoing would fall under divine judgement. A United Methodist Free Churches pastoral letter of 1897 urged members to work strenuously against drink. 'Unless we do', it added, 'we may yet perish in the doom that will one day overtake the unreformed British Empire.'[54] Such warnings made political decisions a matter of apocalyptic significance. The calls for action of the campaigns were thoroughly conditioned by the chapel mentality.

The campaigns also had a common method – the technique of agitation. Guttery, the Primitive Methodist, saw himself as an agitator whose business was 'to stir up the minds of the populace, to create a healthy discontent, . . . to make men feel that some things ought not to be tolerated, to incite the people to insist on justice and freedom and right'.[55] Certain Nonconformists, especially among the ministers, became skilled in this art. It was practised chiefly through 'indignation meetings'. They were summoned throughout the country, but the most publicised were those held in London – in St James's Hall for indoor rallies, and in Hyde Park for large-scale outdoor demonstrations. Size was important in drawing attention to the volume of support for the cause. Such rallies have often been favoured by pressure groups as a means of exhibiting strength. But these gatherings were of a peculiar genre. An education demonstration in 1896 was described by the Nonconformist press as displaying 'the highest order of eloquence – that which springs from passion at glowing heat and inspires answering passion'.[56] This kind of meeting was designed for enjoyment and excitement. Resolutions were carried, but people came for the speeches. Rallies were a suitably moral substitute for the theatre among those who, by and large, would still refuse to see any play. The meetings had the further functions of confirming the allegiance of the convinced and of persuading waverers, both amongst those who attended and those who learned of them from the newspapers. The speeches therefore insisted that the iniquity they denounced was so grim that there must be whole-hearted commitment to the cause. The platform of a protest rally was not the place for a carefully qualified argument. A militant tone predominated, and jibes at political opponents could often creep in. It is no wonder that the Nonconformist conscience seemed to a critic in 1903 'by nature and training belligerent'.[57]

Not all Nonconformist political activity in the period, however, was so assertive. The work of the Liberation Society was conducted from the 1870s onwards in a low key. Its criticisms of abuses in the Established Church were sober, matter-of-fact statements. Far from pressing forward its principle of disestablishment without regard to the circumstances, it was repeatedly prepared to defer the attainment of its objects at the request of Liberal leaders. It lacked bite. This is surprising, for the campaign to achieve religious equality by putting an end to the privileges of the Church of England had long been, as we have seen, the main political aim of Nonconformity. A disgruntled Nonconformist minister commented on this strange state of affairs in 1909:

> The point is this – that organized and corporate action in the political field, for the disestablishment of the Established Church, is the one form of political activity in which Nonconformity is entitled, if not bound, to engage. And the correlative statement, forced upon us by an all-round view of the current situation, is, curiously enough, that this one legitimate form of political activity is precisely the one for which modern Nonconformity, at any rate in recent years, has seemed to care the least.[58]

The disestablishment campaign forms a striking exception to the normal pattern of Nonconformist agitations. Why did the quest for religious equality lack the vigour of most Nonconformist political activity in this period?

2 The Quest for Religious Equality

This generation can scarcely understand the enthusiasm with which we, who were young ministers in the forties, looked upon the leaders of the Anti-State Church movement. (Alexander Maclaren, minister of Union Chapel, Manchester, 1884)[1]

At the start of the 1870s the chief political campaign sponsored by Nonconformity was the one embodied in the Liberation Society. It was designed to separate the Church of England from the state – thus 'liberating' religion from secular influence – and to end all discrimination on grounds of creed. It drew the mass of its supporters from Dissenters who were no longer prepared to tolerate being regarded by the mainstream of society as outsiders. To terminate the privileges of the Established Church seemed the best way of throwing off their own feeling of inferior status. Only when there was full religious equality would they be able to hold their heads high in all walks of life. Furthermore, they believed that in abolishing the artificial props to Anglicanism they were opening the way for free competition between the denominations in which their own brand of Christianity would inevitably triumph. A decision to join a religious body should be purely voluntary, the outcome of weighing up the claims of the various denominations and not a consequence of seeing the social and political attractions of attending the parish church. The Church of England and all other established churches must be stripped of their unfair advantages. Most articulate Congregationalists and Baptists held these views, which they summed up as 'the voluntary principle'. The movement had been gathering strength since the 1840s and now, at last, their convictions seemed to be gaining a hearing in the highest circles. In 1868 Gladstone had carried the abolition of compulsory church rates, so that they no longer had to pay the deeply resented imposts for the maintenance of the parish churches. In 1869, to their great delight, he disestablished the Anglican Church in Ireland. Even if the Liberal education measure of 1870 was unsatisfactory, the march of events appeared to be manifestly in the direction of full religious equality. Edward Miall, the chief spokesman for political Dissent and now MP for Bradford, proposed a Commons motion in favour of general disestablishment on 9 May 1871. Although it was defeated by 374 to 89 votes, it was the holding of the debate rather than its outcome that mattered. For the first time, the case against the Established Church had been directly presented in Parliament.[2] It seemed that the cause of the Liberation Society was advancing triumphantly and that disestablishment in England was only a matter of time.

Never again, however, did the society feel itself to be so near its goal. Debates on similar motions in 1872 and 1873 were much less successful.[3] The Conservative victory at the 1874 general election meant that raising debates would only demonstrate the parliamentary weakness of Liberationism. The society therefore concentrated on propagating its views through its network of agents and lecturers. Public attention, however, was diverted to the Eastern Question from 1876 onwards and the society found the task of arousing support increasingly difficult. By the early 1880s, with a Liberal government again in office, it was thought possible to renew a general agitation. A religious equality committee of five MPs was set up to watch measures in the Commons, plans were laid for a resolution in favour of English disestablishment and a series of supporting meetings up and down the country was organised for the autumn of 1883.[4] It all came to very little, as no time was found for the resolution and the campaign petered out. The regular work of the society dwindled. Between 1874 and 1879 it held an average of 856 meetings a year, but between 1879 and 1889 only about 300. As a special report noted gloomily in 1889, 'dissatisfaction is beginning to prevail at the limited character of the Society's operations'.[5] Subscribers were not renewing. The disestablishment campaign was running out of steam.

Leadership was concentrated in a few hands. After the retirement of Edward Miall from Parliament in 1874, Henry Richard, ex-Congregational minister and MP for the Merthyr Boroughs, acted as spokesman in the Commons for political Dissent. Richard was chairman from 1875 of the Protestant Dissenting Deputies, a body of lay representatives of London congregations dating from the early eighteenth century, which by Richard's time concentrated almost exclusively on giving legal advice to Dissenters about their rights. But the chairmanship gave him an opportunity for delivering an annual manifesto of Nonconformist demands for religious equality.[6] Richard was regularly consulted over parliamentary tactics by the Liberation Society, but he gave much more of his time and energy to the affairs of Wales and the Peace Society, of which he was the secretary. The public man most identified with the Liberation Society was therefore Alfred Illingworth, MP for Knaresborough from 1868 to 1874 and for Bradford from 1880 to 1895. Illingworth was a Bradford worsted-spinner, the archetype of a sturdy northern industrialist. He was a Baptist, a vice-president of the Peace

Society, an outspoken critic of the idle aristocracy and even of royalty. He was remembered for referring with Yorkshire bluntness to members of the royal family as 'only a set of outdoor paupers'.[7] His mill was to become notorious in 1894, when an industrial dispute arose over a management decision that spinners should mind four rather than three machines for the same pay.[8] In the same year he determined to resign his seat in disgust that the Liberals should be toying with legislation that would limit work to eight hours a day, a measure which, in his view, would be disastrous to British commercial interests.[9] Sidney Webb dismissed him as an old-fashioned individualist.[10] Joseph Chamberlain had been more appreciative of Illingworth twenty years earlier. 'Of all the men I know', Chamberlain wrote in a letter of 1873, 'he is the truest soundest Liberal. His principles are matters of belief & conviction & not the result of pressure.'[11] The disestablishment campaign was the core of his Liberalism. He was treasurer of the Liberation Society from 1872, and joined in framing a blueprint for the separation of Church and state in the mid-1870s.[12] He and his brother gave a lump sum of £5,000 to the society in 1874, and in 1892, in less buoyant times, he responded to an appeal to save the society from legal proceedings for debt with an immediate loan of £1,000.[13] He was its chairman from 1886 until into the twentieth century. Disestablishment, he declared in 1895, was 'the passion of his life'.[14] The weakness of the Liberation Society was due to no neglect on the part of Alfred Illingworth.

Behind the scenes there was an even more indefatigable Liberationist, John Carvell Williams. Brought up at the historic Stepney Meeting, Carvell Williams was an active church member at Claremont Congregational Church, Pentonville, became a deacon at Surbiton and later supported the building of a church at Stroud Green. His service to the churches, as much as his political work, was honoured by the chairmanship of the Congregational Union in 1900. He was elected to Parliament for South Nottingham in 1885, and again for Mansfield from 1892 to 1900. Carvell Williams had been a member of the Liberation Society since its inception in 1844. He brought to it invaluable expertise in the technicalities of the Established Church for he was trained in ecclesiastical law at Doctors' Commons. From 1865, when he became chairman of its parliamentary committee, he was both the strategist and the day-to-day organiser of the society's affairs.[15] His devotion to duty knew no bounds. He was not an affluent man, yet in the late 1890s, after a reduction of his notional salary from £600 to £400, he was still prepared to draw an average of only £213 a year to ease the society's financial problems.[16] The society owed most of its remaining energy in the 1870s to his direction. But by the 1880s Williams was in his 60s, very deaf and suffering from a harsh cough that was probably the result of sitting long hours amidst his legal tomes in a dusty office.[17] He remained capable of hard work, but not of the incisive thinking needed for an effective propaganda campaign. The structure of the society did not change after the 1860s. Carvell Williams's devotion was of the kind tenacious of tried methods and inimical to the training of successors. Some responsibility for the decay of the society must be laid at his door. But the problems were beyond the power of an individual to solve.

The reason most commonly cited by Carvell Williams himself for the failure of the disestablishment campaign to make more impact was unfavourable political circumstances. From 1877, he claimed, there 'occurred a series of events which necessarily contracted the Society's operations – the wars in Eastern Europe, in Afghanistan & South Africa'.[18] Public opinion had been distracted from ecclesiastical questions by the Conservative government's foreign policy. It seemed foolish for the society to attempt an agitation, for the mass of its supporters, by now as much Liberals as Liberationists, were absorbed in denouncing their opponents' war-mongering. The executive therefore actually discouraged Leeds Nonconformist zealots from holding a conference on disestablishment in 1878. At the 1880 election the society urged support for all Liberal candidates, whether or not they were pledged to disestablishment.[19] The removal from office of the Conservatives, however, did not end the flow of distracting events. The state of Ireland engrossed attention, then Egypt. And from 1886 Home Rule did the same. The society was compelled to recognise the fact that the election of that year was fought on Home Rule, not the Established Church.[20] 'With the Irish Question in a most acute form demanding all thought', ran the disestablishment entry in the *Liberal Year Book* for 1887, 'Liberationists have perforce acquiesced in the comparative neglect of their demand for the redress of grievances arising from our ecclesiastical organizations.'[21] There was no section at all on disestablishment in the *Liberal Year Book* for 1888. Even Illingworth was distracted to the Home Rule crusade, admitting to the society's annual meeting in 1888 that present political complications had hampered its operations.[22] Furthermore, the society forfeited some support altogether because of Home Rule. Since the society was closely allied with the Gladstonian Liberals, it was deserted by a number of Liberal Unionists including W. S. Caine, the Liberal Unionist whip, and H. S. Leonard, a regular attender of the committee and its legal adviser.[23] The secretary of the Manchester committee (the only functioning branch of the Liberation Society) reported in 1890 his difficulty in raising money 'consequent upon the division there in the ranks of the Liberal Party'.[24] The emergence of Liberal Unionism must be counted as one of the external factors that hampered the work of the society.

Yet political circumstances formed something of an excuse for a fundamental failure by the society to present its case effectively to the public. This is clear from the events surrounding the election of 1885. The election was fought as much on disestablishment as on any other issue.

The Conservatives seized on some unwary remarks by Chamberlain to the effect that the question of an Established Church would become practical politics in the next Parliament. Salisbury opened the Conservative campaign with a speech on the Church in danger and was echoed and re-echoed by clergy and Conservative candidates alike. There was also a spontaneous surge of anticlerical feeling among the newly enfranchised agricultural labourers.[25] All this came as a total surprise to the Liberation Society, which had done very little to bring the disestablishment issue to the fore. Unlike Chamberlain, it expressed no opinion that disestablishment was imminent. It specifically recommended its supporters to ask candidates their views on Scottish and Welsh disestablishment only. Aggressive electoral tactics were deliberately discouraged. The society's chief efforts were directed towards securing a first declaration in favour of disestablishment by the National Liberal Federation.[26] The explanation is that the society did not want to attract public attention at all. Its aim was to permeate the Liberal Party.

The strategy of working for its goals within Liberalism rather than as an external pressure group had first been recommended in 1877. Charles Miall, brother of Edward, had first urged the policy through *The Nonconformist* newspaper, whose direction he had taken over from his brother. It was adopted with some enthusiasm at the society's triennial conference because it seemed to chime in so well with other developments. The new prominence of Nonconformists in Liberal constituency associations would enable them to exercise a decisive voice in the choice of candidates. The creation of the National Liberal Federation gave them a mechanism through which they could hope to guide party policy. Liberationism could be made integral to Liberalism. A strong Liberal government of the future would be compelled by backbench opinion to separate Church and state. Meanwhile there were other advantages. The Liberation Society could not be accused of selfishly promoting its own interests at the risk of party unity. At the 1880 election its leaders pointed to their restraint by contrast with the divisive pressure exerted by temperance advocates. Conspicuous loyalty might reap a reward in the form of gratitude by party leaders. Gladstone skilfully encouraged this hope in 1880 by applauding Nonconformist willingness not to push forward disestablishment.[27] When Carvell Williams proposed the campaign that led to a series of public meetings in 1883 he showed a slightly guilty awareness that it involved 'dangers such as division in the Liberal Party, embarrassment to the Govern.ᵗ & charges of impracticability &c.'.[28] Perhaps most important of all, the new strategy would avoid losing the support of men whose allegiance to the party might prove stronger than their membership of the society in any conflict between the two. Already during the Liberal administration of 1868 one of the most eminent Nonconformist MPs, Samuel Morley, had resigned from the society partly because of its independent stance.[29] For these reasons agitation outside Liberalism was ruled out. The Liberation Society withdrew from the public eye not so much because of adverse political circumstances as because of a deliberately adopted strategy.

There were only two occasions after the brief campaign of the early 1880s when the society diverged from its normal policy. The first was a by-election in the Horncastle division of Lincolnshire at the beginning of 1894. The Liberal candidate, H. J. Torr, was a High Churchman, prepared to support disestablishment but averse to the use of tithes for secular purposes. His vote might harm the Welsh disestablishment measure that was due in the near future.[30] David Lloyd George, an MP since 1890 and an irregularly attending member of the Liberation Society committee, therefore determined that the society should take some action. He wrote to his wife that he did not see 'why these snob Churchmen should be allowed to ride on Nonconformist votes into the House of Commons to oppose Noncon. principles'.[31] He first secured the admission to the committee of another Welsh MP, Evan Jones, and then insisted that a member of staff should be sent to threaten Torr with Liberationist abstentions if he made no satisfactory pledge. Torr refused, and at a second meeting Lloyd George, again supported by Jones, had the committee issue a circular to every Horncastle voter urging abstention. The committee agreed only when Lloyd George undertook to pay the cost.[32] Torr was defeated, although, as the Liberal vote actually increased, Liberationist abstentions cannot have been the reason. Nevertheless the Liberal press roundly condemned the society for disloyalty to the party. An embarrassed Carvell Williams, now himself a Liberal MP, far from using the incident to claim that candidates should be sound on disestablishment, tried in a public statement to minimise what the society had done.[33] 'The Liberation Society folk', Lloyd George wrote home after the second committee meeting, 'are quite terrified at their daring.'[34] Some of the society's supporters, notably in Wales, were delighted by its uncharacteristic vigour; others wrote in disapproval.[35] Horncastle, apart from revealing the potential of Lloyd George as a Nonconformist politician, illustrates how averse the Liberationist leadership had become to public divergence from the Liberal Party.

The only other occasion on which the Liberation Society took issue with the Liberals attracted no publicity, but was otherwise remarkably similar. In June 1895, as the Welsh Disestablishment Bill was passing through the Commons, Lloyd George was eager to amend it so that surrendered Church property should be administered by a Welsh national council. For the first time since the Horncastle by-election he attended the Liberation Society committee. He had already arranged that Herbert Lewis, a fellow Welsh MP, should write to the committee urging it to declare in favour of the proposed amendment. The committee once more succumbed to Lloyd George, resolving that

Carvell Williams should urge the amendment on Asquith, who as Home Secretary was promoting the Bill.[36] The society was stepping beyond its normal self-imposed limits by calling for a significant change in a government measure. The letter was written, but Carvell Williams added a concluding sentence on his own initiative. 'The committee', he assured Asquith, 'do not desire to take, or to sanction, any steps in regard to this matter which may either endanger the Bill, or increase the difficulties of the Government . . . '[37] Liberal morale was low in the House, and attempts to modify the Bill were dangerous opportunities for the Conservatives. Carvell Williams was carefully avoiding the odium that shortly afterwards rested on Lloyd George when his pressing of this very amendment helped to bring about the government's defeat and resignation.[38] The Liberation Society wanted to escape repeating its embarrassments over Horncastle. It had become, and wished to remain, a satellite of the Liberal Party.

How successful was this strategy? A booklet published by the society to mark its jubilee in 1894 was well satisfied with the results:

> By a prudent electoral policy they [the Liberationists] have done much to prevent disunity, and to win over the timid and the hesitating, and, as their reward, they have now the entire Liberal party at one with them in promoting Disestablishment in Wales and Scotland; while the great majority of that party are prepared to adopt the same policy for England also.[39]

It is true that the number of MPs endorsing disestablishment had increased. In 1868, of 382 Liberal MPs, only 95 were opponents of a state Church. In 1885, of 333 Liberal MPs, the figure had climbed to 171. By 1895, of 175, as many as 162 accepted the policy of general disestablishment.[40] Announcement of support at the hustings, however, did not entail commitment to the cause. When in 1897 a general disestablishment resolution was moved in the Commons, only 86 of the 162 troubled to vote for it, despite a whip issued by the society. In opposing the resolution, Balfour could point to an array of empty Liberal benches.[41] The adherence of many MPs was purely formal, and party managers recognised this. By 1901 Carvell Williams was complaining to the press that the National Liberal Federation had boycotted the discussion of disestablishment.[42] There were, it is true, side-benefits derived from loyalty to the party. Carvell Williams was able to build up a special relationship with Liberal leaders. He enjoyed access to John Morley, a former Liberationist, and so was able to clarify the religious equality sections of the second Home Rule Bill.[43] He was also able to propose to Asquith, a former Nonconformist, several technical details in the Welsh Disestablishment Bill.[44] Loyalty, however, meant self-denial as well as privilege. There was little hope of burials legislation unless it was made a government measure. In 1894, however, the society's committee resolved not even to request the government to take up the issue, since it was hard pressed for parliamentary time.[45] Nor did loyalty reap the rewards it sought. In 1899 the society decided that it could reasonably expect disestablishment to become official party policy at last. A deputation visited Campbell-Bannerman, the party leader, on 12 June. No reply was forthcoming. When pressed, Campbell-Bannerman announced on 1 August merely that it was inexpedient for the party to take a stand, although individuals might speak out.[46] The Liberation Society could safely be ignored because it packed no punch. Sober allegiance to the party gained no more than nominal support from the bulk of its backbenchers. The strategy of permeating Liberalism was self-defeating.

The ossification of the society's political impact was possible because of an underlying decay of popular support. This was evident in the society's income. Special fund-raising efforts managed to draw in a very satisfactory average of £13,000 a year between 1874 and 1880, but between 1880 and 1883 the average fell to £9,700. Of that, £4,000 each year came from accumulated legacies.[47] The society, that is to say, was depending on dead supporters to maintain its ordinary operations. From 1886 onwards the society carried a permanent debt that fluctuated around £1,500 and suffered periodic financial crises.[48] Efforts to raise income fell flat. A projected general appeal was abandoned in 1885 when hardly any of seventy specially selected men made promises.[49] The cause became heavily dependent on a handful of the rich. Three gatherings of wealthy friends of the society in the north elicited promises of £1,500 in 1886, and a London dinner in the following year produced £700.[50] Regular giving fell. Around 1890 the average was £5,300; around 1900 it was £4,300.[51] People were becoming less willing to contribute to the society. Time as well as money was withheld. In 1874 the society had 130 voluntary helpers; by 1886, only 33.[52] The annual and triennial meetings, originally designed to demonstrate the society's strength, became increasingly sorry spectacles. At the 1901 triennial meetings, with the octogenarian Carvell Williams in the chair, an 'Old Guard of greyheads' was said to be in the majority.[53] Later that year the society launched an attempt to gain the allegiance of younger men by creating a Young People's Liberationist League, but this organisation soon passed into oblivion.[54] Carvell Williams lamented that 'unhappily a very large number of young men have gone to the football or cricket field, to the golf links or the cycling track, and the appeals which stirred their fathers fall unheeded'.[55] The generation of men devoted to disestablishment was passing away.

The primary explanation of the society's declining appeal is that the cause no longer touched the Evangelical conscience as it had done in the past. When it began, in the 1840s, the society had appealed directly to religious convictions. Its early title, the Anti-State Church Association, proclaimed it to be a typical negative crusade. Like the vigorous campaigns of the end of the century, its method was agitation and its target was wickedness. Edward Miall resigned his pastorate in 1839 to concentrate on advocating the voluntary principle. His reasons, he announced, were two: the connection of Church and state was an obstacle to the gospel; and it was 'impious in principle'. By his first point he meant to draw attention to the existence within the Church of England of lazy, unconverted clergy and of Puseyite, Romanising clergy. Both classes, he held, far from being zealous evangelists, gave erroneous teaching that drew people away from Christ. Yet the state was attracting such men to a clerical career by providing a legally guaranteed income, social privileges and the prospect of preferment. State support for error was wrong. Furthermore, state aid for religion (and this was his second point) implied that religion could not advance of its own accord. Evangelical Christianity, however, had demonstrated its capacity for expansion in the early years of the century. To insist on the need for state patronage was to cast aspersions on the work of Christ himself.[56] In an identical vein the Baptist Union resolved in 1839 that state establishments of religion were 'a palpable departure from the laws of Christ, a gross reflection on his wisdom and power, and the most formidable obstacle in the land to the diffusion of true piety'.[57] Charles Williams, a young Baptist minister who attended Liberation Society annual meetings regularly from 1847, could regard his desire for the separation of Church and state as an extension of his personal religion.[58] Disestablishment for men such as Williams was the ending of an insult to God and a hindrance to his gospel. It is no wonder that it was a powerful call to action.

Gradually, however, the crusading note was lost. The process can be seen in Edward Miall himself. At a political rally in 1867 he declared: 'When men say to their fellow men "Our religion is superior to yours, and we call in the aid of the law – that law which belongs to all citizens equally, to sustain our religion against yours", they must of necessity . . . be guilty of intolerance. Only put this down and my work is done.' Miall was broadening his case so that it would appeal to all who upheld the liberal value of tolerance. When he proposed his Commons disestablishment motion in 1871 he was anxious to present his argument 'not on the ground of sectarianism, but as one of justice and nationality'.[59] The increasingly secular tone was inevitable if the cause was to impress MPs who were not themselves Nonconformists. But the process went further. The original Evangelical arguments were no longer put forward by the Liberation Society at all. In its handbook of 1894, *The Case for Disestablishment*, the section on 'The Religious Argument' supports the principle that men are responsible in religion to God alone by an appeal to Locke and Guizot.[60] The society's literature had to be acceptable to all its supporters. They included from the 1870s Liberal intellectuals like

John Morley and Lyulph Stanley who were agnostics. Accordingly speakers on Liberationist platforms concentrated on contending that all groups in the state should have equal rights and equal access to public places. Disendowment also loomed large. Speakers for the Society for the Liberation of Religion from State Patronage and Control (its full title), quipped a critic in 1892, seemed 'more interested in the liberation of national funds from their present wasteful application'.[61] The society had ceased to make a religious appeal. Significantly by the 1880s its meetings no longer began and ended in prayer.[62] Only older Nonconformists could remember its religious basis. It steadily lost touch with its natural constituency.

The effect was to make some Nonconformists wary of the Liberation Society. Among them was R. W. Dale, minister of Carr's Lane Congregational Church, Birmingham, and probably the greatest intellect of the late nineteenth-century Nonconformist pulpit. Dale joined the society in about 1860, but by the early 1870s found speaking on its behalf uncongenial. He could not talk freely of his religious convictions in the company of some of the other Liberationist orators. Accordingly, in the winters of 1875 and 1876, Dale and his friend Guinness Rogers mounted a speaking tour of the cities of England and Wales outside the auspices of the Liberation Society. The campaign owed much of its success to the high tone consistently maintained by the two speakers. The work, Dale agreed with Rogers, was 'a part of the service to which Christ has called us – with the one object present to us always of getting His will done on earth as it is done in Heaven'.[63] Dale's objection to serving under the Liberation Society banner was not that it was becoming too ensnared in worldly politics. He believed passionately that all areas of life, including the political sphere, should be brought under the authority of Christ. But Dale also believed that the religious should never be subordinate to the secular. The hallmark of his thought was the exaltation of the church as the community of true believers. His rationale for disestablishment was that the affairs of the church of Christ should not be controlled by a secular state. He could no longer discuss the issue in such terms on a Liberation Society platform. He also disagreed with the plan for disestablishment and disendowment drawn up by Illingworth and his circle for the society in 1876. It amounted, in his view, to spoliation. Yet he did not break entirely with the society. With its principles he continued to concur. It was its increasingly secular tone that kept him at a distance.[64] Dale and Guinness Rogers, the most influential Congregationalists of their day, must have aroused similar reservations in the minds of many Nonconformists.

The secularisation of the society was to be challenged more directly. Joseph Parker, the minister of the City Temple in central London, announced in 1883 that he had no wish to join infidels in the work of disestablishment.[65] He himself, he insisted, was a religious and not a political Dissenter. Highly strung and eccentric, Parker stood aloof from his fellow-Congregationalists.[66] He called himself a 'child of impulse',[67] and the incident tended to be dismissed as one of his characteristic vagaries. In 1889, however, he returned to the theme by explaining that he was refusing to address the Liberation Society's triennial conference because he would not co-operate with non-religious men in a religious cause. This time the issue was magnified by an undignified squabble. Charles Berry, a rising star in the Congregational ministry, criticised Parker's decision; Parker declared that he would henceforward regard Berry with 'repugnance and disgust'; and it was even reported that in a fit of pique Parker erased Berry's name from the City Temple record of preachers.[68] All this ensured that the topic was kept before the public. Parker's enthusiasm for disestablishment had not waned. In a novel published in 1898 he clearly shows his sympathy for the hero, the country minister Paterson, whose 'prayers had a political tone, and his hopes of heaven owed not a little to the certainty that the Act of Uniformity would be done away with'.[69] Parker's objection to the society was similar to Dale's, a reluctance to compromise the religious basis of his dissent from the state Church. More serious than Parker's statements for the Liberation Society was the defection of C. H. Spurgeon, the widely esteemed Baptist pastor of the Metropolitan Tabernacle. The Tabernacle was regularly used for the society's annual meetings. When in 1886 it was impractical to hold them there, Spurgeon was careful to reaffirm his loyalty to the society.[70] By 1891, however, Spurgeon had decided to discontinue his subscription.[71] 'We will not', he wrote in his widely circulated magazine, 'be brought into apparent union with those from whom we differ in the very core of our souls upon matters vital to Christianity.'[72] The deacons forbade the use of the Tabernacle for the 'political' purposes of the Liberation Society.[73] Being turned out of its usual premises was a damaging rebuff to the society. Spurgeon's withdrawal must have been imitated by many lesser figures in these years. The secular image of the Liberation Society was its greatest handicap.

Some of the society's supporters realised this. Charles Williams, the Baptist minister at Accrington who had given the society yeoman service over the decades, wrote to the committee in 1891 urging the importance of advocating its case on religious grounds.[74] Charles Berry, Joseph Parker's antagonist, advised exactly the same course in 1895.[75] The committee tried to respond to such appeals. As early as 1887 it decided on a change of tack. 'Without any diminution of political action', ran the minute, 'the Society might probably with advantage appeal more than it has done in recent years to the religious feeling which most strongly influenced the early supporters of the Society.'[76] Over the next few years circulars regularly went out requesting ministers to mention disestablishment in the pulpit or else to preach on 'the Spirituality of

Christ's kingdom'.[77] One of the society's staff thought up the idea of a Free Church Sunday when services should concentrate on the theme each year.[78] Sermons were included in the programme of the annual meetings from 1892 and prayer was reintroduced from 1894.[79] And from the platform there was an attempt to draw on anti-Catholic attitudes. The society began in the 1890s to commend disestablishment as the remedy for the advancing tide of Anglo-Catholicism within the Church of England, what Nonconformists usually called 'sacerdotalism'.[80] Other bodies, however, were making more plausible claims to provide the antidote to ritualism and the society gained little benefit. None of these techniques, in fact, enjoyed any significant success for they were too superficial. The Liberation Society did not look like a religious crusade.

The society was consequently failing to secure the allegiance of younger ministers. The 1901 triennial meetings heard with dismay that no ministers in Leicester, the original centre of Edward Miall's movement, would join in aggressive Liberation work.[81] The problem was that the younger generation was not convinced that there was a well-founded case against state patronage of Christianity. In 1894, for instance, Edward Poole-Connor, the 22-year-old Baptist pastor at Aldershot, requested official recognition of his position as chaplain to Baptist troops together with a capitation grant from the state. He was criticised by more traditional Nonconformists for seeking Caesar's aid in Christ's work. If the state paid him as a chaplain, they argued, it could claim to control him. Poole-Connor replied that the Baptist proportion of the army was similar to the Baptist proportion of the population. Hence the tax-payer would be charged only for services rendered to men of his own denomination. His own religious liberty, according to Poole-Connor, would not be compromised by the state.[82] Here was a reasoned justification of state support for religion. The essential thing in Poole-Connor's eyes was to ensure that Christian teaching was brought to bear on the army. The chapels should not be inhibited by outmoded scruples. Poole-Connor was not alone. Younger Nonconformists took a similar position over chaplains in workhouses. They argued that there should be paid chaplains from the Free Churches as well as from the Church of England. A sharp dispute arose when the secretary of the Metropolitan Free Church Council, John Matthews, endorsed this proposal in 1897. Public support for workhouse chaplains should be extended to all denominations rather than, as the more traditional held, eliminated altogether. If Matthews's argument was correct, commented the *Christian World*, then Nonconformists should never have refused church rates.[83] The growth of a new attitude was also evident in the eagerness of Nonconformists to play a part in state ceremonial. At Queen Victoria's Diamond Jubilee, for example, their protests were not at the part played by dignitaries of the state Church, but at the grudging allocation to Free

Church leaders of places merely on the steps outside rather than inside St Paul's Cathedral.[84] Some Nonconformists were prepared to go so far as to waive all objection to an Established Church. J. H. Shakespeare, appointed secretary of the Baptist Union in 1898, had assured an audience of Church Evangelicals two years earlier that he did not hold the connection of Church and state to be essentially wrong.[85] Without the commitment of their spiritual mentors, laymen were unlikely to throw themselves into the disestablishment movement as a religious campaign. The secularisation of the Liberation Society ensured its decline.

The society also found it hard to recruit new members for a second reason: the removal of the practical disabilities of Nonconformists. The secretary of the Liberation Society, David Caird, pointed in 1908 to the disappearance of grievances as an explanation for neglect of the disestablishment cause.[86] Nonconformists earlier in the century had been spurred to action by incidents that seemed either to exclude them from positions for which they were qualified or to stamp them with the badge of social inferiority. Thus Howard Evans, editor of the Liberation Society's publications in the Edwardian years, had been told in the 1850s that if he wished to obtain an Oxford scholarship he must conform to the Established Church. He refused. 'Ever since then', he recalled, 'I have done my best to avenge that wrong, and have taken a keen delight in standing by other victims of priestly arrogance, which does the devil's work in the outraged name of the God of all goodness.'[87] Similarly Charles Williams of Accrington joined the Liberation Society after resisting a demand for Easter dues to his parish church.[88] Rising businessmen like Samuel Morley resented the stigma attached to Dissent and wanted Nonconformists to 'take their proper place'.[89] Social discrimination roused strong feelings. But successive pieces of legislation gradually abolished the causes of resentment. In 1880 a Burials Act, sponsored by the government, granted Nonconformists the right to have their own ministers and orders of service at interments in parish graveyards. This did away with the last of the major grievances canvassed in the 1830s.[90] After 1880 there was little to complain of in the towns, where nearly all the more prosperous and influential Nonconformists lived. When at Harwich in 1894 a Nonconformist Justice of the Peace was summoned for non-payment of a church rate under an unrepealed special Act of 1829, it was an isolated case.[91] The Liberation Society Council was forced to recognise in 1901 that it faced apathy in the towns.[92] By the turn of the century discrimination no longer induced urban Nonconformists to join the society.

The position in the countryside, however, was often different. There were occasional threats to Nonconformists, often with political overtones. After the 1900 general election, Lord Hastings served notice to quit on tenants in North Norfolk for voting Liberal and for hostility to the Church of England.[93] Such incidents involving landlords strengthened the political resolve of Nonconformists, but they were comparatively rare. Perhaps the most publicised issue was the refusal by Lord Salisbury to sell land for a chapel to the Wesleyans at Hatfield. They were compelled to worship in a small converted cowshed that gained celebrity as 'Moo-Cow Chapel'. Salisbury later offered a site, but it was unacceptable, allegedly because it was close to a sewage farm. Eventually a chapel was built off Salisbury's property. Stories about these events made good propaganda against the Conservative leader and so were bandied about for years.[94] More common were cases of apparent clerical intolerance, usually, in the 1870s, over burials. The best-known was probably a case at Akenham in Suffolk in 1878. The 2-year-old son of a farm labourer died without baptism since the parents were attenders of Zoar Baptist Chapel in Ipswich, four miles away. The ritualist clergyman, Father Drury, directed that the child should be buried in ground reserved for the unbaptised and, according to the parents, declined to take the service. The Congregational minister therefore conducted the funeral. But Drury intervened in the service to urge immediate burial without a Bible reading on the grounds that the ceremony was late. An indecorous altercation ensued. The case was given publicity by the Liberal *East Anglian Daily News* and gained even more when Drury sued the newspaper proprietor for libel. He especially objected to the remark that his rectory and the associated nunnery were very different places from heaven. The jury returned a verdict in favour of Drury, but with only 40s damages. The case helped to convince the Liberal government, which assumed office shortly afterwards, of the need to change the burials law.[95] But the 1880 Act did not end disputes over burials as a number of irritating anomalies survived. The parochial incumbent remained entitled to fees for interments even if he had not officiated, and consecrated ground in new cemeteries was subject to the same condition. Furthermore, clergymen were sometimes reluctant to observe the 1880 Act. The most ventilated case took place at Tarporley in Cheshire in 1886. The child of the Wesleyan minister died. The bereaved father gave notice to the rector that he would himself conduct the service under the Burials Act. The rector, however, appealed to him to withdraw the notice. Methodists had traditionally been buried by the clergyman: why should they allow their unhappy ecclesiastical divisions to extend to the dead? The Wesleyan minister declined to withdraw and claimed that he was put to inconvenience in choosing a site for a grave. The case was blown up, rather unfairly, into a symbol of clerical arrogance. The Liberal *Daily News*, for instance, criticised the 'peremptory summons' of the father to the rectory.[96] Such burial scandals were especially galling because they occurred when the suffering parties were feeling least able to maintain their rights. They did much to keep alive the resentments of rural Nonconformists against the Church of England.

The Liberation Society undoubtedly profited from such feelings. Carvell Williams was able to exploit the Tarporley case in the Commons. Questions were put to the Home Secretary, Childers, over the affair. When Childers claimed, on the authority of the rector, that the father was satisfied with the proceedings, Carvell Williams was able to score a well-publicised point by demonstrating that he was not.[97] Yet the Liberation Society could not achieve a settlement of the burials question. Churchmen in the Commons resisted private member's Bills on the subject and the Liberal administration of 1892 found no time to act on the society's request for legislation.[98] It was eventually a Unionist government which, by the Burial Grounds Act of 1900, following a Select Committee report, ended the grievance. Consecration of part of a cemetery was no longer compulsory, chapels were not to be reserved for one denomination and fees were to be paid to clergy only for services rendered.[99] The Liberation Society could claim no credit. All it gained tangibly from the burials issue was an increasing measure of Wesleyan sympathy. A survey of Methodism published in 1879 declared that if petty clerical intolerance continued, especially over burials, then Wesleyans would soon flock into the society.[100] The denominational authorities still prohibited political activity by Wesleyan ministers but the rule had recently been successfully breached. In 1875 a minister, John Bond, spoke at the Liberation Society annual meeting. At the following Wesleyan Conference he was charged with having infringed the principle of 'no politics', but he defended himself capably and remained a member of the society. Conference merely resolved that ministers must avoid public pronouncements that might embarrass their colleagues.[101] By 1881 Bond was a Wesleyan official, and so it was clear that Liberationism was no bar to promotion. Stirred by their continuing grievances, Wesleyans seemed on the brink of infusing new life into the society.

When the Wesleyans began to seek redress, however, it was not through the Liberation Society. They made use of the connexional Committee of Privileges, which had existed since the beginning of the century for defending Methodist interests against impending legislation. In 1883 the committee was authorised to take the initiative in trying to abolish their remaining grievances. Robert Perks, appointed the first lay secretary of the committee in the previous year, was the driving force.[102] Perks was the legal partner of Henry Fowler, the Wesleyan member of the 1892 Liberal Cabinet, and was to become a railway and civil engineering promoter on a vast scale. In 1907, for instance, he inaugurated the St Lawrence ship canal scheme in Canada. He was a self-made, energetic and astute man whose biographer has to admit his 'harshness' and 'curt manner'. He was also a devoted Methodist: the son of a Wesleyan president, one of the first laymen admitted to Conference in 1878 and later the inventor of the Methodist Million Guineas Fund to greet the new century. From 1892 he was Liberal MP for Louth, 'the Member for Methodism'.[103] It was Perks who guided the Committee of Privileges into concentrating, from 1888, on the removal of Nonconformist grievances over marriage ceremonies. Carvell Williams had achieved the Liberation Society's last legislative victory when in 1886 he carried a Bill extending permitted hours for Nonconformist marriages from noon to 3 p.m.[104] It was still, however, compulsory at Nonconformist weddings, but not at Anglican weddings, to have the presence of a registrar, and this, as a Wesleyan minister put it in 1893, was felt to be a 'stigma of inferiority'.[105] Perks pressed the question insistently. He informed the Liberation Society in 1888 that the Committee of Privileges was, in effect, taking the issue out of the society's hands.[106] Fowler introduced a Bill in that year, but it was given no time. It fared better once Perks was in the Commons. In 1893 a Select Committee endorsed the principles of his Bill, and thereafter he had a case that carried weight with both parties.[107] The Bill next had a chance in 1898. Perks drummed up letters from Nonconformists to all MPs and secured sufficient Conservative support for the Bill to ensure its passage. Chapels were now allowed to have their own 'registered persons' to record marriages.[108] The Act of 1898 showed that the society had been brushed aside as the champion of Nonconformist rights.

Control of the Welsh disestablishment movement was similarly wrested from the society. Carvell Williams wanted to exploit the predominantly Nonconformist population of Wales as a lever for advancing the cause of separating the entire Church of England from the state. In 1881 he argued that a distinct Welsh campaign was timely. 'It is not suggested', he observed, 'that this w^d result in the passing of a Welsh Disest. Bill, but it would be a new & powerful demonstration against the English Establishment as a whole . . . '[109] Others, however, were interested in the Welsh disestablishment issue for an entirely different reason, as a means of rousing national sentiment in Wales. In particular, this was the aim of Stuart Rendel, the well-to-do MP for Montgomeryshire. Disestablishment for him was not based on religious principle at all (he was not a Nonconformist), but a protest against 'all Anglicising influence in Wales'.[110] His object was to swing the Liberal Party behind the Welsh cause. He joined loyally in a Welsh campaign organised by the Liberation Society in 1884, but by 1886 he was demanding that a whole session of the triennial conference should be devoted to Wales.[111] Carvell Williams would not go so far, but compromised by allowing the subject greater prominence. At the meeting Rendel spoke from the chair of the 'paramount importance' of Welsh disestablishment.[112] Soon afterwards he decided that there must be a break with the Liberation Society. 'We *must* be free in Wales', Rendel wrote, 'to make it a Welsh question pure & simple and to deny effectively that it is from our point of view the thin edge of the wedge of the Liberation Society.'[113] He discerned that the national argument alone might persuade his friend and neighbour Gladstone to declare in favour of the Welsh demand, but that Gladstone would never call in question the English Established Church. Accordingly, in February 1887, directly after election as president of the North Wales Liberal Federation, he issued a circular to the Welsh MPs urging that the Welsh disestablishment campaign should be independent of the society. Rendel feared that most Welsh MPs, while agreeing in private, would not be prepared 'to disestablish the L. S. for Wales whatever their serious inclinations as to the Church'.[114] Rendel's efforts, however, were seconded by the growth of Welsh national feeling in the later 1880s, not least in Nonconformity. There was popular approval for Rendel's strengthening of the organisation of Welsh MPs in the Commons in 1888. Younger Welsh MPs like T. E. Ellis were beginning to take pride in the principality.[115] As Rendel persisted in his policy, there was decreasing resistance to separation of the national cause from the Liberation Society. In 1888 he refused to take the chair at a session of the society's annual meeting; in 1889 he declined a request from Carvell Williams for an interview over tactics; and in 1890 he resisted several proposals from Welsh supporters for a renewed alliance with the society.[116] When in 1892 Carvell Williams tried to discover the nature of Welsh plans, Rendel deliberately avoided giving any information.[117] The Liberation Society had been bypassed.

The society became remarkably divorced from events in Wales. It stood aside almost entirely from the 'Tithe War' that spread over rural Wales in the later 1880s, although it was fought on an issue of religious equality. The 'war' began as a series of requests for the reduction of tithe in a period of agricultural depression, but increasingly challenged, in biblically charged rhetoric, the right of the Established Church to impose tithes at all. Farmers refused payment, and the legal process of distraint and auction provided opportunities for the denunciation of ecclesiastical exactions.[118] The Liberation Society considered taking an interest late in 1886, but decided that it would be imprudent to risk association with illegality. A tentative modification of this policy in 1889 led to the resignation of the society's legal adviser, and little further action was taken.[119] The society gave no effective assistance to the Welsh Tithe Bills in the Commons which were becoming occasions for declarations of nationhood rather than the principles of religious equality. Nor did the society deserve any credit for providing public support when Welsh disestablishment became a possibility during the Liberal government of 1892. The obscurity of Rendel's intentions at first made the society decide to do nothing. Later the growth of a Church defence movement directed against Welsh disestablishment convinced the society that it must take action.[120] So little activity reached the public eye, however, that the *British Weekly* judged the society to be 'stone dead' as a political force.[121] In the summer of 1893 when Welsh MPs were insisting that there should be a government Disestablishment Bill in the following session, Lloyd George pushed through a committee minute for transmission to the government that the Welsh cause was urgent.[122] Yet no widespread agitation was attempted by the society. In similar circumstances a year later, the *British Weekly* was demanding that the Liberation Society must show some reason for its existence.[123] It lacked the political will to intensify the lukewarm feeling in England, where its writ still ran. In Wales disestablishment was creating unprecedented enthusiasm, but the society was no longer in a position to harness it.

Two issues brought some improvement to the society in the early twentieth century. The Conservative Education Act of 1902 was a wholesale infringement of the principle of religious equality. Nonconformists regrouped for a vigorous attack on the government that is analysed in Chapter 7. In the process Carvell Williams was swept from the chair of the executive committee of the Liberation Society, Lloyd George was installed as vice-president and John Clifford, the leader in the education controversy, became president.[124] There was a series of northern rallies addressed by Clifford in the winter of 1903.[125] The Liberal victory of 1906 that seemed to presage an education settlement gave a further fillip to the society. The annual meetings of that year included Lloyd George, now a Cabinet minister, as the star speaker and were the best attended for many years.[126] There followed, on 1 March 1907, a parliamentary motion in favour of disestablishment of the Church of England that was carried by 198 votes to 90.[127] Later that year, the society moved its premises to Westminster so as to be nearer Parliament.[128] But all this meant no fundamental change in the society's fortunes. The education battle, as will be seen, was fought by other organisations. The Liberation Society was being carried forward in their slipstream. At the 1904 annual meetings Clifford had to admit that there was still 'a prevalent air of antiquity' about the organisation.[129] Again, the revival of the Welsh disestablishment campaign after 1906 gave the society a fresh sense of purpose. A new secretary, David Caird, conceding that disestablishment had not been very much before the average Nonconformist in recent years, set about reactivating its organisation after 1908.[130] He was able to report the accession of 2,000 new members less than a year later, and by 1913 had raised membership to about 12,000.[131] He also pushed up the number of meetings held by the society. Over the three years up to 1910 the figure was 1,700; in less than a year, in 1911–12, there were more than 1,000.[132] This period, when Welsh disestablishment was coming before the Commons, witnessed more activity than for many years. Yet the feeling raised in England by the society was mediocre in comparison with the passionate intensity of Wales on the question. The *Christian World* approved the Welsh Disestablishment Bill as just and generous, but showed no special concern for the measure.[133] The opinion was freely expressed that English Nonconformists were almost silent about it. That Welsh disestablishment reached the statute book in 1914 and was implemented in 1920 owed virtually nothing to the Liberation Society. It drew some vitality from the debate on the issue, but took no initiative over it and certainly exercised no influence over government on its behalf. The day of the Liberation Society was past.

Its decay had two causes. One was the steady whittling away of the disabilities that had once branded Nonconformists with social inferiority. The disestablishment movement was a way of asserting that Nonconformists should no longer be treated as second-class citizens. Success in securing the removal of disabilities inevitably led to the weakening of the campaign. Yet in the late nineteenth century, grievances had by no means been eliminated. In the countryside there were still restrictions on Nonconformists who wished to have free access to rites of passage in their own way, and in Wales national feeling powerfully reinforced the demand for disestablishment itself. The Liberation Society became enfeebled well before it might have done because it failed to champion those whose resentments were still strong. The Wesleyans took up the marriage question and the Welsh their disestablishment, in both cases displacing the society. Even over burials, which remained its own care, the society allowed the settlement of the question to be taken out of its hands. The society had its own irresolute policy to blame for its weakness on these questions. That is why the second reason for the decline of the society is the more important. It was ceasing to have the characteristics of an Evangelical crusade. It did not arouse religious passion, it did not use the technique of agitation and it did not set its face against compromise. This again was the result of success. The campaign attracted the support of people who did not share the religious convictions of the mass of early disestablishers. The society had to frame a case to convince Liberals who had no sympathy with Nonconformists as such. And as the society became more integrated into Liberalism, its policy-makers became increasingly reluctant to do anything that might embarrass the party leaders. Liberationism was blunted as it neared the seat of power. It no longer claimed to be struggling against wickedness. This had been its original appeal, and older men remembered it. Younger Nonconformists, however, abandoned its principle altogether. Religious equality ceased to be a popular question primarily because it was no longer seen as an assault on outright wrong. Campaigns that did attack evils were supplanting the Liberation Society among a new generation of Nonconformists. Some of the most popular were in the field of social questions.

3 The Problems of Society

At the back of all the world's trouble and the social and economic distress, there lay the fact of sin. (J. D. Jones, minister of Richmond Hill Congregational Church, Bournemouth, to the Baptist Union Assembly, April 1908)[1]

Charitable work was part of the nineteenth-century way of life. Giving to philanthropic organisations reached remarkable heights. In 1861, for example, when the net national income was £717 million, voluntary charities in the London area alone enjoyed an income of £2·4 million. Nonconformists played their full part.[2] Samuel Morley, the millionaire Congregationalist hosiery manufacturer, was a prince among them. He delighted to distribute his money to causes like the Dalrymple Home for Inebriates, the Hospital Saturday Fund, the Orphan Working School and the Provident Association of Warehousemen and Clerks, as well as to more strictly religious societies. Individuals would write soliciting his generosity. Then, as his biographer put it, 'Mr Morley was often the means of confirming the belief of his correspondents in the doctrine of a particular Providence . . . '[3] Liberality was not confined to the rich for bodies like the Stockwell Orphanage, founded by C. H. Spurgeon, depended on a host of small donations. Giving was regarded as a demanding Christian responsibility. Most effort went into interdenom-inational Evangelical bodies such as the Ragged School Union and the Young Men's Christian Association. It has been estimated that roughly three-quarters of the charities of the later nineteenth century were Evangelical in character,[4] and through them attenders of Church and chapel combined to deal with a wide range of social problems. There were organisations for visiting the sick and infirm, for caring for the disabled, for reforming prostitutes, for combating drunkenness. Whatever the field, Nonconformists shared the general belief that the remedy for the ills of society lay in sustained voluntary effort.

In the last two decades of the nineteenth century, attitudes began to change. There was a deepened sense of responsibility for the welfare of the people as the circumstances of the poor were increasingly felt to be intolerable. Philanthropy continued, but it was no longer thought to be sufficient. Conditions of life had to be transformed. There had been too much concentration on cases, it was often said, but what was needed was cures. Hugh Price Hughes, the Wesleyan prophet of this trend of thought, declared that Christians had been 'selfishly individualistic'.[5] They must address themselves directly to the problems of society. The reaction against individualism was far from being confined to Nonconformity. There arose in the later nineteenth century what Beatrice Webb classically described as 'a new consciousness of sin among men of intellect and men of property'.[6] They were increasingly uneasy about the contrast between their own circumstances and the conditions of the mass of the working people. Guilt stirred them to social action. The awakening of a sharper sense of the surrounding deprivation particularly affected the churches. The Christian Social Union, founded in 1889 by Canon Scott Holland and Bishop Westcott to analyse the problems of the day, was its fruit in the Church of England. Cardinal Manning was an influential exponent of the new ideas in the Roman Catholic Church. But the desire to do away with social evils struck deepest roots in Nonconformity, at least up to the first decade of the twentieth century. Nonconformists were prominent in movements to improve the standard of sexual morality, to deal with overcrowded housing conditions, to reduce drunkenness, to restrict gambling, to encourage better industrial relations, to remedy unemployment and to promote Sunday observance. Preoccupation with social problems – or at least with those that seemed to be moral questions – went beyond denominational leaders to take in a high proportion of chapel attenders. The new mood was central to the Nonconformist conscience.

Its beginnings can be traced to the movement for the repeal of the Contagious Diseases Acts. These Acts, passed in 1864, 1866 and 1869, were designed to check the spread of venereal disease in the armed forces. They provided for a compulsory three-monthly examination of prostitutes within fifteen miles of a number of towns where the army or navy was stationed. They attracted little attention during their passage, largely because most MPs believed that they were intended to deal with contagious diseases not among women but among animals. Opposition began late in 1869 with the formation of a National Association for the Repeal of the Contagious Diseases Acts. As the movement gained strength during the 1870s, the greatest impetus came from its female counterpart, the Ladies' National Association. Mrs Josephine Butler, the wife of a Liverpool clergyman, put all her energies into the campaign. The repealers' case had distinctly feminist overtones. They stood for the rejection of the double standard inherent in legislation that regulated prostitutes but protected their male clients. The repealers also objected to the use of a morals police on the French model and argued that the measures were ineffective antidotes to disease anyhow. But their central plank was that the state was condoning sexual immorality, because regulation implied toleration or even approval. Repealers liked to tell stories about prostitutes who regarded their trade as specially favoured by the queen. The state was countenancing wrong. Such arguments had some appeal for traditional radicals opposed to state interference in social life. The essentially moral case for repeal, however, always drew most support from the Christian public.[7]

The Quakers, who were used to taking up questions of social reform corporately, were the first to associate themselves with the campaign. As early as 1870 their annual meeting instructed subordinate meetings to press for repeal, and four years later some 90 per cent of the recognised ministers among the Friends expressed their opposition to the Acts.[8] The Church of England, by contrast, gave the movement a mixed reception. Although in 1873 about 1,500 clergy signed a memorial to Parliament for repeal, there was considerable support for the Act among Anglicans. There was also a feeling that the subject was too delicate for public discussion, so that, for instance, Josephine Butler's husband was asked to omit references to the subject from an address to the 1872 Church Congress.[9] The Congregational Union held back from public pronouncements for similar reasons. A small number of prominent laymen like Henry Spicer believed that the Acts had done good in reducing prostitution, and the Congregational Union committee refused to permit discussion of the subject at the assembly, where ladies were present, throughout the 1870s.[10] A group of Congregationalists, however, were dedicated repealers. H. J. Wilson, an attender at Queen Street Congregational Church, Sheffield, was convinced at a public meeting addressed by Josephine Butler in 1871 and became the mastermind of a Northern Counties' Electoral League for repeal. His energetic minister at Queen Street, J. P. Gledstone, was secretary of an unofficial Congregational repeal committee formed in 1875 to change denominational policy.[11] His efforts were eventually crowned with success when, in 1881, a repeal resolution was carried at the Congregational Union assembly by a large majority.[12] It is evident that the restraint of the leadership was not a faithful reflection of Congregational opinion. Gledstone found from a circular sent in 1881 to the 2,549 ministers in England and Wales that 1,950 were for total repeal and only 18 for retention.[13] Likewise, the Baptists and the smaller Methodist connexions overwhelmingly favoured repeal, and their representative bodies spoke out clearly.[14] But the strongest support for repeal was organised among the Wesleyans, who, remarkably, were prepared to lay aside their normal wariness of worldly politics. The Wesleyans, alone among Nonconformists, maintained military chaplains and so took a particular interest in the moral welfare of the armed forces.[15] Their Conference condemned the Acts in 1871, and three years later a Wesleyan Society for Securing the Repeal of the Contagious Diseases Acts was formed.[16]

It was the first organisation in Methodist history to prompt overt political action by Wesleyan ministers against existing legislation.[17] They were urged, for instance, to raise the question of repeal with candidates at the 1880 general election.[18] Because, as was frequently stressed, the cause was a matter of principle rather than party, it was thought proper to commend petitions to Parliament from the pulpit.[19] The effect, however, was to encourage open support for Liberal candidates, because most Liberals, but few Conservatives, were prepared to oppose the Acts. There was nevertheless a total absence of dissent from the new cause among the Wesleyans. From 1879 the society's report was read in the Conference itself, a sign that repeal was the policy of the whole Wesleyan body.[20] The cause enjoyed particularly strong support among Nonconformists.

The explanation is that the issue at stake seemed momentous. 'It is whether', declared Morley Punshon, a leading Methodist minister, 'expediency or right is to govern a Christian people.'[21] Scripture, Nonconformist repealers pointed out, condemns fornication, and what we must not do ourselves we must not encourage others to do. Hence state regulation was flying in the face of biblical ethics. As Henry Fowler, the Wesleyan solicitor, declared in 1876, it infringed the principle that 'whatever is morally wrong can never be politically right'.[22] Here, already in use, was one of the war-cries of the Nonconformist conscience. Because it opposed 'wrong', the movement adopted the negative policy of a typical crusade. It explicitly disclaimed all intention of proposing 'constructive legislation'.[23] For the same reason, there could be no thought of compromise. Any substitute for the existing system for minimising venereal disease was entirely unacceptable. The Wesleyan repeal journal depicted the struggle as one between the absolute ethic of Christianity and a 'materialistic utilitarianism directly subversive of the Christian faith . . . There can be no compromise between irreconcilable systems of morality . . .'[24] Again, what was plainly wrong had to be abolished urgently. This explains the insistent tone of the Nonconformist calls for repeal. A memorial to the Prime Minister signed by 700 Wesleyan ministers in 1872 characteristically urged that repeal should be immediate.[25] It was better to do nothing about prostitution than to do wrong. The agitation cultivated an earnest commitment among its adherents, and the very need for discretion seems to have made repealers feel all the more deeply. When occasion offered, pent-up emotions were to be released with powerful effects.

Second to none in devotion to the cause was the editor of the Wesleyan Repeal Society's journal, Hugh Price Hughes. Still in his 20s when he took up the editorship in 1876, Hughes was shaped by his participation in the movement. His subsequent career as the foremost exponent of Nonconformist views on social questions was the direct result of his unsparing advocacy of repeal. Hughes was an emotional man with an impetuous strain that contemporaries attributed to his mixture of Welsh and Jewish blood. His father was a Carmarthen doctor from whom Hughes most obviously inherited an aptitude for administrative work. His mother was the granddaughter of a Jewish banker at Haverfordwest. He was to obtain distinction in the Wesleyan ministry by gaining an MA for work on English philosophy, but his cast of mind was always distinctly practical. At his first station, Dover, between 1869 and 1872, he was influenced by Alderman Rees, another passionate Welsh Methodist, to adopt a Liberal and humanitarian political creed. It was Rees, too, who took him to hear Josephine Butler. Her denunciation of the Contagious Diseases Acts reduced Hughes to tears and he hurried from the platform.[26] The battle against the sexual exploitation of women became the mainspring of his work. As editor of the *Methodist Protest*, he did not attempt to mince matters. One leading article concludes:

> Therefore, let all who desire that thousands and tens of thousands of weak and deluded women should no longer be sacrificed to the lusts of brutal men, all who are shocked by the scandalous injustice which metes out forgiveness to the more culpable man, and infamy to the partner of his sin, all who wish that the cancer of debauchery should not eat its deadly way into the vitals of the young men of England, all who repudiate a doctrine and a class of legislation which make the Bible a lie, and blaspheme Almighty God, come to the help of that handful of devoted men and women who are striving to save their country and their faith from the deadly flood of immorality which threatens to overwhelm both.[27]

Hughes seldom restrained his feelings in print. It was the same on the platform. His shrill, penetrating voice and his ability to grasp the attention with terse, vivid phrases gave him great power over an audience. But his most marked characteristic was always the clamant moralism he acquired in the repeal campaign. He was strident, self-confident, prone to exaggeration – 'a Day of Judgment in breeches'.[28] Hughes is an extreme example of the crusading temper of the period.

It was an upsurge of outraged Christian opinion that eventually sounded the death-knell of the Contagious Diseases Acts. The majority of a parliamentary committee reported late in 1882 in favour of their continuance. Repealers who had awaited the report for three years were indignant that their convictions should be flouted after so long. An interdenominational convention assembled in January 1883 to protest. It called on the churches to let Parliament know their views and petitions flooded into the Commons. 'The Christians', said H. J. Wilson, 'are beginning to be fairly roused at last.'[29] Sufficient MPs were impressed to ensure the carrying, on 20 April, of a resolution that suspended the operation of the Acts. They were not abolished until three years later, but the decisive victory had been won.[30] The controversy, and especially its successful outcome, had significant effects on Christian attitudes. It had shown that the churches could play a major part in demanding action on questions of public morality. The Church of England set up a Social Purity Society to maintain pressure on such matters. The Wesleyans followed by establishing a Conference committee for social purity in 1884, with Hughes as one of the secretaries.[31] Issues involving sexual morality were clearly to become a permanent concern of the churches. The campaign had also induced some repealers to see greater scope for the state in promoting social purity. Supporters of the Acts had argued that repealers wanted the state to wash its hands of the problem of prostitution. Hughes, in particular, had replied that, on the contrary, he wanted repeal to be followed by preventive and reclamatory work in which the powers of the state and of municipal authorities could be invoked. He directly repudiated 'a *laisser faire* policy'.[32] Legislation could be fashioned into an instrument of righteousness. Similar ideas were forming in the mind of the Baptist leader John Clifford, who had played an active part in the final stages of the campaign.[33] The suspension of the Acts left many Nonconformists in a volatile state, prepared to make new departures in public affairs in order to improve the nation's moral tone.

This background explains the enormous impact of a pamphlet that appeared in September 1883, *The Bitter Cry of Outcast London*. It was published by Andrew Mearns, secretary of the London Congregational Union, as an appeal for help in the daunting task of evangelising the inner city. He vividly depicted the poverty and degradation of life in central London, but the key to the stir caused by the pamphlet is what it revealed about sexual behaviour. Mearns could point to a street of 35 houses where 32 were brothels. In another district 43 brothels housed 428 prostitutes, some of them no more than 12 years old. Most horrifying of all, he explained that among families occupying single rooms incest was common.[34] A leading article in the *Christian World* commented in the course of reviewing the pamphlet: 'Regard to the marriage tie is a thing scarcely known; the vilest practices are looked upon with the most matter-of-fact indifference, and no language, we are told, fit to be read, could set forth even a faint indication of the true state of things in this direction.'[35] Although Mearns laid no particular stress on the point, such unspeakable behaviour was deeply disturbing. Yet the pamphlet did not seize public attention until its contents were publicised by W. T. Stead in the *Pall Mall Gazette*. Stead, the son of a Congregational minister and himself a member of Wimbledon Congregational Church, was forever on the lookout for causes to champion. He was a brilliant, if erratic, journalist who pioneered most of the techniques of 'the new journalism' such as interviews and cross-column headlines. Stead, who had just taken over the editorship of the *Pall Mall Gazette*, recognised the potential of the theme of 'outcast London'. From 16 October to 7 November every issue of his newspaper contained at least one item about *The Bitter Cry*. He made effective use of the most sensational of Mearns's evidence about sexual immorality, and from the beginning appealed to the churches for action.[36] On the Sunday following the first series of articles, the subject was taken up in many pulpits. Spurgeon prayed that no spot should be allowed to become 'a fever den and a hot-bed of iniquity'; Guinness Rogers referred in the course of a sermon to the 'horrors of sin and impurity' that no printer would issue.[37] In the following week there was discussion of the matter at the London Baptist Association. The poverty was bad enough, said one speaker, but what went on in single-roomed accommodation was far worse.[38] Stead succeeded in harnessing the social purity feeling that had been aroused in the repeal campaign for an assault on the housing conditions of London.

The overcrowding of urban dwellings became a subject of Nonconformist social concern. In the search for a remedy, the idea that the state should take action came to the fore. There had recently been a significant though tentative piece of legislation: the Cross Act of 1875 had given local authorities limited powers to purchase areas of insanitary dwellings with a view to demolition. Hence it was natural for *The Bitter Cry* to propose that 'the state must . . . secure for the poorest . . . the right to live as something better than the uncleanest of brute beasts'.[39] The *Christian World* echoed its call for state interposition and Guinness Rogers contended that the state had a duty to intervene, if only because of a risk to the social order if such conditions were allowed to continue.[40] The public outcry in which Nonconformists participated so fully led to the setting up of a Royal Commission on the Housing of the Working Classes, with the Prince of Wales as a commissioner, and so to the opening of a new chapter in public housing policy. Once more Christian opinion had exerted a wholesome political influence. It became common for Nonconformist manifestos to urge consideration for the 'Housing Question, so intimately bound up with the physical and moral welfare of the people'.[41] Housing reform reached the category of approved non-party issues on which Wesleyans could properly take action.[42] Hugh Price Hughes argued in 1889 that good housing was the first priority in the battle against disease, which by then he was prepared to list as a social evil alongside lust and drunkenness.[43] But there were no more outbursts of mass feeling in the chapels against housing conditions such as marked 1883, because it necessarily was a field for specialists. Chief among them was C. Fleming Williams, minister of Rectory Road Congregational Church, Stoke Newington. Fleming Williams was on the theologically liberal wing of his denomination and known as 'Flaming Williams' because of his periodic outbursts against the exploitation of working people. But his main work was on the London

County Council, where he was one of the first aldermen. In co-operation with other Progressives, like his fellow-Congregationalist John Wedgwood Benn, Fleming Williams pushed forward the campaign against slum housing.[44] This was work that Nonconformists were often requested to support with their votes. Beyond that, however, it was too much of a technical subject for the rank and file of Nonconformity to take an intelligent interest in it.

By contrast, the subject that originally sparked off an interest in housing reform, social purity, continued to be a mass concern. W. T. Stead created a fresh sensation in the summer of 1885 with a series of articles in the *Pall Mall Gazette* on juvenile prostitution entitled 'The maiden tribute of modern Babylon'. Public opinion rapidly reached white heat and induced Parliament to rush through a Criminal Law Amendment Act raising the age of consent from 13 to 16. Stead had obtained his evidence in a typically melodramatic way, by going in disguise ostensibly to procure a girl for immoral purposes, and he was imprisoned for a technical infringement of the law in the process.[45] The reaction of Nonconformist leaders to all this was predictably mixed. Spurgeon wrote to Stead and Clifford visited him in prison, but Guinness Rogers thought the whole affair scandalous and the Baptist Union Council refused to bring forward a resolution rejoicing at the passing of the Criminal Law Amendment Act.[46] Yet a fresh impulse was given to public concern with matters of sexual morality. Over the twelve months following Stead's revelations one star speaker alone, Mrs Ormiston Chant, addressed more than 400 meetings on the subject. An undenominational Gospel Purity Association and a Congregational social purity organisation were set up. Most important was the National Vigilance Association, inaugurated at a demonstration in Hyde Park on 22 August 1885 and designed to ensure the enforcement of the Criminal Law Amendment Act. By 1888 some 300 local vigilance associations were in existence.[47] The chairman and moving spirit was Percy Bunting, a lawyer who was a member of Hughes's mission, and the committee was predominantly Nonconformist. Its main work was legal, and in three fields. It undertook prosecutions on behalf of girls who had been the victims of criminal assault; it tried to have brothels closed, a procedure that had been immensely facilitated by the 1885 Act; and it launched an offensive against indecency. The best-known case was the successful prosecution of Vizetelly & Co. for translating novels by Zola, the first use of the law of obscene libel against serious literature, begun at the instance of the Presbyterian MP Samuel Smith in 1888 and taken up by the association in the following year. Shortly afterwards the organisation suppressed a display of 'indecent' illustrations of Rabelais and mounted a sustained attack, with Hughes in the vanguard, on aspects of music-hall life such as posing by apparently nude women.[48] The National Vigilance Association also managed to put some legislation on the statute book. An Indecent Advertisements Bill drawn up by its legal subcommittee was carried in 1889[49] and a Bill making incest a crime, introduced regularly on behalf of the association and the National Society for the Prevention of Cruelty to Children, was eventually passed in 1908.[50] The measure that most stirred the public, however, was the so-called White Slave Bill of 1912, directed against procuring for prostitution abroad. Free Church councils urged the government to press it forward and there were rallies in its favour held jointly with Anglicans and Jews. The Bill was passed in a strong form.[51] Powerful feelings fuelled a good deal of activity intended to improve the standard of sexual morality during these years.

The intensity of feeling is well illustrated by the hounding of the politician Sir Charles Dilke after a court had accepted his adultery as grounds for his wife's divorce. Because the case against him came up in 1885–6, hard on the heels of the 'Maiden Tribute' affair, it was watched with close attention. Stead was responsible for much of the campaign in 1886 and again in 1891–2. He claimed that Dilke, as a condemned adulterer, was unfit for Parliament, let alone for office. The agitation did not prevent Dilke's return to Parliament, but it did blight his career.[52] Stead was in step with popular Nonconformist attitudes. A Welsh minister, Ossian Davies, was heard with enthusiastic cheering when he told the Congregational Union Total Abstinence Society in October 1885 that he would not vote for a profligate, however talented.[53] Two years later the restrained Carvell Williams of the Liberation Society was prepared to speak of the need 'to purge the legislature of impure legislators'.[54] The waspish editor of the *British Weekly*, Robertson Nicoll, kept up the harrying. When Tom Ellis, the rising young Welsh MP, appeared on the same platform as Dilke in 1891, Nicoll wrote him a stern letter of rebuke. He wanted to know if Ellis had anything to say in extenuation, before, as he put it, 'publicly condemning you'. Ellis was able to explain that he had agreed to address some of his constituents without knowing they had also invited Dilke, and so avoided the denunciation.[55] In the following year, when Dilke re-entered Parliament, Nicoll threatened official Liberalism with the loss of Nonconformist votes if Dilke were offered a place in government. 'There is no political object, however much desired', he declared, 'that can compare with the maintenance of family life and New Testament morality . . . .'[56] Exactly the same view was taken when the possibility of Dilke's inclusion in the next Liberal administration was considered by the general committee of the National Free Church Council in 1904. It was suggested that eighteen years of public service had atoned for his offence, but Bunting, Clifford and F. B. Meyer, all keen social purity men, roundly refused to tolerate him. Dilke had neither confessed nor been exonerated, and so the ban must remain.[57] The private lives of public men had become a subject of keen Nonconformist attention.

Temperance was another field in which Nonconformists expressed themselves strongly during this period. The struggle against drunkenness had grown from its origins in the 1830s into a large-scale movement. The argument that a liking for strong drink was the greatest obstacle to the gospel had a special appeal for Nonconformists who saw the beer shop on one street corner as the chief counter-attraction to the chapel on the other. Of a sample of 273 teetotal leaders during the period 1833–72, all but 41 turned out to have been Nonconformists.[58] Yet the movement took a long time to gain the sympathies of Nonconformity as a whole. In its early years many of the most Evangelical Christians, both inside and outside the Established Church, believed that teetotalism was setting up an alternative to Christianity, a rival way of salvation. It seemed to hold out as much hope for the man who signed the pledge of total abstinence as for the one who cast his burdens on Jesus. Wesleyans as a body therefore tended to look askance at teetotalism. This explains why only 7 per cent of a list of teetotal ministers in 1866 were Wesleyans, a far lower proportion than might be expected from a large denomination.[59] Prominent Nonconformists at the end of the century were still not abstainers: Dr J. H. Rigg, the chief figure in the Wesleyan ministry, was not one;[60] Guinness Rogers, who could remember a time when a barrel of beer had been made available for the refreshment of delegates at the Congregational Union, never became a teetotaller;[61] and Sir Albert Spicer, the leading Congregational layman, did not give up alcohol until the king took the pledge during the First World War.[62] Attempts by zealots to have total abstinence declared a qualification for office (at the Baptist Union autumn assembly of 1897) or to exclude those in the liquor trade from church membership (at the Wesleyan Conference each year from 1898 to 1901) were firmly rejected.[63] Primitive Methodists had been pioneers of the temperance reformation, but in the other denominations teetotalism was only beginning to make headway in the 1870s. When the Wesleyans first established a permanent temperance committee in 1875, it was clearly laid down that the Wesleyan temperance societies it organised were to be open to those who believed in moderation as well as to total abstainers.[64] Although a Congregational Total Abstinence Society was begun in 1874, it was not given an official place on the assembly agenda until 1885.[65] The editor of the *Baptist Magazine* was still aware in 1874 that he would be criticised for discussing the temperance question in a religious journal.[66] In 1879 only 760 out of some 2,000 Congregational ministers were total abstainers, but by 1904 the proportion had risen to about 2,500 out of 3,000.[67] Similarly only about a sixth of Baptist ministers were said to be abstainers in 1860, but by 1886 the proportion was about 1,100 out of 1,900.[68] Perhaps most significantly, in 1907 it was reported that 211 out of 214 Baptist theological students were teetotallers.[69] It was in the twentieth century, not the nineteenth, that total abstinence was normal. At the peak of the

Nonconformist conscience, temperance still seemed a growing concern, a cause of the future.

Total abstainers were not necessarily advocates of new legislation to curb drinking. Temperance was a field where organisations concentrating on voluntary effort were apparently successful. The Band of Hope, which gave temperance teaching to children, had expanded rapidly to a huge size. The Manchester and Salford District Union began with 10 societies in 1863 and could claim 166 directly affiliated societies only eight years later.[70] The next generation could be expected to be far more sober. Again, the existing law from 1872 onwards permitted interested parties to challenge on several grounds the renewal of a licence for the sale of alcohol at annual 'brewster sessions' of magistrates' courts. Nonconformists made frequent use of their rights, especially through Free Church councils around the turn of the century. In such circumstances fresh legislation could appear superfluous. Samuel Morley, for instance, became the first treasurer of the Congregational Total Abstinence Society in 1874, but was not converted to the need for legislation until 1878.[71] Many older Nonconformists must have shared the reservations of Guinness Rogers about calling in the state. The consequent destruction of liberty, he contended, might be an evil greater than the benefit secured.[72] But the main political arm of the temperance movement, the United Kingdom Alliance, did not entertain such fears. Its members were prohibitionists who believed that the state had a duty to protect society against the colossal 'drink evil'. Regularly from 1862 onwards a 'Permissive Bill' was introduced into the Commons on behalf of the Alliance by Sir Wilfrid Lawson, an Anglican of undenominational Evangelical background. The Bill would have permitted localities to prohibit the sale of alcohol. After 1879 Lawson tried to gain extra support by introducing not a Bill but a resolution, and by making the goal not local prohibition but 'local option', the right of an area to abolish or regulate the drink trade in a variety of ways. Alliance supporters were notorious for single-minded devotion to the measure they proposed, which to them was the self-evident solution to every social problem. They were often prepared to oppose candidates generally sympathetic to temperance and progressive measures if they declined to endorse the Permissive Bill or local option.[73] Nonconformists with inherited Liberal loyalties often resented such erratic electoral behaviour. Guinness Rogers regularly denounced it as 'faddism'. Yet the Alliance was supported chiefly by Nonconformists. Of the members of its executive committee in the period 1872–95 whose religion can be traced, nineteen were Nonconformists and only five Anglicans.[74] When Gladstone's government took up licensing reform in 1871 and again in 1872, Nonconformist inhibitions about state action declined markedly. Alliance subscriptions shot up and the *Baptist Magazine* commented that bringing closing time forward from midnight to 11 p.m. had definitely decreased drunkenness.[75] Some younger Nonconformist leaders, with Hughes and Clifford prominent among them, began to speak for the Alliance. Although active prohibitionism remained very much a minority concern, there was general Nonconformist sympathy for temperance legislation from the 1870s.

Various temperance reforms other than the local veto were mooted. The Baptist Union assembly resolved in 1894 in favour of the abolition of grocers' licences, whose introduction seemed to at least one Primitive Methodist to be the one blot on Gladstone's political record.[76] There was considerable Free Church support for the so-called Children's Bills of 1900 and 1901 that aimed to forbid the sale of intoxicants to children. The *Christian World* went so far as to say that if the 1901 Bill was passed, there would be little need for prohibition.[77] But the most popular temperance measure among Nonconformists was Sunday closing. There were two reasons for this. First, the question successfully yoked the newer concern for temperance with the entrenched Evangelical sabbatarianism of mid-century. Those who resisted the Sunday opening of the Crystal Palace in the 1850s were also prepared to demand the Sunday closure of public houses. Thus the Wesleyans, who numbered relatively few teetotallers in their ranks, contributed 48 per cent of the signatures to a Sunday closing petition in 1863.[78] In 1879 the Wesleyan Conference officially encouraged members to seek 'the discouragement of the habits of intemperance [and] the diminution of temptations thereto, especially on the Lord's day'.[79] Similarly in 1869, the first year when the Congregational Union resolved in favour of temperance legislation, Sunday closing was the measure singled out for particular approval.[80] The second reason for the special attention to this proposal was that there were precedents to cite. Scotland obtained Sunday closing in 1854, Ireland in 1878 and Wales in 1881. What was good for the rest of the United Kingdom, it was argued, was good for England. Charles Garratt, the leading temperance advocate in the Wesleyan ministry, claimed in 1885 that the churches were unanimous on the issue.[81] This was not absolutely true, because some Congregationalists like J. J. Colman still feared that total Sunday closing was too coercive and would provoke a reaction.[82] A series of unsuccessful Sunday Closing Bills for England nevertheless received general Nonconformist endorsement in the later 1880s and 1890s. Robert Perks put forward another English Bill in 1905 and two years later tried to press the cause on Asquith as a suitable piece of legislation for a Liberal government.[83] Once more there was no success. Despite Nonconformist enthusiasm, Sunday closing never became the law of England.

Beyond Sunday closing, however, there was no common mind in Nonconformity about the legislative goal to be pursued. Alongside the local option proposals there existed an alternative policy that was to gain wide support. This was the idea of the municipal control of public houses, the 'Gothenburg system', named after one place where it operated. The idea of the Gothenburg system was that when a local authority administered its own drink outlets the profit motive was eliminated and the supply would be kept within reasonable bounds. From the 1870s onwards Joseph Chamberlain advocated this system of 'disinterested management', which chimed in well with his Birmingham brand of municipal enterprise. It gained little popular following, however, until 1894, when a Public House Reform Association was set up to bring it before the public. Hugh Price Hughes was rapidly convinced, and to the dismay of supporters of the local veto began advocating the Gothenburg system.[84] Hughes's thinking on the subject was shared by A. J. Sherwell, one of his helpers at the West London Mission and later MP for Huddersfield, who wrote an influential book on the subject, *The Temperance Problem and Social Reform*. It was published in 1899 jointly with Joseph Rowntree, the Quaker chocolate manufacturer, who no doubt provided the money for Sherwell's research. By marshalling an array of comparative statistics on conditions in Scandinavia and in Britain, the authors were able to mount a persuasive case for disinterested management. The National Free Church Council, while carefully avoiding explicit approval for the book, commended it to the attention of local councils.[85] There was some stout resistance from local veto enthusiasts. When in June 1900 Clifford included praise for the book in an address to the World's Temperance Congress meeting in London there were cries of 'That's rot!'[86] Yet opinion was swinging in favour of municipal control. F. B. Meyer, like Clifford, accepted it as a practical solution, even if ideally he favoured prohibition.[87] T. P. Whittaker, the chief temperance spokesman in the Commons and a Wesleyan, was converted to municipal control in 1903.[88] The hard core of the temperance societies, and especially the United Kingdom Alliance, alone remained unsympathetic. This division in Free Church opinion lasted into the First World War and dealt a fatal blow to Lloyd George's proposal in 1915 to nationalise public houses.[89] The United Kingdom Alliance could not tolerate a larger-scale variant of the Gothenburg system. The absence of unanimity was a severe handicap to temperance pressure in the years before.

Nonconformists therefore tended to respond to temperance proposals made by governments rather than to initiate them. In practice their policy amounted to opposition to Conservative measures and support for those of the Liberals. They agitated against the liquor licensing clauses of the County Councils Bill of 1888 and again against a scheme introduced in 1890 for decreasing the number of licences. In both cases, the Conservative government intended to compensate publicans when licences were abolished and Nonconformists generally backed the argument of the temperance societies that this would create property rights where none existed. Why should those who encouraged drinking be given public money? Both schemes were dropped in the face of impassioned opposition in the Commons orchestrated by W. S. Caine, who put his temperance loyalties before his position as Liberal Unionist Chief Whip.[90] There was an even greater volume of opposition among Nonconformists to the Conservative Licensing Bill of 1904. Protesters had now come to accept that there must be some compensation for non-renewed licences, but they objected to the generosity of the Bill's terms. Denominational bodies resolved, Free Church councils petitioned and there were mass rallies in the Albert Hall and Hyde Park. F. B. Meyer denounced 'this pro-Beer government'.[91] This time, however, government strength in the Commons allowed the Bill to pass into law. On the other hand, there were many Nonconformist demonstrations in favour of the abortive Liberal legislation of the 1890s, the Local Veto Bill of 1893 (proposing local powers to abolish licences) and the Local Option Bill of 1895 (proposing local powers to decrease the number of licences).[92] Wesleyan enthusiasm in 1895 was specially striking for a supposedly non-political denomination: in the regional synods in May, only six hands were raised, two in Leeds and four in Lincoln, against support for the Bill; and although the Wesleyan president was a Conservative, he was prepared to join the other connexional presidents in calling on all Methodists to rally behind the measure.[93] Attempts at temperance legislation were among the Liberal measures most unanimously endorsed in Nonconformity.

Support for Liberal temperance measures, however, was not confined to Nonconformity. The Church of England Temperance Society took an almost identical line. Since 1883 representatives of the various temperance societies including that of the Church of England had co-ordinated their policy through the National Temperance Federation, of which Caine was president.[94] Co-operation between Nonconformists and Anglicans became even closer following the loss of the 1895 Bill and the display of popular hostility to temperance reform at the ensuing polls. Representatives of all the churches met at London House to work out a joint strategy. As John Clifford admitted, the Anglicans were more likely to carry weight with a Unionist government; and it was a suggestion of Frederick Temple, shortly afterwards Archbishop of Canterbury, that was adopted. The conference decided to request a parliamentary commission to examine the various methods of temperance reform.[95] The government was delighted with a plan that allowed it to postpone action on so thorny a question, and so a commission under Viscount Peel was appointed. Its reports, published in 1899, were complex. Eight commissioners recommended a decrease of licences with substantial compensation to publicans; eight others did not disapprove this plan; Peel and seven others ('the minority') recommended only a small degree of compensation; and five of these also asked for local veto. The Minority Report rapidly became a rallying ground for all but a handful of hardline temperance reformers, even though it entailed accepting a measure of compensation.[96] The Free Church discussions of Rowntree and Sherwell's book also took the Peel minority proposals into consideration, and generally approved them. Nonconformists were therefore well prepared for the Liberal Licensing Bill of 1908 that was based on the Minority Report. When this measure came before Parliament Nonconformists demonstrated vigorously on its behalf. Although the education controversy was at its height, almost always the rallies, like those in the Albert Hall and Hyde Park, included Anglican speakers.[97] Once more the Church of England Temperance Society shared the disappointment of defeat when the Lords threw out the Bill. Temperance was still very much a crusading issue, but it was not a matter of Nonconformist fanaticism, as it is often represented. It was an issue on which Nonconformists were prepared to accept practical solutions; and it was the political question on which there was most co-operation between Church and chapel.

In the late 1880s there arose a fresh target for Nonconformist criticism – the beginnings of mass gambling. Previously gambling had existed, but it had been the preserve of the wealthy. For the first time there was sufficient disposable income among the working classes to make betting possible; and the electric telegraph allowed the rapid communication of starting odds. Betting touts roamed the streets looking for clients, and so the new activity was obtrusive.[98] Hugh Price Hughes first preached against it in June 1888.[99] John Clifford declared in 1894 that whereas twenty years before cases of distress in young men were usually due to drink, over the previous six years they were almost wholly due to gambling.[100] A police raid on two gaming clubs in the spring of 1889 drew a denunciation from the *Christian World* of 'the gambling pestilence'.[101] The annual Wesleyan pastoral letter listed gambling as an evil to be attacked later that year for the first time.[102] Nonconformists had no doubt about the wrongness of the practice. Hughes gave two reasons. First, it promotes gain without merit, and so destroys the vital principle of industry and thrift. Secondly, it promotes gain through another's loss, and so is anti-social.[103] But it was chiefly the effects that Nonconformist leaders cited as evidence of the anti-Christian nature of gambling. F. B. Meyer could tell, for instance, of boys who had stolen in order to place their bets or pay their losses at Leicester races. 'Let the Church of Christ', he concluded, 'lead the crusade against this gigantic evil . . . '[104] Hughes needed no encouragement. In his first sermon on the subject he called for the setting up of an anti-gambling society, and shortly afterwards gave active support to the launching of the National Anti-Gambling League.[105] The league was based at York under Rowntree patronage. Its secretary was an Anglican and the cause enjoyed considerable support from the Evangelical wing of the Church of England, but Nonconformists were to the fore in this campaign. They could point to parish churches where a flutter was encouraged for church funds and could cite Church of England papers arguing that racing was innocent and gambling inevitable.[106] By contrast, the chapels now attempted to banish every trace of games of chance, which had previously been accepted without qualms, from their bazaars. Hostility to gambling became an abiding feature of Nonconformity.

Two incidents revealed the depths of this feeling during the 1890s. In June 1891 one of the Prince of Wales's circle brought a court action over cheating at the illegal game of baccarat at Tranby Croft, near Hull, in the previous year. In giving evidence, the prince admitted that he had himself played baccarat for high stakes.[107] He afterwards complained that a torrent of abuse was immediately loosed on him from 'the Low Church and, especially, the Nonconformists'.[108] The first public act of the London Nonconformist Council was to condemn the prince's conduct.[109] W. T. Stead, who had a strong streak of respect for royalty, tried to defend him, only to be denounced by Hughes for shamelessly whitewashing the prince.[110] The Welsh Baptist Association, which happened to meet shortly after the evidence was given, roundly recorded its regret that 'the future King of England is in the habit of playing cards and gambling, and thereby giving his support to immoral habits among the people'.[111] If the heir to the throne was not exempt from censure, the leader of the Liberal Party could hardly hope to avoid it. Nonconformists voiced their reservations about his horse-racing when Lord Rosebery succeeded Gladstone as Prime Minister in March 1894.[112] Only three months later he had the misfortune to win the Derby with his horse Ladas. This time it was the Methodist New Connexion that held its sessions straight afterwards: a special resolution deprecating Rosebery's attitude to the turf was dispatched to him.[113] The *Christian World* argued that he should not allow the glamour of his name to be connected with the betting ring.[114] The Anti-Gambling League organised a demonstration in the Exeter Hall, and its secretary sent a letter of protest to Rosebery. The reply was characteristically deft. 'My position', wrote Rosebery, ' . . . is simply this: like Oliver Cromwell, whose official position was far higher than mine, and the strictness of whose principles can scarcely be questioned, I possess a few racehorses, and am glad when one of them happens to be a good one.'[115] The matter was not allowed to rest, partly because Rosebery won the Derby again the following year. A London rally in December 1897 commissioned R. F. Horton to entreat Rosebery to discountenance the demoralising influences associated with racing. When Rosebery's reply proved unsatisfactory, Hughes and the secretary of the Anti-Gambling League decided to press the London Nonconformist Council to resolve that no Nonconformist should support political leaders connected with the turf. It was rejected because Robert Perks, who was acting as a kind of unofficial political agent for Rosebery, drummed up pro-Roseberyite Liberals to attend. Although

resentment against Rosebery was no longer intense among Nonconformists, it was widely believed that Gladstone's mantle had fallen on
unworthy shoulders. Rosebery was pained by their attitude, feeling, in
particular, that Hughes's critical articles in the *Methodist Times* were
'distinguished neither by accuracy nor by charity'.[116] Even if there had
been no disagreements with Rosebery over questions of policy, their
opposition to his sporting interests distanced Nonconformists from the
Liberal leader.

The example of great men was thought to be so important in this field
because, by and large, it was believed that gambling could best be
combated by influencing public opinion rather than by legislation. Yet it
is symptomatic of the trend in Nonconformist attitudes that there were
calls to limit the freedom of the press in order to handicap would-be
punters. Hughes urged in 1888 that newspaper publication of betting
odds should be prohibited by law and Perks echoed him on more than
one occasion.[117] George Cadbury, the Quaker cocoa manufacturer,
sympathised so strongly with this proposal that when he took over the
Daily News in 1901 he insisted on taking unilateral action. Betting
advertisements and forecasts were excluded, and so was even racing
news. Circulation plummeted and the experiment had to be abandoned.[118] Proposals for legal prohibition of the publication of betting
information, not surprisingly, did not reach Parliament. In 1906,
however, Nonconformists were pleased with a Street Betting Act which
supplemented existing legislation by imposing penalties for betting in
the open air.[119] The problem now was that the police were reluctant to
enforce the law, both because of popular hostility and because of the
risk of incurring the charge of class bias if the amusements of the masses
were suppressed while those of higher classes went unscathed. Free
Church councils therefore sometimes took legal action themselves or
else tried to stir the authorities into action. In 1906, for instance, the
Rochdale Council interviewed the chief constable and employers of the
town with a view to suppressing gambling, and in 1908 the Blackburn
Council began a crusade against the newly emerging practice of betting
at football matches by sending a deputation to the chief constable.[120]
The very greatest could be induced to lend their backing to the anti-
gambling cause. In 1907, while preaching against betting, E. Aldom
French of the Dome Wesleyan Mission, Brighton, was able to read a
message of support from Edward VII.[121] Perhaps the former Prince of
Wales had recognised how strongly Nonconformists felt about gambling.
The cause had certainly come to loom large in the social attitudes of the
Free Churches.

It was rare for industrial questions to become a focus of Nonconformist concern in the way that social purity, temperance and anti-
gambling so frequently did. In 1889, however, the London dock strike
drew their attention to the relations of capital and labour. The dock

workers were employed on a casual labour system that had allowed their exploitation by middlemen and had ensured the perpetuation of very low wages. In August 1889 they went on strike, demanding the abolition of middlemen and an increase in the basic wage-rate from 5d to 6d an hour. The nation was astonished that hitherto unorganised men should strike in tens of thousands and so bring to a halt the centre of Britain's commerce for a whole month. Nonconformists expressed considerable sympathy with the dockers. The *Christian World* judged the dockers' claim to be extremely reasonable, chapels busied themselves in feeding the strikers' families, and many more contributed to relief funds.[122] But the Nonconformist response was relatively slow because in August most London ministers were out of town.[123] On 13 September, as the first public meeting organised by the chapels in favour of the men's claim was coming to an end, the chairman received a telegram announcing the settlement of the strike. Nonconformist dilatoriness provoked unfavourable press comment and Hughes conceded that they had been caught napping.[124] Furthermore, Nonconformists failed to go beyond sympathy to identification with the workers' cause. The one exception was J. C. Carlile, a young Baptist minister who addressed the south London mass meeting of dockers every day and had a place on the strike committee. Carlile, however, was asked to withdraw from the committee by the secretary of the Baptist Union on the ground that he was compromising his brother ministers. The church, it was felt, should not take sides.[125] Again, when the Congregationalists' central building, the Memorial Hall, was used for a discussion by Nonconformist ministers and office-bearers of what more could be done during the strike, there were protests that the premises should have been employed for such a purpose.[126] Joseph Parker made some well-publicised comments critical of the strikers. The consequence was that Ben Tillett, one of the strike leaders, declared that Nonconformists had been conspicuous by their lukewarmness and dictatorial manner.[127] Cardinal Manning, by contrast, so exerted himself that he was chiefly responsible for the eventual agreement that the men's terms should come into force from November. It was clearly possible for church leaders to show their solidarity with the workers and to achieve a settlement at the same time. Nonconformists felt upstaged. For all their professions of concern for social conditions in the wake of *The Bitter Cry*, they had paid little attention to industrial relations. The dock strike added a fresh dimension of guilt to Nonconformist social idealism.

The effect was to stimulate a flurry of discussion and activity over the next few years. Before 1889 was over, Andrew Mearns of the London Congregational Union took the initiative in requesting the Lord Mayor to form a conciliation committee over a threatened dispute in the coal trade. Mearns and Hughes, sitting with Cardinal Manning, the Bishop of London and Sir John Lubbock, achieved a settlement, and also managed to avert a strike at the South Metropolitan Gas Company.[128] Guinness Rogers, always wary of advanced movements, deprecated ministers without economic expertise playing any fuller part in trades disputes, but Fleming Williams, who had brought to an end a lock-out in the Northampton shoe factories even before the dock strike, wanted the churches to plunge deeper into industrial questions.[129] The division of opinion in the Congregational Union was papered over by the creation in 1891 of a social questions committee under Albert Spicer, but the committee's recommendations hardly went beyond bland opposition to 'sweated labour'.[130] More daring was R. F. Horton who, in 1891, declared in favour of the miners' demand for legislation limiting work to eight hours a day.[131] During industrial disputes, however, Nonconformists normally confined themselves to expressing sympathy for the starving families of strikers, leaving aside the question at issue between employers and employed.[132] Their only specific proposal was industrial arbitration: Congregationalists urged this as the remedy for a seamen's dispute in May 1893, George White commended a National Board of Arbitration to the Baptist Union in 1895 and in 1897 a resolution urging arbitration during an engineers' strike was preferred by Congregationalists to another that seemed to take the side of the men.[133] Nor did a large interdenominational gathering in the Jerusalem Chamber of Westminster Abbey in November 1893, where Hughes spoke in favour of arbitration, take matters any further. After that conference there was a remarkable lull in Nonconformist attention to the subject.[134] Only specialists sustained their interest: Fleming Williams and his circle; George Cadbury, who paid for an Anti-Sweating Exhibition in 1906 that helped lead to the introduction of the first statutory minimum wages in certain minor industries in 1909; and a number of other businessmen such as T. C. Taylor, a Congregationalist woollen manufacturer at Batley, and W. P. Hartley, the Primitive Methodist jam manufacturer, who both practised and preached profit-sharing as a panacea for industrial relations.[135] Only in 1911, as a result of the national railwaymen's strike, was there a revival of more widespread concern with the question. The *British Weekly*, endorsed by Clifford and others, announced its support for a legally enforced minimum wage.[136] But the proposals that Meyer intended to put before the Free Church Council, had the railway strike continued, reflect the Nonconformist consensus more accurately: there should be prayer for a pacific spirit, appeals for arbitration and help for the women and children affected.[137] Rank-and-file attitudes to industrial relations had not changed over the intervening years. Nonconformist opinion was simply in favour of reconciliation.

The problem of unemployment gave rise to some similarly common-place responses among Nonconformists, but also to some more imaginative proposals. Hughes's favourite solution was that well-to-do

Christians should take a personal interest in 'honest, sober, and industrious families in the East End' when the breadwinner was out of work.[138] His implied view that many of the unemployed did not merit help, a belief zealously propagated in these years by the Charity Organisation Society, was widely held. William Cuff, noted for his work among the poor as minister of Shoreditch Baptist Tabernacle, insisted on distinguishing the worthy from the unworthy,[139] and T. C. Taylor, the Congregationalist advocate of profit-sharing, contended that it was wrong to support the idle.[140] It was also generally felt that liberty might be threatened if the state tried to deal with unemployment. A. C. Hill, a minister at Harrogate, assured the Congregational Union autumn assembly in 1906 that if they conceded the right of anyone to have work found for him by the state, they would be on the slippery slope to Plato's Republic with state selection of wives.[141] By far the most popular solution to the question was one which avoided both indiscriminate charity and direct state involvement. It was the idea of resettling the surplus population of the cities in the countryside. 'Back to the Land!' was a common cry – and was even the title of a book published in 1893 by an active Free Churchman.[142] In 1906 George White told the Baptists and Fleming Williams told the Congregationalists that the land question was at the root of unemployment, and in each case others concurred.[143] It was an attractive idea, for if people were transferred to the wide open spaces, urban overcrowding and artificially low wage rates caused by too large a labour pool in the cities would both be remedied along with unemployment. Furthermore, rural population seemed to need a boost. The depression of arable farming was forcing families off the land and leading to a decay of village life. Nonconformists had a special reason for wanting to reverse this process, since it was drastically weakening the chapels, especially in their East Anglian heartland. They were therefore particularly drawn to the notion of rural resettlement as an antidote to the problem of urban unemployment.

One of the most untiring advocates of this approach was J. B. Paton, principal of the Congregational Training Institute at Nottingham. In the 1890s his foremost dream was the setting up of rural labour colonies to transform the urban unemployed into an efficient workforce. His model was a series of colonies for the out-of-work begun under the auspices of the German Protestant Church in 1883. A Christian Council of Social Service, of which Paton was the leading spirit, eventually launched a farm colony at Lingfield in Surrey in 1898 and took over another at Starnthwaite in Westmorland two years later.[144] Unlike the German centres, however, those in England enjoyed no state subsidies and so were starved of funds.[145] It also seems to have been difficult to persuade working men to live under what Paton called 'wise and kindly dis-cipline',[146] so that the colonies rapidly became training establishments for the mentally or physically disabled. There is a recognisable affinity between Paton's project and the better-known scheme outlined in the book *In Darkest England and the Way Out* (1890) by General Booth of the Salvation Army. This is no accident, for most of the book was ghost-written for Booth by W. T. Stead, who was well aware of Paton's ideas.[147] The book proposes that the Salvation Army should administer three sets of colonies – in the city, in the countryside and overseas. The poorest 'submerged tenth' of the population would be drawn into the Army's urban relief agencies. They would then be transferred to the farm colony before eventual settlement in the colony overseas. As a result, one farm colony was successfully established at Hadleigh in Suffolk, where stock and poultry farming and market gardening (which were unprofitable) were combined with brick-making from the clay on the site (which turned out to be profitable). Despite chaotic finances, between 200 and 300 men were given work at a time.[148] Even more visionary, and far more momentous in its effects, was another project generated in the same Nonconformist milieu, the idea of a garden city. Its progenitor, Ebenezer Howard, published his plans in 1898 as *Tomorrow: A Peaceful Path to Real Reform*. Howard was influenced by a stay in America but even more by the circle round Fleming Williams, whose church he joined on his return to England. The kernel of his message was that there must be a fusion of the social advantages of the city with the natural advantages of the countryside to create 'garden cities', which would automatically attract the surplus population.[149] He received encouragement from both W. H. Lever, the Congregational soap manufacturer, and George Cadbury, whose planned suburbs at Port Sunlight and Bournville were parallel attempts to deal with the problems of housing industrial workers. Soon a site was found and the first garden city was declared open at Letchworth in 1903.[150] The garden city tradition, with its long-term influence over government new towns policy and town and country planning worldwide, is the greatest single fruit of the schemes of Nonconformists at the turn of the twentieth century for remedying the problems of industrial Britain.

Widespread attention, however, was still reserved for questions connected more directly with the chapel ethic. Among these, sabbath observance often loomed large. Sunday labour was held to be a breach of the fourth commandment, which Nonconformists generally believed to be binding on everyone. Accordingly they took periodic local action against Sunday trading, which was theoretically illegal under an Act of 1677. After fresh legislation in 1871, however, prosecutions were permitted only with the consent of a chief police officer or two magistrates.[151] Nonconformists therefore tended to rely on what Rishton Free Church Council called 'moral persuasion' of shopkeepers.[152] In 1910, for instance, at Leeds, where the authorities turned a blind eye to Sunday trading because of the large Jewish community, the Free Church council issued a manifesto urging Nonconformists not to patronise shops that were open on Sundays.[153] Similarly there were protests against other forms of sabbath desecration: the running of trams, unnecessary work for local authority employees, town hall concerts and band performances in public parks. Sabbatarian feeling seemed to become less intense in the closing years of the nineteenth century, but it revived markedly during the first decade of the twentieth. By 1908 the secretary of the National Free Church Council was putting the maintenance of Sunday observance in the forefront of the council's work.[154] There were three reasons for the increasing attention paid to this question. First, sabbatarianism was drummed up from 1900 by a lay movement in the Church of England organised by Thomas Kingscote, a cousin of the leading Evangelical Churchman in the Commons, Sir John Kennaway. This body secured the patronage of the Archbishop of Canterbury for the first of a series of interdenominational rallies in 1906; the rallies led on to the issuing of manifestos; and eventually, in 1909, an Imperial Sunday Alliance was set up to sustain concern for this subject in all the churches.[155] Secondly, the decline in Free Church membership after 1906 induced Nonconformists, in particular, to claim Sunday as a day that should be set aside for worship. This, for example, was the main theme of Charles Brown's presidential address to the National Free Church Council in 1911.[156] But the third reason is perhaps the most important. In the early twentieth century organised popular recreations were beginning to spill over from Saturday into Sunday. Thus in 1908 both Winchester and Southampton Free Church Councils urged their town councils to prevent Sunday sports.[157] The greatest worry from 1910 was the growth of Sunday 'cinematograph entertainments', especially in London. Many Nonconformists wanted an end of licences for the showing of Sunday films, but when in 1912 the London County Council declined to impose a total ban, Meyer could only urge local Free Church councils to request that performances should not be permitted until after church service hours and that all films should be 'educative and ennobling'.[158] Sunday cinema was to remain. Nonconformist attempts to protect the peace of Sunday were less successful than some of their other campaigns against 'social evils'.

Sunday observance was typical of the questions that attracted mass support from Nonconformists in that it appealed to their Evangelical conscience. They could define certain behaviour as wrong in the light of biblical criteria. Sunday work, along with sexual immorality, drunkenness and (slightly more ambiguously) gambling, seemed to be outright sins. It was in these fields that it was possible to mount large-scale agitations. For a brief period in 1883–4 housing reform aroused a similar passion, primarily because Stead deliberately linked housing with incest; and likewise in 1889 there was for a while a widespread feeling that wrongs were to be discovered in the lot of the poorly paid. Thereafter, however, questions of housing, industrial relations and unemployment became the concern of a small number of Nonconformists who specialised in proposing remedies in those areas. These were complex subjects demanding an expertise that could hardly be expected of ordinary chapel-goers. Nothing intrinsically sinful was there to simplify the issues involved for the rank and file of the Free Churches. An awareness that the churches had a responsibility in the more technical economic problems survived, but such subjects were relegated to specialist study groups. This was the approach commended in the years immediately before the First World War by A. E. Garvie, principal of the Congregational New College, who was to dominate Nonconformist social thought in the 1920s.[159] The National Free Church Council began sponsoring conferences on social questions from 1908, the Wesleyan Methodist Union for Social Service held a major conference at Oxford in 1910 and the Congregational Union Social Service Committee, revived in 1910, recommended close study of social problems.[160] Nonconformists, with Garvie at their head, were to contribute to the inter-church discussions of social order that culminated in the Birmingham Conference on Christian Politics, Economics and Citizenship (COPEC) in 1924.[161] But this newer intellectual approach was entirely different from the crusading temper embodied in Hugh Price Hughes. The Anti-Contagious Diseases Acts movement had ushered in a period when Nonconformists were prepared to throw themselves without careful thought into struggles against evils in the world around them.

This phase had a profoundly important effect in transforming Nonconformist attitudes to public affairs in general. Their assumption that social problems enshrined wrongs gave them a strong sense of the urgency of their task. What was wrong should not be tolerated a day longer than necessary. It followed that the aid of the law must be invoked, because only the law had the power to deal with problems sufficiently quickly. This explains why Nonconformist policies on social questions so often seem repressive. They did not abandon voluntary efforts, but they were increasingly prepared to call on the state and local authorities to close brothels, to limit liquor licences, to prohibit the publication of betting odds, and so on. H. J. Wilson of Sheffield told his Holmfirth constituents in 1886 that there were two sides to the temperance question, 'one of personal abstinence and persuasion, the other of political, national and legislative work . . . He belonged to both sides'.[162] Wilson was typical of the Nonconformists of his day. This was to embrace a new estimate of the capacity of the state to do good. The traditional inhibitions of Gladstonian Liberals were steadily overcome as Nonconformists were increasingly prepared to demand legislation whenever their eyes were opened to a fresh social problem. Hughes was probably as advanced in his view of the competence of the state as any. Private charity, he argued in 1889, is unable to cope with the growing poverty of London. Hence 'it is both legitimate and necessary for the

State to use all the resources of civilization to abolish Pauperism'.[163] The belief that the state should work for the good of the people meant that Nonconformists, with few exceptions, welcomed the Liberal social policy reforms of the period 1906–11 which laid the foundation of the welfare state. Nonconformity played a large part in creating a ground swell of support for the 'New Liberalism', the Liberalism that saw the state as the potential creator of a better society. Nonconformists had normally been wary of state power, which had been used so often against them. Now that their liberties were assured, however, the role of the state could be extended. Under the influence of their leaders, especially Hughes and Clifford, they were beginning to see state intervention as an opportunity rather than as a threat. An Evangelical conscience unrestrained by caution generated their strident demands for legislation and the enforcement of the law. They were able to make their demands effective through the Free Church councils that sprang up in these years.

4 *The Free Church Council Movement*

By means of these councils and federations they would emphasize the necessity of our national life being dominated by the ethics of Christ. (Hugh Price Hughes to the Free Church Congress, March 1895)[1]

The most important institutional development in Nonconformity in the half-century before the First World War was the growth of the Free Church council movement. All over the country during the 1890s there sprang up local Free Church councils. Each consisted of representatives of chapels of the various denominations in a town or village. Their work was the planning of joint activities, whether evangelistic missions or temperance demonstrations, lectures on Nonconformist principles or school board election campaigns. They were normally grouped together in federations that covered whole counties. Each March delegates from the local councils assembled in a major city for a congress which rapidly became the chief mouthpiece of Nonconformity. During the rest of the year the national organisation was a council of some sixty prominent Nonconformists, the National Council of the Evangelical Free Churches. It, too, could claim to represent the whole chapel-going community of the nation, although its claim was frequently contested. From its origins many of its members aspired to make the organisation a decisive influence in public affairs. The Free Church council movement, according to the *Christian World* in 1895, would render Nonconformity 'a force which no power or party in the State can defy with impunity'.[2] The movement was not primarily a political one, but it early took on a political edge. As the American political scientist A. L. Lowell noted in 1908, the Free Church Federation had brought new power to Nonconformity because it had replaced 'individuals stirred by a common impulse' with 'an organized host'.[3] The National Free Church Council was one of the most significant pressure groups of Edwardian England. It became the chief vehicle of the Nonconformist conscience.

Organised Nonconformist co-operation was primarily an outgrowth of the increased engagement with social questions that marked the 1880s. J. B. Paton, inspired by church projects he had seen on visits to

Germany, had set up as early as 1873 a council representing the various churches and charities of Nottingham to co-ordinate social work.[4] In the later 1880s he was busy behind the scenes in trying to persuade other towns to follow the example of Nottingham. He strongly believed that Christians should demonstrate their essential unity through social work without doctrinal compromise. Paton had a close disciple in Percy Bunting, the chairman of the National Vigilance Association. Bunting was at the heart of the Wesleyan Forward Movement that under Hugh Price Hughes's leadership was dedicated to the new social interests of the day, but his temperament was entirely different from that of Hughes. He was restrained, precise and judicious, and so able to exert a quiet influence over a wide circle.[5] Paton found in him a kindred spirit and installed him as editor of the *Contemporary Review*, which Paton had taken over in order to prevent its policy from drifting into agnosticism.[6] As editor of the *Contemporary*, Bunting enjoyed a wide range of contacts and in the late 1880s he was seconding Paton's attempts to urge the churches to combine for the sake of promoting the welfare of the people. He was probably responsible for persuading Guinness Rogers that the 'welding of the Free Churches into a great friendly federation' was a highly desirable aim.[7] In 1890 Rogers was invited by Hughes to suggest in the *Methodist Times* that there should be a national congress for all Nonconformists, an equivalent of the existing Church Congress of the Established Church. Hughes gathered letters of approval from other Nonconformist leaders and a movement seemed well under way.[8] It proved, however, to be a false start. Guinness Rogers had infused too much antagonism to the Church of England into his proposal for it to be well received in some quarters. The congress seemed likely to become an organ of the Liberation Society, a possibility dreaded by Paton as well as by many Wesleyans. These fears that the congress would be used 'as a basis for political purposes'[9] rather than as a stimulus to social work brought the whole idea of a national organisation to a halt.

Meanwhile, however, there were parallel moves towards co-operation on a local basis. At the end of the 1889 dock strike, Hughes called for the creation of a permanent social committee of the London Free Churches to ensure swift action in any future crisis. Clifford and others agreed, but there were Congregational hesitations and the Wesleyans went ahead alone.[10] The monthly meeting of London Wesleyan ministers agreed to admit laymen with a view to the discussion of social questions. By the end of 1890 a London Methodist Council was in existence, and even being imitated – at Manchester and Hull, for instance.[11] The idea of broader co-operation nevertheless remained attractive. It was raised again at the 1891 annual meeting of the General Body of the Three Denominations, an organisation for London ministers dating back to the early eighteenth century that by this period was usually inert. One of the Congregational members, John Matthews, prompted the secretary to summon a meeting to discuss the formation of an interdenominational council that should watch over the condition of the capital.[12] The new body, the London Nonconformist Council, duly came into being in June 1891, with Matthews as one of the secretaries.[13] Unlike the General Body, which included only Congregationalists, Baptists and Presbyterians, the council was open to Methodists. A circular to all Free Church ministers in England issued in the previous month had urged similar or even greater breadth. Signed by Hughes, Clifford, Paton and others, it recommended 'a Union of Evangelical Churches in each town or district for their mutual aid and encouragement, for the guidance of united counsel, and for the co-operation and power of united action in their social ministries of redeeming love'.[14] The same message was being regularly preached by W. T. Stead, now editor of the *Review of Reviews*. In the wake of the publication of *In Darkest England* in 1890, Stead stumped the country to promote his idea of a 'Civic Church', a non-credal organisation of workers fired by the enthusiasm of humanity.[15] At Rochdale in 1892, for instance, the churches formed a Social Questions Union in response to Stead's call, and soon set about demanding the closure of insanitary cellar dwellings and opposing the renewal of liquor licences.[16] Stead's propaganda helped to popularise the trend towards forming local inter-church councils on social questions.

A second impulse, associated with the first but separable, contributed to the origins of the Free Church council movement. This was the emergence of a desire for church reunion. The difference between Congregationalists and Baptists, in particular, seemed to an increasing number in the 1880s to be too small a thing to warrant institutional separation. The expense of maintaining rival buildings and ministers in places with scanty population was a sharp spur to convergence. A joint session of the assemblies of the Congregational and Baptist Unions in May 1886 heard with enthusiasm a paper deprecating denominational competition, and resolved that there should be a conference on overlapping church provision.[17] Although this initiative came to nothing, 'practical union' was in the air. In a similar way Hughes and Bunting were advocating reunion between the splintered branches of Methodism. As a result of a conversation with Bunting, Henry Lunn, the founder of the travel firm but before that an aide of Hughes's, set up in 1891 a periodical dedicated to promoting inter-church understanding, the *Review of the Churches*. In the following year Lunn master-minded the first of a series of summer conferences between denominational leaders at Grindelwald in the Swiss Alps.[18] The first four presidents of the National Free Church Council were all at the 1892 Grindelwald conference. But the most single-minded advocate of moving towards reunion was Dr Alexander Mackennal, who was to be the first secretary of the National Free Church Council. Mackennal, the cultured minister of Bowdon Downs Congregational Church, Manchester, had treasured the ideal of the unity of the church ever since being impressed, on his marriage tour in 1867, by a friar preaching in Milan Cathedral on 'The Barque of Peter'. He saw to it that reunion was prominent on the agenda of the first International Congregational Council that met in July 1891.[19] Many Congregationalists were persuaded that church unity was a desirable goal. The result was a resolution at the Congregational Union autumn meetings that year appointing a committee to explore again the possibility of a Free Church Congress.[20] These first stirrings of the ecumenical movement were behind the revival of the proposal for a national Nonconformist gathering.

The new initiative began with a meeting of Free Church leaders at the home of Percy Bunting. There were some fears, especially in the mind of R. W. Dale, that the proposed congress would have too large a scope. Dale seems to have believed that Mackennal's idea of discussing questions of church order would turn out to be fruitless. There was general agreement, however, that it would be useful to consider the possibilities of co-operation in meeting the religious and social problems of town and country.[21] Accordingly, Mackennal was commissioned to make plans, a preliminary public meeting was held at Manchester in January 1892 and the first Free Church Congress assembled in the same city in November. It was open to any Evangelical Nonconformist who wished to attend. Although the separate Congregational Union scheme for summoning a congress had been dropped, the impetus given to the idea of Free Church co-operation by the International Congregational Council was reflected in attendance figures. Three hundred and twenty-five of the 370 attenders gave their denomination. Of these, as many as 145 were Congregationalists, while there were 53 Wesleyans, 34 Free Methodists, 31 Primitives, 30 Baptists and smaller numbers from the lesser denominations.[22] The tone was set by Mackennal. Their object, he wrote in advance, was 'to present an idea of the Church of Christ held in common by the Evangelical communities . . . They will be in no hurry to formulate plans for corporate union, but their faces are turned that way . . . '[23] The topics discussed on the first day were the church, the ministry, the sacraments and fellowship. Bunting's influence helped to ensure that moral questions had their fair share of time. He declared that they must give a great commission to the Nonconformist MPs returned at the recent election to exert an influence for good on the nation. Hughes harangued the congress on the aims of the temperance party, denounced gambling and 'thoroughly aroused the enthusiasm of the Congress' by stating the principle that no notoriously immoral man should sit in the Commons. Some attention was also given to peace, arbitration and industrial relations.[24] Nonconformists were substantially at one in their desire for ecclesiastical *rapprochement* and engagement with social questions. In the two areas of concern that gave rise to the congress, discussion revealed a large measure of agreement.

A sharp difference of opinion, however, emerged over disestablishment. Wesleyans like Bunting and Hughes were personally sympathetic to disestablishment, but they knew that the more traditional Wesleyans would never risk contamination by so partisan a political issue. The 1890 initiative had been wrecked on this very rock. Bunting therefore persuaded the January planning meeting that although they would have to take into account the existence of clerical antagonism to Nonconformity, disestablishment itself should not appear on the congress programme.[25] From the time when this decision was announced, however, Robertson Nicoll kept up a running protest in the *British Weekly*;[26] and J. H. Hollowell, a Congregational minister at Rochdale who was a religious equality zealot, gave advance notice of a congress motion that sacramentarianism in the Church of England made disestablishment desirable.[27] Hollowell's motion was relegated to a reference committee, which held a stormy two-hour session on the second day of the congress. Hughes, claiming to represent Methodism, insisted that the resolution should not be put. A large majority of the reference committee was concluding that disestablishment was too hot a potato for them to touch when an obscure Manchester Primitive Methodist layman, William Windsor, objected.[28] 'As the son of a village Methodist who was boycotted in his business for his fidelity to Methodism', Windsor wrote afterwards, ' . . . I felt indignant at Mr Hughes' speech.'[29] Why should Hughes speak for Methodism as a whole? Windsor refused to let disestablishment be dropped. Eventually a subcommittee produced a compromise resolution that was carried with only two dissentients. Congress urged 'all such efforts after absolute religious equality before the law as shall commend themselves to the judgement of their several communities'.[30] Guinness Rogers was satisfied with the outcome, but the London Nonconformist Council rejected a proposal to send the congress a congratulatory telegram on the ground that its attitude to disestablishment was too weak.[31] The subject of religious equality was to remain a serious handicap to the Free Church council movement. Wesleyans thought the movement veered too close to Liberal politics by considering the issue at all, and so many stayed aloof. Others believed that so serious a matter of Nonconformist principle should not be scouted. A division with political overtones marked the movement from its beginnings.

The threefold mixture at the congress of strictly religious subjects, social concern and (with more reservations) the religious equality question was also to be seen in the local Free Church councils that were emerging in these years. A few were designed to deal with all three subjects, but most originally concentrated their efforts in one field. The impulse towards taking up social questions was usually behind the creation of councils during the early 1890s. At a meeting designed to launch united Free Church work at Ashton-under-Lyne in 1891, for instance, a local speaker said 'he thought they were living in the midst of a great and widespread religious revival which took the form of a profound conviction that the Christian Church did not sufficiently sympathise with the vast masses of the people'.[32] Temperance work was commonly in the forefront of council activities. 'The Brewster Sessions', reported the *Christian World* in September 1898, 'are giving the Councils a splendid opportunity of proving their strength.'[33] It could list thirteen that were trying to decrease the number of licences in their areas. The councils often promoted temperance demonstrations and passed resolutions about temperance legislation. Sunday observance, gambling and social purity were staple areas of concern, and a wide range of other activities could fall within their province. Wrexham Council employed trained nurses to visit the sick; Rotherham Council protested against an 'incursion of pugilism'; the Council for the Eastern Valleys of Monmouthshire launched a crusade against rabbit coursing; and Spalding Council resolved its opposition to archery tournaments, because they allegedly fostered 'the gambling spirit'.[34] Attention to social questions was probably the most popular concern of the councils throughout the 1890s.

A smaller number of Free Church councils existed primarily to promote religious equality. The earliest bodies with a claim to fulfilling the role of Free Church councils seem to have been a group of Nonconformist associations in Hampshire. The first was begun at Southampton in 1877, a second was in existence at Portsmouth by 1885 and a third came into being at Newport on the Isle of Wight by 1891.[35] Together they ran a magazine, the *Christian Citizen*, to promote Free Church principles and in 1891 they organised a series of addresses by Carvell Williams of the Liberation Society.[36] These councils set up, in 1893, the first county federation of Nonconformist councils, with the primary objects of providing lectures on Free Church history, giving advice in cases of oppression and holding services in villages dominated by the state Church.[37] The Hampshire Federation was one of the rural Free Church bodies that organised village meetings to select suitable candidates when parish councils first began in 1894.[38] Mackennal commented that since 'ecclesiastical and social pressure to crush out dissent is more employed in the country than in the large towns, the note of mutual defence is more pronounced'.[39] Free Church councils in the towns normally held lectures on the past disabilities of Nonconformists rather than dealing with current grievances. The Trowbridge Council, for instance, began a series of lectures on the history and principles of Nonconformity with one on 'The testimony and sufferings of Nonconformists in the reign of Queen Elizabeth'.[40] One dimension of religious equality, however, was of pressing importance in both town and countryside: the education question. The immediate object of the Barnsley Council was to secure adequate representation on the school board (together with the board of guardians);[41] branches of the London Nonconformist Council were formed specifically to fight the school board election of 1894;[42] and the Nonconformists of Guernsey united in 1895 to protest against legislation that allowed Anglican religious instruction to be supported out of the rates.[43] In the later 1890s and afterwards Free Church councils were to throw themselves into the education fray. Such activities help explain why the Conservatives expressed the belief in 1896 that the Blackburn Free Church Council was 'only another Radical organisation with a name intended to give the cause an "odour of sanctity"'.[44] Support for religious equality, especially in the schools, rapidly made many councils seem to be political caucuses.

Other councils were distinctly religious in object. The Bristol Free Church Council put evangelism first on its list of priorities,[45] and the Hartlepool Council was founded 'to promote the spiritual life of the churches, by cultivating a closer fellowship and by adopting united evangelistic action'.[46] A major inspiration of the whole movement was the pattern of concerted evangelism first put into practice at Bradford early in 1892. The main feature was the division of a town into 'Free Church parishes', each of which was assigned to a chapel for house-to-house visitation.[47] According to J. R. Bailey, the Halifax Congregational minister who first suggested using parishes as a basis for visitation, the system meant that 'Nonconformist Churches, as a whole, are capable of asserting and justifying their claim to be considered, not National Churches, but a National Church, and to have a message to deliver to, and a work to do for, the nation at large'.[48] The scheme seized the imagination of younger ministers like Silvester Horne[49] and it was soon imitated elsewhere. In particular, it was taken up by the Birmingham Free Churches on the initiative of George Cadbury, who approved both its businesslike approach and the interdenominational co-operation that it entailed. The Birmingham visitation in May 1893 was a well-publicised success, and a Free Church council was formed there in November to carry on the work.[50] The inception of parochial visitation among the Free Churches, according to Hugh Price Hughes, marked a turning-point in modern English Christianity. It proved, he wrote, 'that the great Evangelical and Protestant churches of this country have at last realised their essential unity'.[51] Following the Bradford experiment and the Birmingham confirmation of its success, Free Church councils were commonly started with the co-ordination of visitation evangelism as their chief aim.

The variety of objects is evidence of the spontaneity of what was properly called a movement. In the early years the councils were formed by demand from below, not by direction from above. Mackennal pointed out early in 1895 that up till then there had been virtually no guidance given either by the Free Church Congress or by himself.[52] The idea of creating councils for joint work was popular with the chapels. The movement steadily gained momentum up to 1896. According to the National Council's own figures, there were 4 councils in existence by the end of 1889; 5 began in 1890; 5 in 1891; 21 in 1892; 41 in 1893; 54 in 1894 and up March 1895; 79 in the year up to March 1896; and 175 in the year up to March 1897. After the peak of 1896–7 the number of new councils began to fall. There were 106 in the year 1897–8, and 99 in 1898–9.[53] These figures can give no more than an impression of the growth of the movement, for an individual council might represent any strength between the 154 Free Churches of Birmingham and the 2 chapels in the village of Ringstead, Northamptonshire.[54] Some of the new councils listed, especially in London, were not so much autonomous bodies as branches of a larger council.[55] Others were previously existing organisations transforming themselves into Free Church councils. At Rochdale, for example, the Social Questions Union, formed under Stead's influence in 1892, turned itself into a regular Free Church council four years later.[56] Once again variety was a consequence of spontaneity. By and large the county federations that linked local councils were less vigorous bodies. They were slow to develop and often collapsed through lack of support. By May 1896 only three were operational.[57] Most of the country, however, was swept by the fashion for local councils. Wales, despite its Nonconformist strength, was an exception. There were only nine Welsh Free Church councils by March 1896, primarily because of scruples on the part of Baptists in Wales over joining in interdenominational communion services.[58] The other areas where Free Church councils were slow to take root were rural counties, especially where Nonconformity was weak. By March 1896 there was no Free Church council within the boundaries of only five English counties: Dorset, Rutland, Shropshire, Westmorland and (more surprisingly, in view of Nonconformist strength) Huntingdonshire.[59] The degree of nationwide support for such new and uncoordinated organisations was remarkable.

There was far less impetus behind the national congress. Representatives of Leeds Free Churches invited Mackennal to organise a second congress there in March 1894, but the response to his invitations to attend was so meagre that he contemplated abandoning the enterprise. He believed that it was essential to secure representatives from the various Nonconformist denominations, but he gained no official encouragement for the plan.[60] At a time when prospects seemed gloomy, the position was transformed by George Cadbury. In January 1894 the first meeting of the Birmingham Free Church Council, with Cadbury in the chair, issued an invitation for a congress to be held in the city in 1895.[61] The invitation, according to Mackennal, 'saved the Congress'.[62] He determined to go ahead with the Leeds meetings and realised that he must forget the idea of denominational representation.[63] Instead, as Hughes proposed at Leeds, county federations and large urban councils would be encouraged to send representatives to future congresses to sit alongside the personal members who were still allowed to come on payment of a 5s subscription.[64] This decision was important, for it ensured that the congress became not a colloquy of church leaders but an organ of the popular enthusiasms of the chapels. During the 1895 congress Cadbury took another crucial step. He offered to give not less than a total of £1,000 over the next four years for an organisation fund. Less than a year later he increased his promise to £600 a year for five years, and his brother Richard did the same.[65] The national body now enjoyed financial security. The Cadbury money enabled an organising committee to be established, and the paid secretary of the Birmingham Council, James Rutherford, was seconded to the work as assistant to the organising secretary.[66] For the first time Free Church councils were promoted from above. Towns without councils were approached with the offer of eminent speakers such as Hughes and Mackennal who would address meetings on the value of joint Free Church action.[67] The constitutions of local councils were increasingly formalised, with all ministers ex officio members and churches represented by one layman per 50 or 100 members.[68] New councils set up from the autumn of 1895 began to have a standard list of objects. A permanent link was forged between the national congress and the local councils.

The man put in charge of the new bureaucratic arrangements was Thomas Law, a 40-year-old minister of the United Methodist Free Churches. He was selected as organising secretary of the movement because during a ministry in Bradford he had been responsible for the parochial visitation there.[69] For about a year he served in a part-time capacity while continuing an ordinary ministry in Birmingham, but from the spring of 1896 he was installed in London at the Memorial Hall as full-time secretary.[70] 'He was a man of medium height', J. C. Carlile recalled, 'of strong frame, and clear vision, genial and self-possessed, with boundless confidence in the new enterprise and its secretary.'[71] He believed in magnifying his office and soon came to exude an air of self-consequence and pomposity.[72] He had few intellectual claims and indeed had the reputation of possessing no hobbies.[73] He lived for the Free Church Council, so that the personality was eclipsed by the job, and people found it difficult to penetrate to the real man. Law's organising genius, however, was undoubted. He brought business techniques to his task and to many seemed too calculating for the agent of a religious body. According to Joseph Compton Rickett, later treasurer of the Free Church Council, Law 'could engineer an enthusiasm which I do not think he always shared, though appreciating its practical effect'.[74] He was, in fact, a backstairs politician of enormous potential. Yet he was a man of sincere Evangelical conviction. Spurgeon was said to have been a seat-holder at one of his early churches.[75] Law always insisted that the Free Church council movement was spiritual in purpose. 'It is a mighty Evangelical revival', he wrote, 'an organised effort, guided by the Great Divine Spirit, to lay hold on the vast masses of people who are outside all religious communities.'[76] Unlike Mackennal, to whom he remained technically responsible until 1898, Law was not aiming for organic reunion.[77] He was content that the chapels should co-operate through his organisation as it stood. He was also happy that the variety that had marked the early years of the movement should continue. This was partly because for two or three years after his appointment he had no choice. As he put it in 1897, the leaders were 'not so much leading the movement as the movement is leading us'.[78] But in later years when he enjoyed greater powers of initiative Law made no obvious effort to direct the councils towards a particular goal or away from others. As might be expected of a man of his temperament, he was not averse to politics. His regular argument was that the more political activities of the organisation were permissible so long as spiritual concerns bulked larger. Law's overriding aim was that the movement should succeed in whatever it took up.

The movement gained not only an organiser but an ideology. In the new, more concerted phase of the life of the Free Church councils that began in 1895, they became the bearer of a new message. The speakers who advocated Free Church co-operation needed to offer some theological justification for it. They presented the idea of 'Free Churchmanship', the substance of the ecclesiastical convictions shared by all Nonconformists. Its originator was Charles Berry, the Congregational minister of Queen Street, Wolverhampton, who had leapt to fame when in 1887 at the age of only 34 he was invited to succeed the eminent American preacher Henry Ward Beecher in Brooklyn.[79] Berry was a man of charm, a great raconteur with a gift for friendship.[80] He had imbibed a high doctrine of the church from Dale and at the Grindelwald discussion in 1893 had been stung by Anglo-Catholic claims into asserting a place for Congregationalism in 'the great Catholic Church'.[81] Hughes, whose complex character included a strong strand of ecclesiasticism, warmed to Berry's words as he heard them. The two men struck up a close accord and from the winter of 1895–6 began to argue that Nonconformists represented a 'scriptural Catholicism', as opposed to the less pure Roman and Anglican versions.[82] 'They had always been Churchmen', Berry told the 1896 congress, 'they were High Churchmen, they were the only High Churchmen in England to-day. So high were they that they would not allow Pope or monarch to take the place of Christ.'[83] They were Free Churchmen, with their own positive principles, rather than Nonconformists, those who did not conform to the Church of England. This propaganda had an immediate appeal. On the one hand, it asked Nonconformists to surrender nothing. As the *Home Counties Baptist Association Report* for 1896 put it, the movement 'substitutes *inter*-denominationalism for *un*-denominationalism, and therefore offers all the advantages of Christian brotherhood *without any sacrifice or suppression* of distinctive principles' (italics in original).[84] Baptists and Congregationalists, Methodists and Presbyterians, were already one in their common Free Churchmanship. On the other hand, the new message buttressed Nonconformist self-esteem. The Nonconformist mayor of Nottingham assured a meeting during the 1896 congress that he did not believe in the term 'Nonconformist': 'He much preferred the term Free Churchman. He believed in those who would build, erect, construct, not those who would dissent, criticise, pull down, destroy . . . He should, for his own part, be very glad when the time came when Nonconformists and Dissenters would be no more, but when Free Churchmen, as they ought to be, were recognised as such.'[85] There was clearly an attraction for the lay mind. Many Nonconformists left Berry's meetings, according to his biographer, holding their heads higher.[86] They no longer felt stamped with ecclesiastical inferiority. The notion that they were Free Churchmen appealed to their desire for social standing. Existing 'Nonconformist councils' hastened to turn themselves into 'Free Church councils'. 'Free Churchmanship' helped consolidate the movement in the later 1890s as the initial populist impetus was beginning to wane.

The new ecclesiastical claims set a limit on the extent of Nonconformist co-operation. In the early days of the councils, representatives of the Salvation Army, Plymouth Brethren, Unitarians and Swedenborgians were all on occasion admitted without demur.[87] After the exposition of Free Churchmanship and the regimentation of the councils by Law such borderline groups began to be discarded on the ground that they could not be recognised either as sufficiently churchly or as sufficiently orthodox. The first principle dictated the exclusion of the Salvation Army,[88] which disclaimed at this period being either a church or a part of any, and of the Plymouth Brethren. Perhaps surprisingly, Quaker membership of the councils was never questioned, despite their rejection of sacraments. Cadbury's support for the movement is no doubt a primary explanation. The second principle entailed the severance of ties with the Swedenborgians[89] and the Unitarians, since neither group accepted a Trinitarian theology. The breach with the Unitarians was specially important for after their divergence from Evangelicalism, the orthodox had normally maintained traditional co-operation with them in social and political activity. There had sometimes been co-operation even in the religious field: Unitarians had participated in the Bradford visitation scheme.[90] There were Unitarian protests when they were not invited to the original Free Church Congress, but Mackennal knew that many of the orthodox, and especially the Wesleyans, would refuse to have anything to do with them.[91] The Birmingham Free Church Council similarly excluded Unitarians from the beginning because, as Cadbury explained, they denied the doctrine of the atonement that effectively united the other participants.[92] Hughes, who was said to loathe Unitarians,[93] insisted in 1895 that no council could include them. Co-operation was possible in social and ethical work, he wrote, but 'the primary object of the Evangelical Councils and the Free Church Congress is neither social nor ethical, but spiritual and religious; and the divinity of our Lord is an essential feature of our spiritual and religious life'.[94] Law reported in 1897 that most of the councils had adopted the exclusion policy of the National Council.[95] All but a few simply added the word 'Evangelical' to the title of the council to advertise that Unitarians need not apply for membership. By the beginning of the new century, the movement consisted solely of the mainstream Evangelical Free Churches.

The sharpest debates in the movement took place over its political role. There were particularly strong fears about its tendencies in Birmingham, where Nonconformists were probably more divided than anywhere else between Liberalism and Unionism. R. W. Dale, himself a Unionist, recognised that the Free Church councils were likely to adopt a partisan stance and so disrupt the life of the chapels. He refused to have anything to do with the movement.[96] George Cadbury made his support for the Birmingham Free Church Council conditional on its avoidance of political questions and tried to press a similar policy on the National Council.[97] He looked askance on Law's move to London, away from his own immediate sphere of influence, and so stipulated that only £400 of the £1,200 contributed by his brother and himself should be used for the general purposes of the London office. The remainder was to be spent on particular purposes he approved.[98] His worries were justified, because the London leadership had settled on an entirely different policy. At a gathering in the home of Robert Perks in May 1895 the relation of the movement to politics was thoroughly thrashed out. Monro Gibson, minister of St John's Wood Presbyterian Church, urged that they should dissociate themselves from politics. Gibson, who was to follow Hughes as president of the National Council in 1896 and Mackennal as its secretary in 1898, was a Unionist, though an unobtrusive one. They were not agreed on politics, he pointed out, and the Presbyterian Church could not join in a political movement. John Clifford, who had entered during Gibson's speech, rose dramatically to declare that their commitment to righteousness must lead them into politics. Percy Bunting agreed. 'The reason why the Tories win London elections', he opined, 'is because there are not enough converted people about . . . '[99] Monro Gibson was driven to explain that he objected not to politics, but to party politics; but if one party happened to take up a righteous cause, like temperance, they must support it. That was to concede the whole case. Two months later, Gibson warned the new Willesden Free Church Council not to become a kind of Liberation Society, but he admitted that disestablishment must be faced if it arose again.[100] Despite Gibson's reservations, he was unable to place an absolute bar on any subject that was likely to be taken up by the Free Church councils. The London leadership was deciding that political involvement was legitimate and necessary; and it was the London leaders rather than Cadbury who set the tone of the whole movement.

Accordingly, the Free Church councils rapidly evolved into the chief political arm of Nonconformity. Whenever a political issue seized the imagination of Nonconformists in the later 1890s the councils voiced their sentiments. The feeling was genuine, but its expression was encouraged and co-ordinated from the centre. The National Council of the Evangelical Free Churches was finally constituted as a standing organisation at the 1896 congress. Immediately afterwards there took place the first concerted outburst of Nonconformist indignation. The target was a government Education Bill. The National Council issued a manifesto against the measure, called on local councils to hold public meetings and exhorted them to write to their MPs.[101] There was a widespread response. The pattern was to be repeated frequently as Nonconformists protested against aspects of Conservative policy. In particular, there was immense resentment at the failure of the government to protect the Christian subjects of the Turkish Empire from outrage; and Free Church interests seemed to be directly challenged by measures (like the Bill of 1896) designed to help the schools of the Church of England. These two subjects of foreign policy and education will be examined in Chapters 6 and 7, but the lengths to which partisanship could run is illustrated by an incident in another field. In 1898, John Matthews, secretary of the Metropolitan Council of Evangelical Free Churches (as the London Nonconformist Council had become), issued a manifesto on its behalf urging votes for the Progressives on the London County Council. Matthews's organisation had endorsed the Progressives' policies of social reform in 1892 and 1895, but this time the manifesto commended the Progressives on the ground that they wanted self-government for London as a whole to replace the existing subdivision of the city into ten or twenty boroughs.[102] Cadbury deplored taking sides on such an issue. 'It is just one of those questions', he told the Birmingham Free Church Council, 'whereon the members of our different churches are quite entitled to hold different opinions, and therefore should not be committed by such a manifesto to either silence or withdrawal from the council.'[103] Joseph Parker condemned the manifesto, Marylebone Free Church Council disavowed it, and Perks informed the press that, though treasurer of the Metropolitan Council, he knew nothing of the manifesto before its publication.[104] Matthews tendered his resignation.[105] He had become too accustomed to endorsing the proposals of one side in London politics. Partisanship had become second nature.

Yet there were internal limits on the freedom of the councils to express political opinions. One was the existence within them of a number of Unionists like Monro Gibson. What they could achieve is shown by the response of the 1897 meetings of the National Council to the Cretan crisis. Nonconformist feeling against the British government's leniency towards Turkish repression was high. Hughes wanted a strong resolution condemning government inaction on what he classified as a moral issue. Others on the committee of the National Council, however, believed that this would amount to party politics. They were probably led by J. Oswald Dykes, principal of the Presbyterian Westminster College, Cambridge – a Unionist. Dykes eventually seconded a mild compromise resolution desiring that God would guide statesmen to secure the safety of Cretan and other Christian populations without further bloodshed.[106] Hughes had evidently capitulated. 'We must never split on a political rock', he declared in proposing the resolution. 'That is our great peril in the future. Let us have unanimity or silence on public questions. We can never forget that our first object is to promote the interests of the Church of God.'[107] Unionists could exploit the general desire for unanimity in order to avoid a partisan stand. The other check on political outbursts came from the Wesleyans. The loyalty of Wesleyans to the Free Church councils was at best doubtful. Only the section that looked on Hughes as its leader gave wholehearted support. Others were suspicious of an organisation that seemed to engage in many activities besides saving souls. Hughes hailed the fact that Charles Berry died in 1899 while speaking in a Wesleyan chapel as a symbol of Free Church unity, but a council secretary suggested that many Free Church council functions were held on Wesleyan premises purely to ensure the presence of the Wesleyan minister.[108] Whenever the councils touched on questions of religious equality there was a risk of Wesleyan secessions. At Crewe in 1900, for instance, the Wesleyans wished to avoid discussion of the education issue, and withdrew from the council when the other representatives insisted on proceeding.[109] The effect of the Wesleyan attitude was to make Free Church councils wary of outright commitment to the principle of religious equality. Under pressure from the *British Weekly*, Mackennal included a Welsh disestablishment resolution on the programme of the 1895 congress,[110] but the Liberation Society was right to be worried by the weakness of the movement's attachment to the cause.[111] 'Some Free Church Councils regarded it as their duty to promote Free Church principles', Carvell Williams told the Liberation Society in 1901, 'but others held that their action should be strictly religious and regarded promotion of disestablishment as political or semi-political . . .'[112] This was largely the doing of the Wesleyans. There were definite restrictions on the political scope of the Free Church councils.

This was why, in 1898, there was an attempt to create a parallel organisation without inhibitions over partisanship or disestablishment, the Nonconformist Political Council. The idea was that Nonconformist MPs should band together to secure total religious equality. They would be supported by a council of representative ministers and laymen and by a network of local branches so that the whole of Nonconformity would be welded into a compact political machine.[113] Lloyd George, who became vice-president, took the original initiative. He had determined to end the 'Anglican regime in the Liberal party', he told his wife, for 'Dissenters have too long been the doormats'.[114] Perks, the pushing Wesleyan MP, took up the suggestion, laid the plans and became president of the new body. During his campaign in favour of the Nonconformist Marriages Bill, Perks had become aware that the religious equality parliamentary committee of the Liberation Society was severely handicapped by its lack of contacts in the country.[115] The new organisation, he hoped, would formulate Nonconformist claims which local groups could press on candidates before another general election. Hirst Hollowell, the extreme disestablisher at the 1892 Free Church Congress, was appointed secretary, John Clifford and other leaders gave the project their blessing and twenty-three MPs were appointed to the preliminary committee.[116] Perks secured a commendation for the movement from the presidents of all the main denominations except the Wesleyans (for whom C. H. Kelly, an ex-president sympathetic with Perks, signed) and the Presbyterians (for whom nobody signed).[117] But the Political Council failed to gain mass support. Perks appealed for all Free Church congregations and organisations to be represented at an inaugural London conference in November 1898, yet when it was due to commence only four or five rows of seats were occupied.[118] A series of conferences was held over the next twenty months in Leeds, Cardiff and Birmingham,[119] but the vision of branches voluntarily affiliating to the council did not materialise.[120] At the Birmingham conference in July 1900, Perks admitted, with a sidelong glance at Lloyd George, that they had absolutely divergent views over the Boer War, and no more was heard of the organisation afterwards.[121] The Nonconformist Political Council seemed superfluous. It was primarily designed for the removal of grievances, but the Liberation Society already existed for that purpose. The issue that most roused its audiences was always the Romanising movement in the state Church, but it failed to tap the religious enthusiasms of Nonconformity. It admitted Unitarians and even Jews.[122] The inaugural conference did not begin with prayer, and there was no concern with questions of public morality. It could not hope to replace the Free Church council movement as the chief organ for expressing the political views of Nonconformists.

The Free Church councils were, therefore, responsible for the greatest Nonconformist agitation of these years – the campaign against the 1902 Education Act which made ratepayers liable for the support of Anglican and Catholic schools. The course of the controversy will be discussed in

Chapter 7, but it is important to stress the extent to which it politicised the councils. Unionists and Wesleyans, by and large, fell into line against a proposal that seemed to threaten the interests of all Nonconformists. On 15 April the National Free Church Council organised a protest rally in London at St James's Hall where Law proudly announced that there were present 1,100 accredited delegates from the local councils in England and Wales representing about eight million Free Church adherents.[123] Already many of the local councils had organised indignation meetings. Within five months of the publication of the Bill, the Leeds Council, which was in the vanguard of opposition, held no fewer than sixty-four protest meetings.[124] The Free Church councils were masterminding a sustained campaign of opposition to the government measure. Every Nonconformist minister in the land was summoned to secure a resolution against the Bill from his congregation either at a special meeting or at a Sunday service.[125] But in the midst of all this politicking, the Free Church councils did not cease to be religious bodies. They were still arranging joint services and evangelistic missions. Inevitably their religious temper entered into their political meetings. When the Leeds Council resolved in favour of refusing to pay rates for denominational education, according to a member present: 'We opened with prayer, and before we went to the vote we had prayer again. The spirit of moral earnestness was a real means of grace.'[126] The sacred not only infused the secular: the reverse was true. During the 1903 annual meetings of the National Free Church Council news arrived of the defeat of the government candidate in a by-election at Woolwich. The president's announcement was greeted with wild cheering followed by the doxology.[127] The movement had become the bearer of strong feelings that straddled the borderline between religion and politics.

The Free Church Council soon became enmeshed in Liberal Party efforts to prepare for a general election. The process began with the idea of Silvester Horne that the Free Churches should put up 100 candidates of their own to ensure an educational settlement along acceptable lines. Horne was a warm-hearted, idealistic minister, only 38 but seemingly even younger, who was then moving from the influential Allen Street Congregational Church, Kensington, to the superintendency of Whitefields Mission in the heart of London.[128] His *Popular History of the Free Churches* (1903) showed him to be an ardent admirer of the Commonwealth, for then Nonconformists had ruled the land. He had been an active supporter of the Nonconformist Political Council, and had grown deeply dissatisfied with Liberal education policy by 1900. 'We want a new party', he had written.[129] In 1903 he commissioned Arthur Porritt, a journalist on the *Christian World*, to discover whether Herbert Gladstone, the Liberal Chief Whip, would accept Free Churchmen for constituencies as yet without candidates. Gladstone had reservations. He was happy that Horne should exert pressure on good potential candidates but, Porritt thought, was wary of taking on any but 'a thorough-going party Liberal'.[130] At this stage the Free Church Council was drawn into Horne's scheme. Law sent out a letter to a number of leading Free Churchmen pressing them to stand for Parliament, and shortly afterwards called on Herbert Gladstone himself. Only about thirty constituencies, Gladstone explained to Law, had no candidate, but in other places existing prospective candidates might be prepared to make way for a Nonconformist.[131] That was quite sufficient encouragement. Horne made a public appeal for men of wealth and leisure to come forward, the Free Church Council opened an election fund designed to raise £50,000 and Law wrote to every minister requesting his support for the fund.[132] Law, together with others, paid more visits to Gladstone. Twenty-five constituencies were allocated for Free Churchmen to fight, and Gladstone agreed to contribute £5,000 to election expenses.[133] It has been pointed out that Gladstone ran rings around Law, who was given 'hopeless' constituencies and had asked for £25,000.[134] Yet when it came to the election, Liberal gains were so sweeping that some of the extremely forlorn hopes, including Brentford and Cheltenham, were actually to be won by the candidates approached by the Free Church Council; and, more important, Law secured from Gladstone the promise that the first work of an incoming Liberal government would be to amend the Education Act.[135] Gladstone clearly treated this as a serious undertaking, for he subsequently referred in a private letter to Campbell-Bannerman to this 'concordat' with the Nonconformists.[136] Law felt he was becoming a power in the land. 'What we must aim at', he said, 'is to secure effective ascendancy in the Liberal Party.'[137] The Free Church Council had become a pressure group with high ambitions.

From the summer of 1903 onwards the whole organisation was kept in a state of readiness for a general election. At by-elections the local Free Church council sprang into action. At Brighton in April 1905, for instance, a newly appointed member of the government was unseated (in the opinion of the successful Liberal) because of Free Trade and the Free Churches.[138] As soon as the government resigned, in December 1905, Law marshalled his forces. He arranged to address the fifty or so secretaries of Free Church Federations at five conferences up and down the country. Law explained something of his message: 'At all the secretaries' and other Conferences which I have addressed, I have strongly urged that all ordinary Church and other meetings should be given up during the time of the Election. I maintain that the most godly work that can be done during January will be to return godly men to St Stephen's.'[139] Each federation secretary was given detailed instructions to pass on to the secretaries of the local councils in his area. They were told to establish a local election fund; to form a joint electoral committee where there was more than one council in a constituency; to ensure an acceptable pledge to educational reform from the candidate (only anti-

Conservatives were likely to give one); to watch election addresses to see that the candidate declared his education commitment; to distribute the council's own millions of leaflets; to organise meetings in consultation with the federation secretary; and to liaise with the National Free Church Council.[140] Many Free Church councils also heeded a call to organise bands of canvassers in co-operation with Liberal agents.[141] Most spectacular were the Free Church motor tours. General Booth had recently drawn attention to the Salvation Army by travelling through the country by car, the first ever seen in some parts, and Law seized on the idea. Prominent Free Church leaders in pairs were dispatched in different directions. Clifford and Campbell Morgan in East Anglia had to abandon two cars that broke down and send for a third from London;[142] Meyer and the Congregationalist Thomas Yates suffered three punctures before they reached their first meeting, and arrived at Reading three and a half hours late because a wire snapped, a petrol pipe choked and a sparking plug failed to operate.[143] But it was all good publicity. Meyer, with a reputation for otherworldiness, told stories about a man who fell on his head and therefore voted Conservative.[144] 'I am quite sure', he declared at North Petherton in Devon, 'that the men with the clearest heads and the purest hearts will vote Liberal.'[145] This was the peak of a mountain of Free Church Council electioneering. Nonconformists, commented the *Church Times*, had 'automobilised their pulpits in order to preach those doctrines of party politics which have become to so great an extent the religion of dissent'.[146] The 1906 general election marks the climax of the political involvement of the Free Church councils.

The overwhelming Liberal victory of 1906 cannot be attributed to the work of the councils. The zeal of their members helped to boost Liberal morale, but Herbert Gladstone believed that their special concern, education, came as low as fifth on the list of issues that had caught votes.[147] The election was won because the Liberals, in taking up the fiscal question, were the party of cheap food. Yet Nonconformists were justifiably elated. 'The great fact about the new political situation', according to Silvester Horne, 'is that more English and Welsh Free Churchmen have been returned to Parliament than members of the Tory party.'[148] There were only 156 Unionists, but the *Christian World* put the number of Free Church MPs at 181.[149] Nearly a hundred of them attended a celebration dinner in March 1906 at the Hotel Cecil.[150] The jubilation was natural; but so was criticism of the Free Church Council's contribution to the triumph. Law had already formulated his defence as he prepared for the election:

> The Free Church Federation Movement is one with spiritual objects, but . . . the situation is extraordinary and extraordinary measures must be taken. The National Council can take no part in

ordinary politics such as the Fiscal Question, having in its ranks men of all political parties. On the question of Education, however, we are all united, and have been impelled to make it a test question for the election.[151]

His case was sufficiently satisfying so long as Nonconformists were confident that their educational grievances could be remedied speedily. Their 'extraordinary' incursion into the heartland of politics could be regarded as temporary. When it became clear that the government, despite the size of its majority, did not have the power to impose an educational settlement, disillusionment with politics started to set in. The victory of 1906 was the prelude to disenchantment with what the Free Church councils had been doing.

The process began among the Wesleyans. Early in 1907 their long-standing suspicions of Free Church councils broke out with renewed force. Sir John Randles, a Wesleyan Unionist MP, argued for the political neutrality of his church; there were revelations in the *Methodist Recorder* that in Derbyshire a Free Church council had paid half the expenses of a meeting organised jointly with a Liberal Association; and soon a Wesleyan teacher in Manchester published *The Nonconformist Conscience a Persecuting Force*, a vigorous denunciation of the councils for being overbearing, partisan and hypocritical.[152] The criticisms were not confined to Unionists. Robert Perks, who was increasingly out of sympathy with what he regarded as the spendthrift policy of the Progressives on the London County Council, insisted that the Metropolitan Free Church Council should issue a more neutral manifesto for the 1907 LCC elections than had been intended.[153] The sharpest Wesleyan controversy came at the end of 1908 when Scott Lidgett, the minister in the denomination most fully identified with the Free Church Council after Hughes's death in 1902, declared as president of Conference that Wesleyans would neither forget nor forgive the Lords' rejection of the government Licensing Bill. Many thought this too partisan for the denominational leader.[154] Qualms began to appear elsewhere about excessive political involvement by the Free Church councils. By the 1909 annual meetings it had become necessary to hold a session when Meyer and Horne tried to argue that political activity, within reasonable limits, was a legitimate concern of the councils.[155] But a retreat from party politics gathered force. It was a marked feature of the general elections of 1910. There was every reason for renewed Free Church Council electioneering, for the education grievance remained unsettled and the Lords' veto on Liberal legislation, the central election issue, had also prevented the Licensing Bill from reaching the statute book. But Robert Perks, who was implacably opposed to Lloyd George's budget,[156] actively discouraged a partisan statement by the Free Church Council and it was rumoured that it was intending to stand aside from the contest altogether. Eventually Joseph Compton Rickett, Perks's colleague as treasurer of the Free Church Council, announced that, although in changed circumstances there would be no attempt to find Free Church candidates, the Free Church Council would issue a manifesto and arrange speakers for demonstrations. The initiative, however, would be left to local councils.[157] The effect was that organised Free Church electoral work paled into insignificance. By the time of the second election campaign of 1910, the new secretary of the movement, F. B. Meyer, frankly recognised that organised intervention was impracticable. Although the Free Church Council manifesto supported the Liberal position on education, Welsh disestablishment and social reform, Meyer explained, in many local councils there was a strong minority opposed to entering the fight. In those places it would be wise for the councils to leave electoral work to individuals.[158] The contrast with 1906 could hardly have been more marked.

From 1910 the Free Church Council was deliberately steered away from the political arena. The greatest change was in the secretaryship. In April 1910 Thomas Law was found drowned in the sea off Brighton. He had been seen two days before, standing in the water at the outer end of Brighton pier, his breath smelling of spirits, and although sent back to London, he had returned to the town to meet his unhappy end.[159] Law had by no means recovered from a nervous breakdown in the previous autumn when he was told in March that he would have to resign. The prospect of severance from the organisation he had created made sleepless depression deepen into a suicidal condition.[160] The general committee had decided that Law must go because of a 'deep misgiving' that local evangelism had been eclipsed by political activities. Even before his death, it directed him to reactivate the parochial visitation that had lapsed almost entirely for a whole decade.[161] It is not surprising, therefore, that Law was replaced, at first on a temporary basis, by the man in the movement most closely identified with spiritual work, F. B. Meyer.[162] There was an extraordinary versatility about Meyer that stemmed from a pent-up reservoir of nervous energy. He was the only son of a highly strung father, and was himself described as 'gentle and yielding, almost womanly in his consideration for others'.[163] His father, a London merchant of German descent, gave him a social background possessed by few Nonconformist divines. His gentlemanly manner attracted professional families to the two London churches both of whose pastorates he held twice: Regent's Park Baptist Church and Christ Church (Congregational/Baptist), Westminster Bridge Road.[164] Again unusually among Nonconformists during this period, he regularly attended the Keswick conventions with their message that a 'higher life' was attainable by faith alone.[165] He stood close to many Anglican Evangelicals and wrote numerous devotional works of a conservative theological cast. Yet he was dedicated to organised social concern: his earlier ministry at Melbourne Hall, Leicester, was marked by a whole range of schemes such as those for reducing the number of grocer's licences and rehabilitating ex-prisoners;[166] he co-operated with Paton in his Lingfield colony for the unemployed;[167] and he paid from his own pocket for a full-time agent to do vigilance work under the auspices of the Central South London Free Church Council.[168] He had travelled widely, visiting the sultan in Constantinople[169] and, in South Africa in 1908, perceiving the remarkable potential of Gandhi as a leader of men.[170] When the political work of the Free Church Council had been under attack in 1909, he had advocated persistence in pursuing all causes for 'the betterment of the people' into the political sphere, but (despite his stories in 1906) had been critical of blindly following the line of a single party.[171] Meyer seemed the man for the hour.

He set out his programme for the Free Church councils straight after assuming office. He intended to tighten the organisation; to reinspire confidence in many devout people alienated by the excessive political emphasis of recent years; to return to earlier features like house-to-house visitation; to act in great national crises in concert with the Established Church; and to give proof of their sympathy to Wales.[172] The last item was a standing administrative headache for Meyer: with Welsh disestablishment on the horizon, the councils in Wales demanded stronger support from the whole movement for the cause, and eventually, in July 1914, formed a separate National Union of Welsh Free Churches.[173] Otherwise he was able to achieve considerable success. He compiled a table showing how many of the eight hundred or so councils had undertaken various types of activity during his first year of office:

House-to-house visitation	63
Special missions	118
Open-air evangelism	444
Defence of Protestant principles	244
Temperance work	400
Anti-gambling	145
Social purity and other social work	225
Sunday observance	306
Co-operation with Anglicans	280
Services in workhouses and hospitals	328

Religious work was going ahead, as all wished; popular social questions were to the fore; and Meyer's special emphasis of co-operation with the Established Church was gaining ground.[174] Yet the controversy over their political role had knocked the stuffing out of many local councils. Some were doing humdrum work without enthusiasm; one was said by a member to exist only to hold its annual meetings.[175] Meyer knew that this state of affairs would be transformed by a vigorous national agitation. This knowledge, it has been shown, was partly what induced him to lead an agitation that formed the most exciting incident of his secretaryship. In September 1911 Meyer initiated a public protest against the world heavyweight boxing championship match announced for the following month at Earl's Court. Boxing had seldom been a target of Nonconformist campaigns, but in the previous year there had been sporadic objections to the showing of a film of the last world heavyweight fight as brutal and demoralising.[176] These two world championship matches attracted particular attention because the world champion, Jack Johnson, was black, and his challengers, Jeffries in 1910 and Wells in 1911, were white. There were fears that the Wells match would arouse racial tension in the empire, especially if, as in the previous year, the black champion knocked out his white opponent. Meyer did not mention the race issue in his first protest against the Johnson–Wells bout, but increasingly the spate of public discussion centred on this question. Bishops rallied to Meyer's side, a memorial against the match was widely signed and the Home Secretary, Winston Churchill, was prevailed upon to authorise proceedings against the match promoter. Before the case had concluded, the owners of the freehold of Earl's Court decided to stop the match. The fortnight's campaign was successful.[177] At a critical moment the Free Church Council had done exactly what Meyer had hoped: divisive political issues had been set aside, there had been co-operation with Anglican leaders and the local councils had been revitalised by what Meyer called an 'intense moral outburst'.[178] The Free Church Council had been vindicated as the bearer of the national conscience.

Such crusades, Meyer rightly believed, were the true *métier* of the Free Church council movement. The councils were most active when they were taking the field against sin. The popular campaigns were of two types: evangelism against personal sin and demonstrations against national sin. The Simultaneous Mission mounted by the councils at the beginning of 1901, with its well-known evangelists like Gipsy Smith and its favourite choruses like 'Count your blessings' stirred genuine fervour nationwide.[179] Similarly the great indignation meetings of the 1890s gave vent to what was strongly felt in the chapels. The councils owed their existence to a spontaneous wave of enthusiasm for co-operation in evangelistic enterprise and the struggle against social evils. The difficulties of the movement arose from the third ingredient: the desire for religious equality. Despite the fears of the Wesleyans and the warnings of Dale and Cadbury, many Nonconformists insisted that any organisation expressing their views must take a stand on disestablishment and allied questions. Hence the Free Church councils paid a great deal of attention to successive government attempts to help Anglican schools and when, in 1902, the schools received rate aid, the councils became the vehicle of the passionate Nonconformist protest. Mere declarations in favour of religious equality entailed alignment with the Liberal Party, but the struggle against the 1902 Act brought about close co-ordination with the party and earnest support at the 1906 general election. The Free Church Council was going the way of the Liberation Society, for the same reasons but over a much shorter space of time. Secularisation was evident in such details as the perfunctoriness of devotional exercises at the beginning of council meetings, but even more in the decay of evangelistic campaigns organised by the council after 1901. Furthermore, because the Free Church councils were so much closer to the life of the chapels than the Liberation Society, the process began to contribute to the sapping of the religious vitality of Nonconformity. Week-night services were abandoned in favour of political demonstrations; ministers were even known to ignore preaching engagements for the sake of speaking for the Liberal Party.[180] Some commentators began to connect declining membership after 1906 with politicisation.[181] Alarm began to spread and in 1910 there was a sharp change of direction. Law, who had been so involved in the day-to-day administration of the council as to be blind to the trend, was replaced by Meyer, whose eyes were fully open to the danger. 'They say that I have saved the FCC by God's blessing', he wrote in 1912,[182] but it proved impossible to recapture the buoyant spirit of the 1890s. The heyday of the Free Church Council was brief. For a while, however, it was a permanent organisation that could give rapid expression to the views of ordinary chapel-goers. It was the authentic voice of the earnest hopes and deep-seated prejudices of Nonconformity. The mixture of hopes and prejudices is very evident in the Nonconformist attitude to the Irish question over these years.

5 *The Irish Question*

Home Rule is to me one form of the Golden Rule. (Hugh
Price Hughes, May 1888)[1]

For a decade after the introduction of Gladstone's first Home Rule Bill
in 1886, the Irish question was the main issue of British politics. Because
religious divisions were so significant in Ireland, Nonconformity was
drawn into the centre of the debate. Before 1886, however, Nonconformists had paid little attention to the Irish question. Their only
conviction was that the demands of the Irish Nationalists for self-
government should be rejected. Home Rule, observed the *Baptist
Magazine* at the 1874 election, 'is but another name for the repeal of the
Union, and the introduction of universal anarchy into Ireland'.[2] Like
most other Englishmen, Nonconformists regarded the maintenance of
the Union with Ireland as a matter beyond discussion. There was less
unanimity over what policy would best preserve the Union. Conciliatory
measures were normally preferred, but the spread of disorder in Ireland
made most Nonconformists acquiesce in Gladstone's introduction of
coercion in 1881.[3] The subsequent truculence of Parnell, the leader of
the Irish national movement, convinced Guinness Rogers that 'between
his friends and any English party a real alliance can never be established'[4]
– an ironical comment in view of Rogers's later efforts to cement a bond
between Parnell's followers and the Liberal Party. When the Conservatives made overtures to Parnell in 1885, Nonconformists saw it as an
instance of the unscrupulousness of both sides.[5] They were totally
unprepared for Gladstone to take up Home Rule. When it was first
rumoured that he favoured the Irish cause, an editorial in the *Christian
World* under the heading 'A threatened treason' warned that no
statesman should seek to rob the British Parliament of its supremacy.[6] It
maintained its stance when Gladstone's Bill came before Parliament in
the spring of 1886, and it was joined in rejecting the proposals by *The
Baptist*, the *Baptist Magazine* and the *Methodist Recorder*. Nonconformity had no history of sympathy for the cause of Home Rule.

Yet the mass of Nonconformists gave their support to Gladstone's
Bill. The annual meetings of the area Baptist associations, most of which
happened to be held during the crisis in the May and June of 1886, afford
a good touchstone of opinion. The majority passed resolutions of

support for Gladstone and his attempt to solve the Irish question without endorsing the specific provisions of the Bill. The few like the Shropshire Association that excluded the subject for fear of controversy were counterbalanced by others like the Northamptonshire Association that went so far as to sanction the Home Rule Bill as it stood.[7] Baptists were clearly overwhelmingly in its favour. The general opinion of Congregational ministers in Lancashire, Cheshire and Derbyshire was said to support the Bill, and those in North Lancashire specifically recorded their gratitude to Gladstone for his efforts to bring justice to Ireland.[8] This was the more remarkable because Unionist defections from the Liberal Party were considerable in Lancashire. At Nottingham, J. B. Paton, who was an opponent of the Bill, collected the names of sixteen ministers for a memorial deprecating any form of Home Rule beyond a local administrative body,[9] but the riposte was far more significant. J. H. Hollowell, whose ministry was then at Nottingham, organised a counter-memorial to Gladstone in favour of Home Rule. He obtained thirty-eight signatures from ministers in the town, while eight others expressed agreement but declined to sign a political manifesto.[10] Although Joseph Chamberlain, a Unitarian pledged to disestablishment, was a leading opponent of the Bill, he did not carry the bulk of Nonconformists with him. Instead he was vilified as a traitor: H. J. Wilson wrote 'Judas from Birmingham' on the back of Chamberlain's photograph.[11] Alfred Illingworth represented rank-and-file Nonconformist opinion far more accurately than Chamberlain. He was dedicated to Home Rule, what he called 'the cause'. Illingworth was one of those who ensured that the Committee of the National Liberal Federation, Chamberlain's own creation, swung behind Gladstone rather than Chamberlain.[12] A week later Illingworth chaired a meeting of fifty Liberal MPs that planned the backbench speeches in favour of the Bill and he unsuccessfully urged on Gladstone the need for a gathering of the whole party to rally waverers.[13] Despite the rejection of the Bill and the subsequent defeat of the Liberal Party at the polls, most Nonconformists, like Illingworth, became convinced Home Rulers.

The sudden Nonconformist acceptance of Home Rule calls for an explanation. It was frequently said at the time, especially by Unionists, that Nonconformists stayed with the Liberal Party because they expected disestablishment as their reward. 'It is not right', declared Chamberlain a few years later, 'to purchase the Disestablishment of the Church at the price of the Disintegration of Empire ...'[14] Such an analysis may have been valid for a few. It was probably true of Joseph Parker, who extracted from Gladstone in November 1886 a statement favourable to disestablishment with the bait that it would 'do more to unify nonc[on]f[ormi]ty on the Irish question than anything I know of'.[15] *The Times*, which published Gladstone's statement at Parker's request, commented that it revealed how Nonconformists were trading their

political support for the promise of religious equality.[16] Parker, however, was an idiosyncratic man whose opinions could never be taken as
representative. Yet a similar impression was given by the editor of *The
Baptist*, T. H. Stockwell, in February 1887. Stockwell wrote to Gladstone and Chamberlain, urging them to reunite on a programme of
Welsh disestablishment.[17] His allegiance, it seemed, depended on the
preparedness of the leaders to advance the cause of religious equality.
Chamberlain's reply, insisting that plans for settling the Irish question
must be laid aside, was important in leading to the termination of
negotiations for Liberal reunion; Gladstone, on the other hand, argued
that Ireland blocked the way for any other legislation.[18] Stockwell's idea
came to nothing. It did not reflect the mood of the chapels. Guinness
Rogers was at pains to reassure Gladstone that his Nonconformist
supporters had no sympathy for Stockwell's suggestion. Nonconformists, he went on, recognised with Gladstone that Ireland must have
priority, 'and our one desire is that you may have the honour of settling
the problem which stands in the way of all other legislation'.[19] The
general Nonconformist enthusiasm for Home Rule was not a consequence of calculating which side would offer most. Concern for religious
equality, as Chapter 2 has shown, was ceasing to be a primary
determinant of the political direction of Nonconformity. Support for
Home Rule was not a matter of rational calculation at all, but the result
of traditional allegiance.

   Nonconformists had become entrenched in the Liberal Party. At the
Home Rule split there could be no doubt which section represented
authentic Liberalism, for Gladstone symbolised party continuity. Devotion to Gladstone intensified now he was assailed by erstwhile friends.
At a united session of the Congregational and Baptist Unions held
between the first and second readings of the Home Rule Bill, a chance
mention of Gladstone's name called forth 'an irresistible storm of
applause'.[20] The decision over Home Rule boiled down to a matter of
loyalty to Gladstone. This was partly because, as *The Baptist* suggested,
most men who could not study national affairs closely were overawed by
the stature of the Liberal leader and so lost their power of independent
judgement.[21] Even so seasoned a politician as Samuel Morley felt
compelled to accept Gladstone's guidance on trust. 'He did not
advocate the Bill now before Parliament', he said at Leigh near
Tonbridge in April, 'and he did not profess even to understand it, but he
knew that many of the best men in England believed there was essential
justice in the measure.' One man in particular was in his mind. 'He
expressed his unabated confidence in Mr Gladstone ...'[22] When this
was Morley's position, informed judgements could not be expected from
those further from the centre of politics. Chamberlain recognised the
power of Gladstone's popular appeal. He explained privately in April
that the current was running in favour of Home Rule for three reasons:

Liberal feeling in favour of self-government, an impatient wish to be rid of the Irish question and the personality of Gladstone. 'The last of these', he wrote, 'has had the greatest effect in causing Liberals to accept the proposals without careful personal investigation of them. They have assumed that the details must be all right because they are recommended by Mr Gladstone's great name.'[23] Likewise Guinness Rogers was convinced from his testing of opinion among Nonconformists even before the Bill was given to the nation that 'the issue would ultimately be reduced to one of confidence in Mr Gladstone'.[24]

Guinness Rogers himself found the Home Rule crisis peculiarly testing. His choice of sides was likely to be influential, for he had emerged from the shadow of R. W. Dale in the late 1870s to occupy the foremost place among politically active ministers in Nonconformity. He was a master of rhetoric, whether in print or on the platform, capable of turning any political event to the advantage of the causes he represented. James Guinness Rogers was an Ulsterman, his second name bearing testimony to a link with the brewing family, but he was taken to England when only 3 years old.[25] Although by 1886 he was in his mid-60s, he retained an Irish impetuosity that had once earned him the soubriquet of 'Fergus Froth'.[26] Underneath there was a humble private character, a strain of deep seriousness and a passion for reading anything and everything from patriotic literature to penny novelettes.[27] From 1865 he was minister of Grafton Square Congregational Church, Clapham, probably the congregation of the highest social standing in the denomination,[28] which no doubt encouraged his reservations about novel social enthusiasms that might offend propriety or cultivate a class spirit. Yet Rogers was a Liberal to the marrow. He wrote a monumental amount of political commentary for Liberal periodicals as well as for the *Christian World*, the weekly *Independent and Nonconformist* (of which he was to be consulting editor), the monthly *Congregationalist* and its successor the *Congregational Review* (which he edited from 1879 to 1891). His main message since 1874 had been that Nonconformists must trust the Liberal leaders, especially Gladstone. When Home Rule divided the leadership, Rogers faced an unprecedented problem. He told the Cornwall Congregational Association in April 1886 that he deeply regretted the separation between Gladstone and Chamberlain, 'the one the present, and the other the future leader of the Liberal party'.[29] Rogers saw the force of Chamberlain's argument that the Home Rule Bill threatened the unity of the empire and had his own doubts about the safety of the Protestants of Ulster.[30] Yet he could not bring himself to dissociate himself from the Liberal Party. By the general election he was speaking in defence of Gladstone's policy while continuing to hope for the reunion of the party.[31] Five years later Chamberlain was assured that Rogers had for him 'the kind of feeling that a woman has for her lover after she has quarrelled with him and yet loves him still'.[32] But it was

Gladstone whom Rogers still loved with his whole heart. In the 1890s attenders at the Congregational Union assemblies used to count the sentences of Rogers's speeches until the first mention of Gladstone.[33] The magic of Gladstone kept back Rogers from the brink of opposing Home Rule.

There were, however, some within Nonconformity whose loyalty to Gladstone was not sufficient to stop them deserting the Liberal Party. Such Nonconformist Unionists call for careful analysis. Two groups among them were relatively small. One section consisted of those who followed Joseph Chamberlain out of the Liberal Party in 1886. Chamberlain's influence was decisive for the Unitarian MPs of Birmingham, for some of the ministers in the town and for many in their congregations. He swayed few outside Birmingham. The only non-Birmingham Nonconformist MP to follow him was W. S. Caine, the temperance leader who returned to Gladstone's party in 1890.[34] There was also a handful of men who became Liberal Unionists in the town but then moved elsewhere. Thus F. W. Macdonald, a Wesleyan theological tutor at Handsworth, remained opposed to Home Rule when in 1891 he became a London secretary of the Wesleyan Missionary Society;[35] and Arthur Mursell, who was called from a ministry in Birmingham to Stockwell Baptist Church in 1887, continued to regard Chamberlain as 'the most patriotic statesman of his time'.[36] Although he privately renounced any special concern for Nonconformist questions in 1891,[37] Chamberlain still had high hopes of attracting Nonconformist votes at the 1892 and 1895 elections. It was rare, however, for his influence to be acknowledged after 1886 as a reason for changing sides. A second class of anti-Home Rule Nonconformists was a set of older ministers and laymen who saw Gladstone's measure as a breach of Liberal principles. Benefits, they believed, should never be conferred on lawbreakers. They held attitudes similar to those of John Bright, the veteran Quaker statesman, who remained obdurately opposed to concessions to Irish 'rebels' until his death in 1889.[38] 'As a Liberal', wrote Newman Hall in retrospect, 'I felt I could not sanction coercion by an irresponsible and secret conspiracy ...'[39] These men formed the intellectual élite of Nonconformity. Like Liberal intellectuals in the universities, they swung against Home Rule because they were capable of independent political assessment and saw no reason to abandon their previous estimate of the Irish demand. The ministers among them had usually risen to eminence in their denomination: Henry Allon, Robert Bruce, Newman Hall, J. B. Paton, John Stoughton and J. Radford Thompson in Congregationalism, Oswald Dykes and Monro Gibson among the Presbyterians and J. R. Wood among the Baptists. Unionist speakers made great play with their names, but they themselves seldom expressed their convictions in public. Newman Hall told Gladstone that he suffered 'the *daily grief* of remaining unconvinced' (italics in original) by his arguments for Home

Rule, and had deliberately kept silent.[40] Reluctance to speak out meant that such men exercised little influence over the rank and file, even though they were leading figures. Like Chamberlain's entourage, they formed a small group of men who diverged from the Nonconformist mainstream.

The man of greatest standing in both these groups was R. W. Dale. As minister of Carr's Lane Congregational Church, Birmingham, he came within Chamberlain's orbit; and as the leading theorist in Congregationalism he remained unconvinced by the case for Home Rule. Dale judged that if Ireland was to have a Parliament, there must be security for its loyalty through keeping Irish representation at Westminster. Otherwise the Irish might take up the old American colonial cry of no taxation without representation. Dale successfully proposed a resolution to this effect at the Birmingham Liberal organisation in April 1886, pressed similar considerations by letter on Gladstone a few days later and, when this appeal was rejected, urged that the question of Irish representation should be left open. He was desperately eager to heal the breach in the party. At the general election he announced his opposition to Home Rule, yet supported the Gladstonian candidate for East Birmingham out of continuing loyalty to the Liberal cause.[41] It was Dale who, through approaches to John Morley and Sir William Harcourt and pressure on Chamberlain, was responsible for beginning the attempt at reconciliation at the turn of 1887, the so-called Round Table Conference.[42] At this stage 'his voice trembled with emotion as he spoke on the subject. "I never", he said, "believed it possible that I should forsake Mr Gladstone" ...'[43] Even after the collapse of the Round Table Conference Dale still hoped for reunion. This made an incident at the 1888 autumn assembly of the Congregational Union peculiarly painful. Edward Crossley, MP, a keen Home Ruler, in seconding a motion of gratitude to Dale for his services on the Education Commission, referred to the Liberal Unionists as being 'chained to the Tory chariot'. It seemed that Crossley was questioning the sincerity of Dale's Liberalism, and Dale was deeply hurt. He declined to reply and never returned to the Congregational Union.[44] He also withdrew from active politics. 'The suffering', he wrote in 1890, 'has become less keen as a result of my detachedness from political affairs but even now it returns in spasms.'[45] Later that year, in the aftermath of the Parnell affair, he made a final fruitless overture to Chamberlain for an attempt at reunion.[46] At the 1892 election he wrote a short letter to the denominational newspaper commending Liberal Unionist opposition to Home Rule but incorporating a tribute to the genius of Gladstone.[47] The case of Dale poignantly illustrates the difficulties of those Nonconformists whose minds were drawn to Unionism while their hearts remained Gladstonian.

A third, and much larger, category of Nonconformists opposed to

Home Rule consisted of those whose redoubtable Protestantism made them fearful of any concessions to Roman Catholics. Best known among them was C. H. Spurgeon, the immensely popular Baptist pastor of the Metropolitan Tabernacle. Since he first burst on the capital as a boy evangelist from the Fens in the 1850s, Spurgeon's blend of common sense, orthodox Calvinism and playful humour had consolidated his position as the greatest preacher of the age. His influence was more deeply felt because of the wide circulation of his weekly published sermons and the hundreds of men sent into the Baptist ministry from the Pastors' College he founded.[48] Guinness Rogers told Gladstone that Spurgeon's 'political influence is in inverse ratio to his spiritual & religious force',[49] but Home Rule was a question that many were inclined to treat primarily as a religious issue. Both sides thought his name was worth some effort to secure. A Whig opponent of Home Rule, Albert Grey, reported to Earl Grey in May 1886 that he was trying to catch Spurgeon for the Liberal Unionists,[50] and later that month Gladstone invited him to dinner. Spurgeon, however, did not wish to declare himself publicly. He declined Gladstone's invitation on the ground of ill health and similarly excused himself from expressing an opinion on Home Rule in *The Baptist* because of indisposition.[51] Privately, he was dismayed at the threat to Irish Protestants. 'As to Ireland', he wrote to a Cardiff Liberal, 'I am altogether at one with you; especially I feel the wrong proposed to be done to our Ulster brethren. What have they done to be thus cast off? The whole scheme is as full of dangers and absurdities as if it came from a madman.'[52] This letter was leaked to the press, the Unionists saw their chance and soon Bristol was placarded with the assertion that Spurgeon had charged Gladstone with madness.[53] Spurgeon regretted the letter and explained that 'I must be mad myself if I thought Mr Gladstone mad'.[54] During the 1886 election campaign he had his secretary issue a denial that he had written on the side of the Tories.[55] Yet Spurgeon did express in his church magazine fears of Catholic ambitions in Ireland should Home Rule pass into law.[56] 'The real secret of his extraordinary utterances', Rogers reassured Gladstone, 'is gout.'[57] Spurgeon seems to have exerted no special influence over the men he had trained for the ministry. At the 1892 election, when a group of Nonconformist ministers issued a memorial against Home Rule, of the fourteen Baptist signatories, only three were men trained at his college.[58] Yet at that time Liberal Unionists still expected his judgement of Home Rule to carry weight. They knew that the political Protestantism that determined Spurgeon's response affected many other Nonconformists.

The reason was that anti-Catholicism had put down deep roots in Nonconformity. Roman Catholicism was seen as a rival faith, a perverted system of doctrine that misled souls about the way of salvation. Catholicism seemed to stand condemned by scripture. Opposition to it had fuelled many an Evangelical protest movement of mid-century, especially the outcries against the Maynooth grant in 1845 and against the restoration of the Catholic hierarchy in 1851. What is more, Catholicism seemed utterly illiberal. The Catholic Church, it was supposed, was prepared to use power unscrupulously to impose its beliefs on others. Gladstone himself had warned in his Vaticanism pamphlets of the mid-1870s that a loyal Roman Catholic must put allegiance to the pope before duty to the Crown. Fears of this sinister alien force were reinforced by the national myths of Bloody Mary, the Spanish Armada, Guy Fawkes and Jesuitry. It is hardly surprising, therefore, that the proposal of Home Rule unleashed a rash of 'no popery' among many Nonconformists. 'There can be no doubt', affirmed *The Baptist*, 'that the agitation in Ireland has been encouraged by the Jesuits.'[59] 'We know', wrote an 'English Nonconformist' to the *Christian World*, 'that as soon as the Catholics have their own Parliament, the bitterest persecution will commence . . . Centuries of Popish rule have taught us that we can never trust them when once they have power in their hands.'[60] The most rational form of this Protestant feeling was the fear that an Irish government would recognise and endow the Roman Catholic Church and its schools. More common than this specific fear, however, was a general apprehension that Home Rule would mean disaster for Protestants in Ireland. There was a stark logic about what J. Hiles Hitchens, a Congregational minister, wrote to the *Christian World* during the 1886 general election: 'to support a separatist candidate is to play into the hands of the Pope . . . '[61]

Such attitudes were encouraged by the alarm of Protestants in Ireland itself. Protestant solidarity against Home Rule was almost total. A few Dublin Baptists and Cork Congregationalists were known Home Rulers,[62] but in Ulster the policy was rejected nearly unanimously. At the 1892 General Assembly of the Presbyterian Church in Ireland, the largest Protestant denomination in Ulster, only eleven commissioners out of several hundred failed to support an anti-Home Rule resolution, and not all of them were Home Rulers.[63] The Wesleyans were sufficiently unanimous in 1886 for their Committee of Privileges to petition the Crown against a measure designed 'to hand over the loyal minority to the control of the disloyal majority without adequate security for property, liberty or life'.[64] The non-Episcopalian Protestants, as Irish Nonconformists had to call themselves after disestablishment in 1869, did their utmost to persuade the Protestants of Britain to reject Home Rule. So long as the issue was before the country, there was a long series of memorials and appeals to the British churches, with the Irish Wesleyan lobby always particularly active. Two Irish Wesleyans travelled round the country during the 1886 general election, stirring up feeling against Gladstone's proposals, and ministers of several denominations even came over for some by-elections.[65] Larger numbers arrived for the

1892 general election and in 1893, the year of the second Home Rule Bill, there was what Guinness Rogers called 'another Ulster Presbyterian invasion'.[66] The Irish effort was seconded by forthright Nonconformists with strong Irish connections. Such a man was John de Kewer Williams, a Congregationalist who had begun his ministry at Limerick in the 1840s and who announced in 1886 that he preferred Cromwell's forceful method of settling the Irish question to Gladstone's timid conciliation.[67] Another was Sir William McArthur, a Wesleyan ex-Lord Mayor of London with roots in Londonderry, for whom Home Rule was merely 'absurd'.[68] And a third was William Arthur, an ex-president of the Wesleyan Conference, the Irish author of *The Pope, the Kings and the People* (1877), 'an exposure of that vast Jesuit conspiracy against the intellectual and spiritual liberties of mankind which . . . is being promoted to-day in every land under heaven'.[69] Arthur was so enraged by the proposal of Home Rule that he flouted the connexional 'no politics' rule by electioneering against it in 1886. The stern Irish brand of political Protestantism, which even had its representatives in the chapels of England, made a powerful appeal to Nonconformity.

The Wesleyans were most responsive. Since early in the century Irish Methodists had encouraged their sister church in England to exert political pressure against Roman Catholic interests on their behalf. Anti-Catholicism had become a major component of Wesleyan public attitudes. At the 1892 election two replies to an Irish Protestant appeal were opened for signature by Nonconformist ministers, one favouring Home Rule, the other opposing it. Only 6 of the 102 pro-Home Rule signatories were Wesleyans; but 38 of the 79 anti-Home Rulers, virtually half, were Wesleyans.[70] The 'no politics' rule undoubtedly inhibited many pro-Home Rule Wesleyans from signing, but it is remarkable that so many opponents felt sufficiently strongly to overcome the same inhibition. Wesleyans formed the backbone of Nonconformist Unionism. There were marked electoral effects where Wesleyans were numerous. Their power was felt in Lincolnshire, the English county with the second highest proportion of Wesleyans in the population. It is significant that in Lincolnshire there was a remarkably high swing from Liberalism to Unionism between 1885 and 1892.[71] But the greatest impact of Wesleyan political Protestantism was in the south-west, where they were at their strongest. In Devon and Cornwall there was, between 1885 and 1892, a swing against Liberalism twice as large as the average for Britain as a whole. It was not, as has been suggested, a threat posed by Home Rule to the fishing interests of the region that was responsible for the swing,[72] but the threat to Protestant interests in Ireland as perceived by Wesleyans. At Whitsuntide 1889 Gladstone toured the south-west, and at Truro reassured his audience that there was no risk that the events of the reign of Queen Mary would be re-enacted in an Ireland under Home Rule.[73] Four months later

Chamberlain argued at Bodmin that, on the contrary, the Catholic threat was real.[74] The agent of the Devon and Cornwall Liberal Unionist Federation reported in 1890 that 'our Nonconformist supporters, who are specially numerous, are as devoted and hearty as can be desired'.[75] Anti-Catholicism was responsible for creating, specially among the Wesleyans, a considerable groundswell of Unionism.

The fourth and final category of Nonconformists opposed to Home Rule consisted of those influenced chiefly by social conservatism. For them the Irish question was far less a concrete reason for Unionism than a welcome opportunity for shedding their Liberalism. Some Nonconformists were among the prosperous Liberals who were increasingly dismayed by the radical proposals emerging from the party. Illiterate agricultural workers were enfranchised by the 1884 Reform Act; Chamberlain's *Radical Programme* for the 1885 election appeared to presage the legislative redistribution of wealth; and Gladstone seemed to be losing control of the course of events. Nonconformists with this outlook were in Guinness Rogers's mind in October 1885 when he commented that their Liberalism was wearing thin. 'The strain upon the loyalty of some of them at present may be severe', he wrote, 'for Conservative instincts affect them as they affect all, and many may regard with some anxiety the advance of democratic ideas.'[76] Such men were predisposed to reject Home Rule. A good number of Wesleyan businessmen were Conservatives even before 1886, a phenomenon, as one of them explained to Lord Salisbury, connected with the fact that Wesleyans 'belong to a much higher social class than used to be the case'.[77] The Conservative Party was increasingly an institution of middle-class defence. The industrial tensions of the 1890s accelerated the tendency to see it in that light, so that, it was generally agreed, more Nonconformists supported Unionist candidates at the 1895 election than ever before.[78] The trend was specially marked in London and its environs. According to E. G. Gange, president of the Baptist Union in 1897, there were many Conservatives in his own Regent's Park Baptist Church;[79] and Robertson Nicoll, himself a well-informed Presbyterian, guessed in 1894 that London Presbyterians would divide two to one in favour of Unionism.[80] At Guildford, a feature of the 1892 election was the number of Nonconformists who declared for the Unionist candidate, and in 1906 when the Free Church motor-car speakers reached the same town they were dismayed to discover Wesleyans canvassing for the Unionist.[81] In the London area the tendency for politics to become polarised on class lines had progressed further than elsewhere, and Nonconformists were far from immune. 'Villa Toryism' captured many of them for Unionism.

Opposition to Home Rule among Nonconformists was sufficiently strong for them to be able to form a Nonconformist Unionist Association (NUA). A group of Unionists, several of them lawyers, became dismayed that a wave of public meetings during 1887 had created the impression that all Nonconformists were Home Rulers. Eleven of them decided in January 1888 to send out circulars inviting ministers and laymen to sign a denunciation of Gladstone's Irish policy.[82] Some 1,500 signatures, an encouragingly large number, were received, and the group agreed to launch a permanent organisation. Accordingly, the N U A was formally inaugurated at a meeting in the Cannon Street Hotel on 17 April 1888. Although only about sixty attended, the meeting made its intended point: nobody could thereafter claim Nonconformist solidarity for Home Rule.[83] An even more significant point was made in the autumn. A Home Rule address had been presented to Gladstone by English Nonconformist ministers, and so the N U A determined to show that their Irish equivalents were of the opposite opinion. Eight hundred and sixty-four of the 990 non-Episcopalian ministers of Ireland were persuaded to sign an anti-Home Rule address that was presented to Lord Salisbury and Lord Hartington at a grand banquet in November. There were speeches by the Moderator of the General Assembly of the Presbyterian Church in Ireland and by a leading Irish minister from each of the Methodist, Congregational and Baptist denominations. 'This', Salisbury observed, 'is the expression of the only organized loyal opinion we have in Ireland.'[84] That is why, no doubt, Salisbury thought it worthwhile to attend the occasion. The address presented to him at the banquet was regularly cited in Unionist speeches up to, and including, the 1892 election as the true voice of the people of Ireland. The N U A had found a considerable role in mainstream politics, to act as a sounding board in Britain for Irish Unionism.

The chairman at the banquet was Sir George Hayter Chubb, the leading spirit in the N U A. Born in 1848, Chubb was tall, spare and black-bearded, a man of immense energy. He was a partner and then managing director of Chubb & Son's Lock and Safe Company for seventy-four years, from his father's death in 1872 until his own in 1946.[85] Chubb was one of the first laymen admitted to the Wesleyan Conference in 1878; his brother was a Wesleyan minister; and his father had married, as his second wife, a cousin of Percy Bunting. He shared something of the social concern, though not the Liberalism, of the Forward Movement. He had his firm erect a block of workmen's dwellings with a coffee tavern and reading room, which, according to Lord Shaftesbury at its opening, was the first attempt to improve working-class housing in the wake of *The Bitter Cry*. Chubb's philanthropy concentrated on providing facilities for the armed forces, especially through the Royal United Service Institution and the Buckingham Palace Road Soldiers' Home. These were also avenues into high society. In 1893, for instance, he supplied an elaborate casket for the foundation stone of the Royal United Service Institution laid by the Prince of Wales. Eventually, in 1928, he was to enter the peerage as Lord

Hayter. Chubb was a life-long Conservative, several times, and at least once by party headquarters, being pressed to become a parliamentary candidate. Much of his public life was dedicated to bringing together Conservatism and Wesleyanism. In 1883 he unsuccessfully tried to induce the Wesleyan Conference to petition against the Liberal Affirmation Bill which was designed to permit Charles Bradlaugh, the secularist, to take a seat in Parliament.[86] In 1884 Chubb publicly defended Salisbury against the charge of refusing land for a Wesleyan chapel at Hatfield.[87] In June 1885 he wrote to draw Salisbury's attention to the strong Conservative element among the Wesleyans, adding that 'it would be of great present & future benefit if your lordship & the Government which I rejoice to think will soon be in power, by some act or appointment recognizes the fact'.[88] Salisbury took the hint. A month and a half later, ostensibly on account of his efforts to improve the material and moral condition of the working classes, Chubb was recommended by Salisbury for a knighthood. He became the youngest knight bachelor in the land. Salisbury perceived his promise as a Conservative stalwart.

Chubb organised, and no doubt paid for, the main activities sponsored by the NUA after 1888. These were gatherings addressed by well-known Unionist politicians at times when they were likely to capture public attention. In May 1889 a conversazione was held during the Congregational Union assembly to dispel the effect of a gathering addressed by Gladstone at the same point in the previous year. Arthur Balfour, as Irish Secretary, was the main speaker. The Nonconformists of England, he said, were divided by Home Rule, but the Nonconformists of Ireland were united, and they were on the spot.[89] Another meeting was held in March 1892, on the eve of a general election campaign. This time Joseph Chamberlain was the star speaker. He introduced himself not just as a Unionist politician but also as 'one of yourselves and a Nonconformist', and went on to stress the case of the Irish Protestants.[90] In November 1892 a dinner was held on the day following the Lord Mayor's banquet, where Gladstone had been expected to speak, so that Salisbury could reply.[91] Gladstone did not speak, and so Salisbury dealt with matters of his own choosing. He assured his hearers of the association's importance, 'not merely on the ground of the influence which Nonconformists might exercise on the political opinions of their countrymen, but because through . . . your necessary sympathy for the Protestants of Ireland, you are an organisation for the communication of their opinions . . . to an extent which no other body can claim'.[92] In June 1894 Balfour addressed an NUA banquet,[93] and Salisbury again showed the value he set on the association when he accepted an invitation at very short notice for January 1896.[94] In 1901 there was a final meeting addressed by Salisbury that was intended to win over Nonconformist Liberal imperialists,[95] and in 1903 Balfour attended a gathering with a similar object.[96] In 1905, however, Balfour declined an invitation from Chubb to attend an NUA dinner on the advice of the Chief Whip, who dismissed the association as 'mostly a self-advertising lot'.[97] Self-advertisement, however, was precisely what the NUA banquets were about. They gave publicity to the Irish Protestant case while Home Rule was to the fore, and afterwards continued to fulfil their other role of demonstrating that Nonconformists need not be Liberals. The NUA succeeded in providing an avenue into Unionism for Liberals who at first hesitated to oppose Gladstone. The list of well-known ministers appearing at, or sending apologies for absence to, NUA meetings steadily grew over the years. Well-reported meetings were the best means of keeping the ball rolling.

The NUA claimed to do a great deal more than hold exclusive gatherings in London. In the wake of the 1892 election there was talk of setting up branches throughout the country.[98] When interviewed in 1893, Chubb spoke of branches at London, Chester, Hull, Birmingham, Wolverhampton and 'other towns'.[99] Apart from the parent body in London, however, only the organisation at Hull, where Wesleyans were particularly strong, seems to have held a public meeting.[100] Chubb himself explained why there was so little provincial organisation. The outlay, he said, was not worthwhile, 'as there are Liberal Unionist Associations about half the members of which are Nonconformists'.[101] There was only a little more substance to the appearance of electoral activity by the association. In 1892 the NUA dispatched a manifesto from Ulster Protestants to all Nonconformist ministers in Britain;[102] Chubb and A. W. Groser, the association's secretary, wrote letters to the press on the strength of the Nonconformist Unionist vote;[103] and a file was opened of occasions when Nonconformist congregations 'persecuted' their ministers for being Unionists – as when the Wesleyan minister at Pateley Bridge was prayed against at his own Saturday evening prayer meeting.[104] At several junctures during the struggle over the second Home Rule Bill, Chubb spoke on behalf of the NUA in a number of constituencies.[105] Apart from Chubb, however, there is evidence of only three men having spoken on behalf of the NUA during the two campaigns of 1892 and 1895.[106] At the 1900 and 1906 elections, when the association merely sent out manifestos, they were issued from Chubb's address.[107] The NUA never appealed for funds during this period and had no paid officials. The impression that the NUA was a one-man band would not be far wrong. The association did little effective work apart from holding banquets, but in giving those banquets Sir George Chubb played a very significant part in national politics.

The great majority of Nonconformists, however, were among the most devoted supporters of Home Rule. The NUA was felt to be necessary precisely because Nonconformity seemed to take up the Home Rule cause with so much fervour. Ministers denounced the wrongs of Ireland with all the vehemence of their attacks on sexual vice or intemperance. The Irish question was a matter not of prudential judgement but of moral principle. The beginning of this mood can be dated precisely. Nonconformists displayed little passion over Ireland in the first eight months after Gladstone's defeat at the general election of July 1886. During this time their hopes still centred on talks aiming for Liberal reunion. But the publication of a Coercion Bill by the Conservative government at the start of April was the signal for an upsurge of feeling. There was a sense of release now that it was possible to turn away from frustrating negotiations to do battle with the Tories. Hugh Price Hughes, as usual, gave vent to the most extreme pronouncements. He took up the subject in an editorial in his own newspaper, the *Methodist Times*:

> The introduction of a savage Coercion Bill has transformed a political discussion, in which we have not intervened, . . . into a religious controversy, in which we must take part or sacrifice all claim to be thoroughgoing disciples of JESUS CHRIST . . . O that GOD would send some brave ELIJAH to awaken the national conscience! Shall we worship JEHOVAH or BAAL? Do we believe in Divine Love or in brute force? Are we heathen men or Christians?[108]

The Crimes Bill, as it was called, provided what had hitherto been lacking, a target that could be attacked as wrong. The government proposed to give powers for the banning of suspect political associations, to allow Irish prisoners to be transferred to England for trial and to make the new arrangements permanent. This was certainly more drastic than what Gladstone had imposed and could be represented as a breach of fundamental Liberal philosophy. It was a Bill, Guinness Rogers told the National Liberal Federation, not for the repression of crime, but for 'the suppression of free thought and free speech'.[109] The most striking demonstration of Nonconformist opinion was a memorial published in the *Daily News* protesting against this exceptional legislation that was signed by as many as 3,200 ministers.[110] The Bill also caused some wavering among Nonconformist opponents of Home Rule, like Dale, and induced the *Christian World* to take its first steps back towards the Gladstonian party.[111] At the spring meetings of denominational bodies, Unionists were often able to resist any outright commitment to Home Rule, but they were forced to yield to the tide of feeling around against coercion. The Baptist Union Council excluded the subject from its assembly programme because of the risk of acrimony, but zealots insisted on a special meeting during the assembly where coercion was condemned with only about ten voting against.[112] Provincial pressure ensured that the Congregational Union assembly debated and carried a similar motion.[113] The introduction of coercion turned Nonconformist support for Home Rule, hitherto a matter of passive loyalty to Gladstone, into a typically energetic moral crusade.

Gladstone noticed this development and took pains to foster it. He had been concerned at the 'want of active support from the Nonconforming Ministry on the great Irish question',[114] and so he was glad to accept an invitation to a luncheon during the Congregational Union assembly of 1887 attended by most Congregational leaders and a sprinkling of Baptists. He devoted most of his speech to Ireland, denouncing government coercion and contending that the Liberals, by contrast, were 'endeavouring to apply the elementary principles of our duty which our blessed Lord and Saviour came to proclaim upon the earth'.[115] The speech had the desired effect. John Clifford noted in his diary:

> Speech from Gladstone of singular lucidity and power on the Irish question. His manner most earnest. The trend of his mind majestic, penetrating, victorious and irresistible. He is a commander of men. Plain of speech and simple, clear and aggressive. The moral momentum immense. It was a contest. The hearer felt he was witnessing a fight for righteousness, for humanity, for God.[116]

Gladstone deliberately created more opportunities for casting a similar spell. At the end of July 1887 he addressed the council of the London Liberal and Radical Union at the Memorial Hall, the headquarters of London Congregationalism.[117] Guinness Rogers wrote from holiday to thank Gladstone for singling out the efforts of Nonconformity to censure the government's Irish policy. 'You know not', he assured Gladstone, 'how hearts throb with passionate interest for you & certainly none more than mine.'[118] Again, in October 1887, during the National Liberal Federation meetings in Nottingham, Gladstone went out of his way to visit the Congregational Institute and to speak of Home Rule as a course which 'the Prince of Peace it may be hoped will recognise and bless. (Loud cheers)'.[119] This careful cultivation fanned the flame of Nonconformist enthusiasm. In February 1888 Rogers, having consulted Gladstone, arranged a conference of London Nonconformist ministers that appointed a committee to keep a critical eye on government policy.[120] The committee was responsible for a Nonconformist Home Rule memorial that was signed by 3,730 ministers and presented to Gladstone during the Congregational Union assembly on 9 May.[121] Gladstone insisted that the presentation must take place in the Memorial Hall so that he could once more refer to the surrounding walls as having been made historic by their struggles against the foreign policy of the Conservative government in the 1870s.[122] As in each of his previous speeches, he called on Nonconformists to champion the principles of justice and humanity once more. Hughes caught the mood, declaring that Home Rule was 'simply applied Christianity'.[123] There were further appeals by Gladstone to Nonconformity alone in 1889 and to the Wesleyans alone in 1890.[124] It was an undisguised attempt to forge the moral enthusiasm of Nonconformity into a spearhead for Home Rule opinion.

The intense Nonconformist partisanship provoked angry reactions. Some began to suggest that the Irish question was too much of a political issue for ministers of religion or denominational bodies to take sides. At the 1887 Congregational Union spring assembly there had been a protest against the very introduction of a resolution on Home Rule.[125] By the autumn assembly of 1888 it was decided that discussion of a resolution condemning coercion should be technically outside the official programme, but even then there was a simultaneous counter-meeting of some seventy-five who objected to the suspension of assembly business for the sake of the Irish question.[126] Among the Baptists, Spurgeon declared that a minister should not meddle in party politics as he should use his power 'alone for the Lord's glory'.[127] He reconciled this advice with his earlier practice of making political pronouncements by saying that his objection was directed against *party* politics. This point of view, though not confined to Unionists, became general among them. Not surprisingly, Sir George Chubb took up the question as it affected the Wesleyans. Hugh Price Hughes, he protested in a letter to *The Times* in April 1887, was attempting to commit the Wesleyan Methodist Church to opposing the Crimes Bill, a purely political question.[128] Chubb assiduously dispatched a set of newspaper cuttings about the resulting controversy to Lord Salisbury,[129] On the day after receiving the package, Salisbury spoke at the Constitutional Club. Just as the Established Church would resent the suggestion that its organisation should be used for advancing political doctrines, he said, so did the Wesleyans. He went on to draw a contrast. 'The great Nonconformist bodies do not hesitate to place their organizations at the disposal of the party from which they hope for political results.'[130] Thereafter criticism of Nonconformist politicking became the stock-in-trade of Unionist politicians. Balfour, for instance, replied to Gladstone's speech of May 1888 by observing that the Nonconformists always suggested base motives for his measures as Irish Secretary. Politics, he concluded, were not elevated by association with religion, but religion debased by association with politics.[131] The Nonconformist part in the campaign was so obtrusive that it became the butt of political criticism itself.

A second charge made against Nonconformist Home Rulers was that, for all their moral claims, they were endorsing immoral developments in Ireland. Controversy turned on the status of the so-called 'Plan of Campaign' mounted by Irish Nationalists. To Unionists, it was the attempt of an illegal organisation to conspire against property rights by encouraging the withholding of rent; to Liberals, it often seemed the last expedient to which despairing Irishmen were driven by ruthless government harassment. Liberal leaders were wary of condoning the plan, which could lead on to boycotting and dynamiting, but excited Nonconformists were less so. The plan 'may be illegal', ran an article in the *Congregational Review*, 'and it is certainly opposed to our English ideas, but . . . it is simply absurd to treat it as though it were a breach of the moral law'.[132] Robert Perks was so proud of a speech defending the plan that he had it separately published.[133] And Nonconformists like H. J. Wilson were prominent among the Liberal MPs who travelled round Ireland collecting evidence of government brutality.[134] All this was repugnant to Unionists. Gladstone had hypnotised Nonconformists, said the Liberal Unionist MP Powell Williams in October 1889, into countenancing theories subversive of morality.[135] This was the context in which *The Times* gave currency to the phrase the 'Nonconformist conscience'. Nonconformist pressure led to the fall of Parnell, the Irish leader, after it had emerged that he was an adulterer. When three weeks later Patrick Egan, one of the heads of the dynamite conspiracy, declared himself an opponent of Parnell as well, *The Times* returned to the phrase that had been coined by a Wesleyan minister. Would the 'Nonconformist conscience' be unmoved while working in league with a dynamiter even though it had protested against an adulterer?[136] The implication was that, for all their show of righteous indignation, Nonconformists had long been winking at crime. 'The inconsistency of "conscience" is glaring', wrote a correspondent in January 1891, 'which demands the shrillest protests against the eviction of a tenant who does not pay his rent, and is absolutely silent on the midnight murder of a tenant who does pay, or his innocent children.'[137] If Nonconformity could be tarred with the brush of double standards, its moralistic clamour would be neutralised. Much of the correspondence printed by *The Times* spelled out the charge that the Nonconformist criterion in selecting subjects for protest was the interest of the Liberal Party.[138] The launching of the phrase the 'Nonconformist conscience' was designed to fix on Nonconformity the stigma of hypocrisy.

The Parnell affair of 1890 was an incident when one Nonconformist crusade was eclipsed by another. The sharp Nonconformist response to the evidence of Parnell's adultery given in the divorce court was fired by the convictions of the social purity movement. 'Men legally convicted of immorality', wrote Clifford to the press on the day after the verdict, 'will not be permitted to lead in the legislation of the Kingdom.'[139] Pressure soon built up. The *Christian World* and Hughes's *Methodist Times* echoed Clifford;[140] then W. T. Stead and Henry Lunn issued a manifesto calling for Parnell's withdrawal;[141] at his Sunday afternoon service Hughes furiously insisted that he must go;[142] and meanwhile at the National Liberal Federation meetings at Sheffield, H. J. Wilson was the first MP to speak in the same vein.[143] All those who spoke out were veterans of the campaigns against sexual immorality. 'Whatever else happens', H. J. Wilson told his son, 'it is a tremendous demonstration in favour of social purity.'[144] Gladstone was at first disinclined to act, both because he was averse to behaving as a censor of morals and because Parnell was the leader of an independent party. He suspected that the campaign against Parnell might be a fuss by a few social purity extremists.[145] He may have heard that Alfred Illingworth, who continued to hold the view of the Nonconformist leaders of the 1870s that sexual morality was not for public discussion, was in favour of Parnell remaining in office.[146] But then Gladstone learned that Guinness Rogers, who had always been cool towards the Anti-Contagious Diseases Acts movement, shared the feelings of those who had already spoken out against Parnell,[147] and J. J. Colman, the respected mustard manufacturer, assured him that the mass of Nonconformist electors would no longer consider Parnell worthy of support.[148] The opinion of these two sober men showed Gladstone that Nonconformity, which he had marshalled so diligently as the vanguard of his Home Rule army, was in danger of rejecting the cause as well as the leader. Within a day of receiving the views of Rogers and Colman, Gladstone wrote a letter for publication avowing the belief that Parnell should cease to head the Irish party. There can be no doubt, as a detailed study of the episode has shown, that Nonconformity was primarily responsible for this decision which eventually led to the repudiation of Parnell by a majority of his followers.[149]

What Gladstone feared, the weakening of Nonconformist allegiance to Home Rule, nevertheless did take place. In his first heady denunciations of Parnell, Hughes went so far as to suggest that Nonconformists might renounce Home Rule.[150] He soon gave up the idea of entirely abandoning Home Rule, but he began to commend, both in public and in private correspondence with Gladstone, a compromise solution that should guarantee the good conduct of the Irish.[151] Even Rogers wavered following Parnell's fall. English Liberalism, he commented circumspectly, would not suffer if, on account of Irish action, Home Rule should cease to be a principal plank in the party platform.[152] Unionists tried to exploit the new hesitations felt by Nonconformists over their alliance with the Irish. They raised the spectre of arbitrary power wielded by Catholic priests. Their opportunity, paradoxically, was the success of the Irish Catholic clergy in ensuring what Nonconformists wanted, the downfall of Parnell. The priests were specially active in the Kilkenny by-election of December 1890 in persuading their people that a follower of the immoral Parnell was to be rejected in favour of an anti-Parnellite candidate. A correspondent of *The Times* called upon Dissenters to heed the threat: 'Monks and priests everywhere . . . These dark-browed gentry know what they are working for – . . . the reconversion of Ireland . . . '[153] Lord Salisbury took up the theme in a series of speeches during 1891 and 1892, knowing that the expression of a traditional English distaste for clerical dictation would confirm Protestant Churchmen in their Conservatism.[154] But a primary aim of the Unionist campaign was to use their ingrained anti-Catholicism to unsettle Nonconformists further in their commitment to Home Rule.

Efforts were redoubled as the 1892 general election approached. Chamberlain decided to make the appeal to Nonconformists over the Ulster question his chief theme.[155] Liberal Unionist headquarters published a torrent of leaflets with such headings as 'Toleration in Ireland: A Word to Nonconformists'.[156] Irish non-Episcopalians issued more calls to Nonconformists to rally against the Catholic threat.[157] On 17 June at the Ulster Convention, a monster meeting drawing on all sections of the northern Irish community opposed to Home Rule, Presbyterians were joined by a Wesleyan millowner and an Independent minister in exhorting English Nonconformists to vote Unionist.[158] Sir George Chubb chaired a London Unionist meeting that acknowledged the Ulster resolutions, and successive speakers spoke hopefully of Unionism spreading among Nonconformists.[159] Gladstone clearly feared that inroads might be made on the Nonconformist vote. He chose to reply to the speeches of the Ulster Convention before a gathering of Nonconformists at the home of Guinness Rogers. He denounced the use of the 'No popery' cry by the Unionists, though, with a touch of Gladstonian casuistry, he justified himself in drawing attention to some truckling to the pope by the Conservative government over the validity of Maltese marriages.[160] An attempt to lever Nonconformity into Unionism was at the heart of the 1892 election campaign. Nor did the efforts cease there. A report on the election in South Meath, published in December, revealed that an anti-Parnellite had been returned only because of improper pressure by priests. Unionists saw to it that this vindication of their warnings was well publicised.[161] The barrage of anti-Catholic propaganda was kept up while the second Home Rule Bill was before the Commons during 1893. By this stage the Nonconformist press was beginning to show sensitivity to little incidents that allegedly revealed the spirit of Catholicism. The *Christian World*, for example, started to give credence to hoary tales of the kidnapping of Irish girls for incarceration in nunneries and expressed alarm when it was reported that the Roman Catholic Lord Mayor of London held a dinner where a toast to the pope preceded the toast to the queen.[162] Guinness Rogers was now treating Home Rule not as a crusade to be preached but as a commitment to be justified.[163] Nonconformist devotion to the cause was weakening under pressure.

The strain on the Irish alliance reached breaking point over the question of education. At the 1895 election the Conservatives stressed the cause of protecting voluntary schools in England, Catholic as well as

Anglican. Cardinal Vaughan urged English Roman Catholics to put their educational interests before Home Rule, and so to vote Conservative. When Tim Healy, the leader of the section of the Irish party closest to the Catholic hierarchy, denounced Nonconformists for resisting Catholic claims for their schools, there were suggestions that Nonconformists might drop Home Rule in retaliation.[164] The mood grew as the new Conservative government prepared to introduce legislation to help the voluntary schools. 'I should never vote again for Home Rule in its old form', declared Perks in March 1896, 'if the Irish party enter into any . . . compact with the Government on education.'[165] Nonconformists felt that due warning had been given. As soon as the Bill was published, two of the three sections of the Irish party, Healy's clericals and the Parnellite rump, announced their support. The Dillonites, on the other hand, hoped to champion Nonconformity against the Church of England. Yet when the second reading came on, even Dillon backed the Bill. At the moment he sat down after speaking, Hughes wrote dramatically, 'Gladstonian Home Rule was dead'. The Irish action, according to Hughes, justified much that had been said by their Ulster kinsmen, with whom close relations must be restored. 'May we not', he asked, 'once more stand shoulder to shoulder in opposition to the principles which have degraded Spain, and in defence of the principles which have made England?'[166] Perks had delivered a similar renunciation of the Irish cause in the Commons debate,[167] and it is clear that Wesleyans, with their special susceptibility to anti-Catholicism, were most forward in the repudiation of Home Rule. Charles Berry at the Congregational Union assembly declared more temperately that, although they would vote for Home Rule when it came up again, the Irish were clearly not putting Home Rule before other questions, and so neither would Nonconformists.[168] The *British Weekly*, never a convinced supporter of Home Rule, followed Hughes's line; the *Christian World*, Berry's.[169] The Liberal daily press argued for the continuation of the Home Rule policy, but did not persuade Nonconformists.[170] They felt betrayed. Lord Rosebery was 'greatly impressed with the strong feeling against the Irish manifested by a number of prominent Nonconformists' at Rochdale, and Lord Tweedmouth had similar experiences at Norwich and Bolton.[171] Revulsion against the Irish cause was general. The *Christian World* commented in 1899 that Home Rule might be right in principle, but they would not submit to dictation by the Nationalists.[172] After 1896 Nonconformist support for Home Rule was (as Robertson Nicoll put in in 1898) as dead as the first edition of the *Encyclopaedia Britannica*.[173]

The Irish question did not come to the fore again until after 1910, when the Liberals found themselves dependent on the Nationalists for a majority in the Commons. This time it did nothing to stir the imagination of Nonconformists. Robertson Nicoll in the *British Weekly* was now prepared to give rather grudging support to Home Rule so long as there was security for religious liberty.[174] When the Bill appeared in April 1912, the *Christian World* merely reported that Nonconformists thought it to be quite satisfactory.[175] John Redmond, the Irish leader, had made a conciliatory gesture by publicly offering to help Nonconformists remove their education grievances,[176] but even so there was no trace of enthusiasm for the Bill. There was, in fact, a tone of resignation about the most publicised Nonconformist statement on the issue. In February 1912 R. F. Horton, who had become well-known as an anti-Catholic controversialist, wrote to *The Times* to explain why he nevertheless supported Home Rule. The regrettable demand of the Irish majority for self-government, he argued, made it unjust to refuse. Home Rule was 'a political necessity, which we Nonconformists cannot help recognising'.[177] The only Nonconformist passion, in fact, was to be found among the few outspoken Unionists. Several found a platform in the NUA, which sprang to life with a fresh series of dinners and luncheons for a new generation of Unionist leaders, Bonar Law, Austen Chamberlain and Sir Edward Carson.[178] Sir George Chubb, now the NUA president, once more took a leading part. He presented an anti-Home Rule memorial to Balfour during the December 1910 election campaign and another at a mass protest rally in June 1912;[179] he wrote regularly to the press urging the Unionist case;[180] and in 1914 he was invited by Carson to be one of the first signatories of the Covenant that announced Ulster's intention of refusing to acquiesce in the implementation of Home Rule.[181] The NUA also became more than a skeleton organisation. It appealed for funds; it appointed a secretary, G. Wilson Moore, a Moravian from Ireland, who occupied a room at the Liberal Unionist office; and it began issuing its own literature.[182] Yet the NUA made far less impact in these years than it had in the 1880s and 1890s. For one thing, the Unionists now had other efficient organisations to publicise the case of loyal Ulster in Britain. For another, it had become well known that Nonconformity was divided in its party loyalties. Perhaps most important, the NUA concentrated on an issue to which Nonconformists no longer paid particular attention. The apolitical mood that seized Nonconformity around 1910 was unresponsive to appeals from either side of the Irish question. Home Rule was left to the politicians.

For a while, however, Home Rule had been the main public issue absorbing the attention of Nonconformists. Between 1887 and 1890 the great majority were convinced that they must bring justice to Ireland. This was a consequence of their discovery, in the coercion introduced by the Conservative government, of a fresh wrong to attack. Home Rule became, as Guinness Rogers put it, an embodiment of 'the fundamental principle of the Gospel which they as Christian ministers preached – that was, to do to others as they would have others do to them'.[183] Gladstone was delighted that Nonconformists should turn their capacity for moral passion on to the question he had taken in hand, and did all in his power to encourage their dedication to the cause. Since allegiance to Gladstone was already the chief reason why Nonconformists supported Home Rule at all, he was highly successful. The Parnell affair was disastrous for Gladstone's strategy. The claims of Ireland never again aroused the same degree of enthusiasm after they had come into collision with social purity attitudes. Formal support for Home Rule continued until 1896, but then opposition by the Irish MPs to deeply felt Nonconformist convictions over education completed the process of disenchantment. Nonconformist suspicions of Roman Catholics, skilfully played on by the Unionists, had done much to sap their commitment to Home Rule. And it was anti-Catholicism that had created the bulk of rank-and-file opposition to Home Rule in the first place. Nonconformist Unionists were outraged that their Liberal brethren were ignoring the claims of Protestant solidarity. This led to the creation of the Nonconformist Unionist Association as a standing witness that not all Nonconformists were so blind. Both sides treated the issue as a matter of taking a public stand against wrong. Home Rule and anti-Catholicism were alike crusades. That is why neither side could understand the other and why there was the degree of bitterness that caused such pain to R. W. Dale. The Irish question raised the temperature of party strife to one of the highest levels of the nineteenth century. Nonconformity contributed a great deal to this highly charged atmosphere by holding the centre of the stage and by injecting religious commitment into political partisanships. Similar emotions on questions of foreign affairs eventually led to a comparable division in Nonconformity.

6 *The Role of Britain in the World*

The Cross of the world's Redeemer was shrouded in the Union Jack. (On Nonconformist opinion during the Boer War)[1]

Between the decades of the 1870s and the 1900s the prevailing attitude of Nonconformists to foreign affairs was transformed. The best index to the change is their attitude to empire, although their views on British intervention and the use of force were also of central importance. In the 1870s most Nonconformists were among the sternest critics of the growth of empire; by the 1900s the majority were dedicated imperialists. In the earlier period Beaconsfield and his government were denounced as adventurers, spendthrifts and war-mongers for pursuing a forward foreign policy on the fringes of Britain's existing territories. By the time of the Boer War at the turn of the century, however, Nonconformists themselves were eager participants in an upsurge of popular imperialism. Occasional calls for peace by a handful of ministers and laymen were drowned in a clamour for the prosecution of the war with greater vigour. Most Nonconformists wanted the Dutch republics of southern Africa to be annexed to the British Empire. Opponents of imperialism deplored the defection of the Nonconformists. Sir Wilfrid Lawson, for instance, declared that the chapels were as active as any other section of the community in fanning the flame of war. 'The Nonconformist conscience', he claimed, 'is as silent as the grave.'[2] Certainly Nonconformists in general were no longer little Englanders standing out against the national trend towards taking greater pride in Britain's imperial mission. Earlier Nonconformist attitudes had been supplanted.

In the middle years of the nineteenth century Nonconformity had been influenced by the ideas associated with the names of Richard Cobden and John Bright, the radicalism of the day on foreign affairs. These men had argued, first and foremost, that there should be no intervention in the affairs of other nations. Contact between governments, they believed, should be minimised. Cobden's favourite toast was 'No foreign politics'. He used to stress that with the decay of inter-governmental feuding there would be increased scope for the spread of commerce and other forms of friendly contact between nations. Bright also preached non-intervention, often so exalting it, especially after Cobden's death in 1865, that it seemed to become an end in itself rather than a means to the end of closer international relations. The two men believed, secondly, in the avoidance of the use of force in international affairs. This conviction came particularly readily to John Bright as a Quaker. Yet neither man went so far as pacifism. Cobden avoided urging that nations should never go to war, and Bright specifically repudiated the doctrine of non-resistance. What they wanted was an end to all but a minimal defensive use of force. The third axiom of their thinking was that there should be no territorial expansion. There was a risk that the growth of empire would embroil Britain in overseas disputes, and it would certainly entail greater government spending and consequently higher taxation. Neither man believed in the dismemberment of empire, but they both hoped that existing colonies would evolve into independent, self-financing nations.[3] All this had great attractions for Nonconformists, and especially for the industrialists among them who recognised the commercial advantages of this set of policies. 'As little as possible interference in foreign affairs', declared J. J. Colman, 'is one of the cardinal points in my creed.'[4] The views of Cobden and Bright were held in high esteem by many of the Nonconformists of the 1870s.

Such attitudes were reinforced by the propaganda of the Peace Society. This organisation adopted a stronger stand than Cobden or Bright, arguing that war was an outright wrong that should be entirely eliminated from the world. Its resolutions in the 1840s had gone beyond calls for non-intervention to demands for disarmament. The society was marked by a tone of Evangelical crusading that was both a cause and a consequence of widespread Nonconformist participation. Of 194 British ministers of religion at the London peace congress in 1851, no fewer than 190 were either identified as 'Nonconformist' or else designated 'minister' rather than 'clergyman'.[5] Support for the movement melted away during the invasion scares and victory celebrations of the 1850s. The high-flown aims of the society were brought to earth and a new realism prevailed. Under the guidance of Henry Richard, the ex-Congregational minister who was secretary from 1848, the society began to concentrate on practicable goals. Richard won a number of parliamentary victories on its behalf, the last and greatest being the carrying against Gladstone's government in 1886 of the principle that it is inexpedient to declare war or to annex territories without consulting Parliament.[6] As in the case of the Liberation Society, however, the shift from idealism to realism was disastrous for recruitment. Richard tried to make the society more attractive by insisting that membership did not entail endorsing 'the Quaker principle, that all fighting, even for our hearths, homes and the lives of those dearest to us, is unlawful to the Christian'.[7] But this strategy meant that the society no longer sounded the clear rallying cry that war in itself is wrong. Few other than Quakers, stirred by their existing convictions, were likely to join. Consequently Quakers tended to predominate as the century wore on. The society complained in 1885 that the 'Church of Christ . . . stands aloof and holds its peace in the presence of this, the most stupendous of all the evils that afflict humanity'.[8] Only Canon W. H. Fremantle, it claimed, publicised his opposition to all war, and the only denomination possessing a peace organisation was the Society of Friends. After Richard's retirement in 1885, the Peace Society was plagued by falling income and falling attendance at its annual meetings.[9] Nonconformity on the whole was failing to supply new members. Militancy in the cause of peace was declining.

The decay of peace principles among Nonconformists in the later nineteenth century was partly the result of the spread among them of another school of thought about foreign relations. This was the much more nebulous view that while peace was no doubt always desirable, force was sometimes necessary in international affairs. Many Nonconformists, such as Robert Vaughan, the Congregational editor of the *British Quarterly Review*, had held this position even during the greatest popularity of Cobdenism. 'The doctrine of non-intervention', he wrote in 1864, 'just and wise as it may be within certain limits, may become the embodiment of a selfishness of the lowest order . . . '[10] Several events drew Nonconformist opinion in this direction. During the Crimean War of the 1850s it was highly unpopular to oppose war altogether. The Indian Mutiny of 1857–8, with its tales of native atrocities, made Nonconformity virtually unanimous in wishing well to British arms. And the American Civil War, apparently a struggle between slavery and anti-slavery, seemed to be a conflict in which Christians should take sides. Even Bright spoke out for the North. Henry Richard wrote despairingly in 1862 that each new war detached some group of friends from the Peace Society.[11] For most Nonconformists non-intervention might remain an ideal, but they believed that moral considerations sometimes demanded military action. That is why Gladstone's Midlothian addresses of 1879 chimed in so closely with their convictions. They applauded Gladstone's censure of Beaconsfield's 'theatrical' foreign policy as expensive and oppressive. Gladstone's condemnation of wanton attacks on weaker nations appealed to their preference for peace, even if they did not understand his concept of public law undergirding the equality of nations. Yet few were disposed to criticise Gladstone for endorsing the principle that sometimes the European powers should exert joint pressure backed up by the threat of force. Here again they no doubt failed to grasp Gladstone's notion that 'the united authority of Europe' represented the distilled wisdom of Christian civilisation, but they agreed with him that the European powers should have coerced Turkey into giving freedom to her Christian subjects.[12]

There can be no doubt that by 1879 Nonconformity's attitude to foreign affairs was more Gladstonian than Cobdenite.

The response of Nonconformity to the foreign policy problems that ensnared Gladstone's 1880 administration confirms this diagnosis. In 1882 the Liberal Cabinet, faced with anarchy that was threatening British lives and interests in Egypt, authorised the bombardment of Alexandria and the occupation of the country. Bright resigned from the government, denouncing the measures as 'a manifest violation of International Law and of the moral Law'.[13] Henry Richard agreed in condemning the whole adventure, but Guinness Rogers could not concur.[14] He believed that though the intervention was regrettable, at the time it was unavoidable. When in 1884 Britain was sucked further into the Egyptian imbroglio and dispatched an expedition southwards into the Sudan, Rogers again defended official policy.[15] The attitude that he and a majority of his fellow Nonconformists displayed was determined primarily by their allegiance to Gladstone's government. The death of Gordon at Khartoum opened the Cabinet to charges of vacillation and incompetence, but still Rogers maintained that 'the spirit and aim' of government policy was right.[16] Similarly, the Gloucester and Hereford Baptist Association, although expressing the hope that future conflict in the Sudan could be avoided, resolved 'its full confidence in Her Majesty's Government both in its Home and Foreign policy'.[17] Richard complained at the 1885 Congregational Union assembly that members of the denomination were subordinating their duty to protest against the Sudan expedition to their admiration for Gladstone.[18] He was not far wrong. It was certainly clear that Nonconformists did not feel bound to stand by the principle of the Peace Society or even the views of John Bright. They still believed themselves to be champions of peace and non-intervention, yet in practice they were prepared to sanction war and annexation. As they were shortly to show over Home Rule, they trusted Gladstone to make difficult decisions for them.

The germ of imperialism can already be detected in these Nonconformist views of the early 1880s. But it was a reluctant form of imperialism, a world apart from the zealous flag-waving of the Boer War. What was responsible for the transformation of attitudes between these two stages? Concern for the welfare of the less privileged, what is usually called humanitarianism, is a strong candidate. This strand in Nonconformist thinking was favourable to government action in foreign and colonial affairs. Only the state, it might appear, was sufficiently powerful to protect native races against exploitation. There was, for instance, the case of the opium trade. Addiction was encouraged in China because the British government failed to prohibit the export of opium grown in India. In 1891, and again in 1906, Commons resolutions condemning the trade were warmly received by Nonconformists.[19] The second resolution, proposed by T. C. Taylor, a Congregationalist MP, contributed to spurring the government into entering the negotiations with China that eventually abolished the official trade in 1913. But opium was not a mass Nonconformist concern. When in 1895 there was a major setback for the cause because a Royal Commission reported in favour of the trade, the *Christian World* was impressed by the evidence that supported its continuation and some Nonconformists, including the Baptist MP, R. L. Everett, were actually convinced by it.[20] The brunt of the battle was borne by the tiny Society for the Suppression of the Opium Trade, which was largely Quaker in support. At a rally it held in 1895, the only representative Nonconformist figure was H. J. Wilson;[21] and at its annual meeting in 1911 there was no prominent speaker from the main Nonconformist denominations.[22] The volume of commitment to the anti-opium cause outside the ranks of the Quakers was so small that it could have little effect on mass Nonconformist attitudes.

A more widespread concern was opposition to slavery and the slave trade. 'Since the days of Wilberforce', declared the *Baptist Magazine* in 1873, 'it has been the special vocation of England to take the field against the slave trade in all parts of the world'.[23] Nonconformists had been persuaded since the 1830s that the whole institution of slavery was not only cruel but an affront to God. Anti-slavery had become a matter of burning conviction. During the 1860s the fires of their hostility had been restoked by sympathy for the North in the American Civil War and they were quite prepared to support fresh onslaughts against it. But at this stage the movement began to run out of targets to attack. The slaves of America, always the main British concern, were now free men. The British takeover of Fiji in 1874 dealt a severe blow to the slave traffic of the South Seas, and in the same year the Chinese coolie trade from Macao to South America also came to an end. There remained only the slave traffic of Arab lands. The British occupation of Egypt in 1882 prompted the presentation of a memorial to Gladstone as Prime Minister urging that Britain should put down slavery in the new territories for which she was responsible and many prominent Nonconformists were among the signatories.[24] But the main focus of attention was Zanzibar. The sultans there were essentially merchant princes, presiding over a network of trade routes penetrating deep into the African interior. Much of the trade was in African slaves, the victims of inter-tribal wars. In theory the slave markets of Zanzibar were closed by a treaty imposed by Britain in 1873, but more or less open trading continued.[25] Zanzibar supplied a target for anti-slavery sentiment, notably in 1896 when Britain intervened to deal with a usurping sultan,[26] but it was a small one. Struggling against slavery on an offshore African island did not have the mass appeal of a worldwide crusade. It is significant that a resolution on the question at the 1895 Free Church Congress recommended not government action but church interest.[27] Quakers formed the backbone of the anti-slavery movement. The small

British and Foreign Anti-Slavery Society was dominated by members of the Society of Friends. In the Commons the cause was championed by the Quakers A. E. Pease and then J. A. Pease. And it was the presence of a deputation from the Friends' Anti-Slavery Committee that led the Baptist Union autumn assembly to declare its abhorrence of the slave traffic in 1894.[28] Anti-slavery remained a considerable latent force among Nonconformists, but the relatively small dimensions of the problem did not encourage profound or persistent concern.

Recrudescences of conditions close to slavery nevertheless continued to attract attention after the turn of the century. Most Nonconformist passion in this field was concentrated on the issue of 'Chinese slavery' in South Africa. In 1904 it became known that Rand mine-owners were bringing in thousands of Chinese from the East as indentured labourers. They were normally confined to their quarters unless they held a permit and forbidden to leave one master for another; they were liable to imprisonment if they failed to work adequately and were to be returned to their place of origin, by force if necessary, at the expiry of their contract. This seemed to amount to slavery in a territory where Britain was responsible for restoring order after the Boer War. As soon as the subject was raised in the Commons, the National Free Church Council drafted a resolution condemning the indentured labour system and had it adopted by many chapel congregations up and down the land.[29] It was the heyday of Free Church Council campaigning. Soon the denominational assemblies fell into line by passing resolutions: the Baptists, the Presbyterians and the Congregationalists in turn.[30] Indignation subsided, but the question resurfaced as a topic of widespread concern shortly before the 1906 election. Nonconformists could complain that the Conservative government had done nothing about the state of the indentured labourers.[31] It had tolerated wrong. Consequently the issue came to the fore during the election campaign.[32] Although it was soon forgotten afterwards, Chinese slavery supplied a useful stick with which to beat the Conservatives. For two brief spells, in early 1904 and in 1905–6, feeling about the treatment of coolies in South Africa assumed the proportions of a crusade.

The other significant issue of these years to draw on the reservoir of anti-slavery sentiment was the Congo question. King Leopold II of Belgium, as personal owner of the Congo Free State, was tolerating what amounted to a system of forced labour. Official traders were permitted to ensure the payment of a weekly rubber tribute by the use of African troops, who were frequently ill-disciplined. Atrocities like the chopping off of hands were common in some districts. The Congo was a Baptist Missionary Society field, but the society showed reluctance to foster an agitation both because its missionaries seldom heard anything more than rumours of cruelties and because it depended on the goodwill of Congo authorities for mission station sites and many services.[33] In

1902, however, a young British journalist specialising in west African affairs, E. D. Morel, launched a campaign to end King Leopold's personal rule, which, he was convinced, was responsible for the continuing inhuman treatment of the Congolese. Fresh evidence induced a number of leading Baptists, including John Clifford, to lend their support to Morel's campaign. His Congo Reform Association, organised in 1904, pressed the British government to insist on changes by King Leopold, and eventually British influence contributed to the decision to transform the Congo into a regular Belgian colony (1908).[34] During these years Morel enjoyed widespread Nonconformist support, culminating, in June 1907, in a Free Church deputation to the Foreign Secretary.[35] It was a struggle that revived the passionate conviction that slaveholding must be accompanied by cruelty. Leopold, according to F. B. Meyer's autumn presidential address to the Baptist Union in 1906, was an 'inhuman monster'.[36] Here was a cause where initial caution was over-ridden by sympathy for the oppressed as soon as the true state of affairs came to the light of public attention.

It is clear that anti-slavery remained a significant component of chapel psychology. But it was a declining force and in none of its chief manifestations did it encourage Nonconformists to advocate more forceful measures by the British government abroad. Other campaigns, however, were potentially more powerful. These were the agitations in which humanitarianism was yoked to missionary interests. Christian missions seldom confined their attention to the spiritual interests of those they served, but busied themselves in meeting their agricultural and medical needs. They went further. Although for most of the nineteenth century missionaries were strongly forbidden by their societies to take part in politics, they could hardly avoid becoming advisers to local rulers on such matters as how to resist aggressive neighbours and slave raiders. The missionaries, and in due course their home constituencies, began to sympathise with the desire of those they served for protection from these scourges. Thus the Aborigines Protection Society, though disproportionately a Quaker body, enjoyed considerable Nonconformist support. The question arises of how far missionary humanitarianism was responsible for the growth of imperialism among Nonconformists. In the Congo pressure on behalf of the natives was at first held back in order to avoid antagonising the authorities against the missionaries. Elsewhere, especially where there was no existing European rule, the interest of the inhabitants and the interest of the missions might seem to coincide. If native peoples needed protection, British suzerainty could appear to be its best guarantee. Study of east Africa has suggested that although there is little evidence of missions trying to draw the government into territories in their wake during the period up to 1885, there was afterwards a great deal of pressure in that direction. The Church of Scotland and the Free Church of Scotland called for a protectorate over Nyasaland and the Anglican Church Missionary Society demanded one over Uganda.[37] How far were Nonconformists similarly swayed by missionary humanitarianism?

Wesleyans were most forward in demanding the extension of British rule to territories where their missionaries were active. Their first and most significant initiative, for the annexation of Fiji, began as early as 1859. The Wesleyan missionaries on Fiji feared that French annexation was likely and that afterwards the work of Protestants would be thwarted by the Catholic preferences of the authorities. The French Catholic threat was stressed in the case for annexation made out by William Arthur, one of the Wesleyan Missionary Society's secretaries and the Ulsterman who was to oppose Home Rule, in his pamphlet *What is Fiji?* The idea of British control was turned down by the government, but it was revived in the early 1870s. William McArthur, the later Wesleyan Lord Mayor of London and brother of a merchant trading to Fiji, brought the claims of the islands before the Commons each year from 1872 to 1874. His case was multi-faceted, dwelling on commercial and strategic advantages but also insisting strongly on humanitarian arguments. The arrival of white planters had led to a serious breakdown of the traditional structure of authority so that life and property were no longer secure and forms of kidnapping that approximated to a slave trade sprang up to supply the new demand for labour. The Aborigines Protection Society joined the Wesleyan Missionary Society and an *ad hoc* Fiji Committee in pressing for British annexation. Gladstone's government would not consider incurring fresh territorial responsibilities, but shortly after a Conservative government took over, in 1874, Fiji became a protectorate.[38] The Fiji missionaries wrote to congratulate McArthur on the success of efforts undertaken 'in the deep interests of humanity, and from motives which move noble-minded Christian men to do battle for the helpless and the enslaved',[39] adding encouragement that he should seek to extend British rule over others. McArthur needed no hint. In 1874 he opposed British withdrawal from the Gold Coast, in 1876 spoke against the exchange with France of The Gambia for some other territory, and in 1886 chaired a committee urging the extension of British authority over Zululand.[40] It is evident that Wesleyans, both in the mission field and at home, felt no Cobdenite compunction about the growth of empire. Even Hugh Price Hughes, one of the most committed Liberals in the connexion, could not bring himself in the 1880s to believe that Britain should evacuate Egypt. He was too strongly convinced of the civilising benefits of British rule.[41] By 1890 he was preaching against Cobden's contention that colonies should evolve towards independence.[42] The opinion of Wesleyan missionaries, according to his daughter, was a major factor in his thinking on this question.[43] The intense Evangelicalism of the Wesleyans, with its corollaries of anti-Catholicism and anti-slavery, made them highly responsive to missionary opinion.

The result was that in their case a mixture of humanitarianism and a desire to defend their missions did lead on to imperialism.

The case of the Congregationalists is more complicated because of a gulf between missionary and domestic opinion. Men in the field representing the London Missionary Society, largely Congregationalist in support, became as eager as Wesleyan missionaries for imperial expansion. In the 1880s and 1890s J. G. Paton and James Chalmers, well-known LMS missionaries, urged a policy of annexation to save the islands of the South Seas from other powers,[44] and from 1868 onwards John Mackenzie, a disciple of Livingstone in southern Africa, wanted to bring the Bechuana under British rule.[45] But Congregationalists at home lagged far behind their missionaries in their attitude to empire. There were two main reasons. First, as they believed that the state had no part to play in the furtherance of the gospel at home, they were disinclined to invoke state aid for missions abroad. 'That Government should be asked to protect either the missionaries or their converts', wrote R. W. Dale to Gladstone in 1883, 'is . . . contrary to the principles of those with whom I am accustomed to act.'[46] Congregational missions, they held, must not become entangled with the government. Secondly, Congregationalists had far greater leanings to Cobdenite principles than the Wesleyans. In 1895 when Madagascar, an LMS field, was being overrun by the French, there were calls by missionaries for the society to insist on action by the British government. The LMS secretary, however, explained that 'a demand for interference would mean that the directors wished the Government in the last resort to defend their missions by force of arms. From any such idea they naturally shrink with horror . . . '[47] For these two reasons Congregational opinion at home was not stimulated by its missionaries into supporting imperial rivalries abroad. There was an apparent exception when in 1882–3 there was Congregational backing for the early stages of a successful campaign mounted by Mackenzie to secure a protectorate over Bechuanaland.[48] But domestic opinion was roused only because the Bechuana had been invaded by Boers who had undertaken in a treaty of the previous year not to molest the tribe: the agitation was originally mounted solely in favour of British intervention to enforce treaty obligations. When it evolved into pressure for annexation, Guinness Rogers repudiated the enterprise as a form of imperialism only a shade less objectionable than 'the vulgar type of the music halls'.[49] Congregationalists had not become agitators for the growth of empire. Nor had most other Nonconformists. During the campaign by the Church Missionary Society for the declaration of a protectorate over Uganda in 1892, the Foreign Office received a representation in favour of annexation from the Wesleyans and three from English Presbyterians (no doubt spurred on by similar recent Scottish campaigns), but none from any other Nonconformists.[50] The preponderant Nonconformist view of the proper role of Britain abroad was not changed by missionary humanitarianism.

The chief solvent of received Nonconformist attitudes was another form of humanitarianism, a sympathy for victims of Turkish repression that emerged in the 1870s. In the late nineteenth century the various Christian nationalities of the Turkish Empire were trying to shake off their irksome allegiance to a Muslim power. In 1876 a rising by Bulgarians was rigorously suppressed by the Turkish authorities, and there was a likelihood of Russia, the natural patron of Orthodox Slavs, coming to their aid. Disraeli's government seemed to be on the point of going to the defence of Turkey against Russian ambitions. There was Liberal dismay that Britain might be plunged into an unnecessary war. At that stage reports in the *Daily News* of atrocities committed by the Turks in Bulgaria had an electrifying effect on public opinion. Nonconformity led an outburst of indignation at the 'horrors' and the government's willingness to support their perpetrators. There was a series of 'atrocity meetings' that began on the initiative of W. T. Stead (at the time editor of the Darlington *Northern Echo*), and protests poured into the Foreign Office from Nonconformist bodies.[51] The sheer cruelty revealed in stories like those of babies being spitted on bayonets did a great deal to move them,[52] but other reasons explain the peculiar depth of feeling expressed by the chapels. First and foremost was their disgust at the sexual assaults that were given some prominence in the *Daily News* reports. A girl of 18 declared that she had been raped by ten soldiers, for instance, and children of 10 and 12 were said to have been treated similarly,[53] Just as in 1883 the discovery of incest was sufficient to stir a crusade against overcrowded housing, so in 1876 publicity for rape was the chief reason for the passionate intensity of the Bulgarian agitation. Secondly, there was hostility to the Turkish troops as Muslims. The *Daily News* article that had the greatest impact explained the mass murders in terms of the 'Mahometan' belief that to kill a certain number of infidels guaranteed admission to Paradise.[54] Dislike for Islam and all its works was strong enough to overcome any prejudice against the errors of Eastern Orthodoxy that might have inhibited sympathy for the Bulgarians. Thirdly, Gladstone spoke out, urging that the Turkish executive power should be expelled, 'bag and baggage', from Bulgaria. Although Gladstone identified himself with the crusade only well after it had been launched, the 'blaze of light shed by his oratory on the simple moral issues of the European crisis' (as *The Nonconformist* put it) dazzled chapel-goers.[55] Esteem for Gladstone gave a fresh impetus to a movement in which Nonconformity was stirred by a powerful blend of emotions. John Bright was troubled by the thought that the logical conclusion of the pro-Bulgarian case, especially as voiced by Gladstone, would be war against the Turks on behalf of their victims.[56] Nonconformists, however, followed Gladstone in not pressing their arguments so far. As usual, their crusade had a negative purpose. Their object was to avert British involvement on the side of the Turks, not to urge British intervention against them. There was no need for worry lest the episode should divert Nonconformists away from peace principles.

When Turkish misrule of Christian subjects next drew widespread public attention, however, the issue was to do more than any other factor to transform Nonconformist attitdes to the use of force. The Eastern Question again assumed a central importance in European diplomacy in the mid-1890s, this time because of the sufferings of the Armenians in the remote north-eastern parts of the Turkish dominions. They had long been the victims of heavy taxation and unchecked depredations by nomadic Kurds, and from the late 1880s, roused by incipient nationalism, they started to offer sporadic resistance.[57] By 1889 news was filtering through to the British press of outrages committed against them and the *Christian World* prophesied that 'the country will speedily make its voice heard as sternly and as loudly as it did in reference to Bulgaria'.[58] Over the next few years, however, information was so scanty as to preclude all but occasional consideration of their plight. It was not until the autumn of 1894, with news of a massacre at Sassoon, that feeling first came to a head. High Church leaders played their part, as they had done in 1876. The most active leader of the protest movement was Canon Malcolm MacColl, and Charles Gore, a future bishop, was prominent, but in April 1895 Gore was upbraiding his fellow Churchmen for leaving the brunt of the agitation to Nonconformists.[59] Denominational bodies passed resolutions, Nonconformists came to the fore in local meetings, and chapels sent representatives to a national protest meeting in May.[60] The Sultan of Turkey himself is said to have dismissed the whole affair as something got up by Nonconformist ministers.[61] The agitation ebbed gradually during 1895 until it suddenly revived in much greater intensity with the arrival in November of reports of fresh atrocities. During this phase Canon MacColl deliberately restrained the chief specialist pressure group, the Anglo-Armenian Association, in the belief that Lord Salisbury was doing all he could for the Armenians.[62] It was also the peak of the period when youthful Free Church councils were eager to hold rallies and pass resolutions. For these two reasons the agitation was very much a Nonconformist-dominated movement. It culminated in a Free Church demonstration at the City Temple on 17 December that was marked by 'fierce anger' and 'burning shame'.[63] But as public attention shifted to other questions the campaign melted away after less than two months. The third and last phase of the Armenian agitation occupied the autumn of 1896. This outburst took place following the seizure of a Constantinople bank by Armenians and a number of retaliatory massacres at the end of August 1896. MacColl could no longer control the tide of feeling and local leaders of Church and chapel communities joined in a series of indignation meetings for about a month before resignation set in.[64] Nonconformist motives during this protracted affair were the same as in 1876: shame at British responsibility for upholding Turkish authority, compassion, disgust, aversion to Islam, and even devotion to Gladstone – for twice he abandoned the silence of retirement to speak on behalf of the Armenians. Again it was a potent brew; and this time it went to their heads.

A gradual change of emphasis took place in Nonconformist declarations during the course of the Armenian agitation. There was a shift away from mere protest towards calls for British intervention. At an isolated pro-Armenian rally in 1893 the Presbyterian MP Samuel Smith was careful to insist that Britain should exert only a moral influence without intervening,[65] and by and large his position was maintained by Nonconformists during the low-key first phase of the campaign in 1894–5. A national demonstration of December 1894 simply insisted on the need for an impartial inquiry and on British responsibility to press Turkey for reforms.[66] There was general acceptance that progress could be made only through joint diplomatic representations by the European powers. As the campaign wore on, however, there were occasional calls for more drastic action. In May 1895 Alexander Maclaren, a distinguished Baptist minister, told a rally in Manchester that if we had to put things right in Turkey ourselves, 'let us go!'[67] By the autumn of 1895 such unilateral intervention was commonly proposed as the solution to the ills of Armenia. In September the *Christian World* declared that, if need be, Britain must go to war on behalf of the Armenians. 'Christianity,' it claimed, 'is no more opposed to a right use of armaments than to the right use of a police force.'[68] The speakers at the City Temple demonstration in December made similar avowals. War was a curse, said John Clifford, but not the greatest curse: 'this wholesale butchery and robbery, this ravishing of maidens that was going on against the Armenians was worse than war . . .'[69] The excitement of the campaign was undermining Nonconformist inhibitions about the use of force, but at this stage statements on the subject were usually couched in reluctant terms and hedged about with reservations. The *Christian World* in September treated British intervention as only a last resort, for the government should be anxious to avert war.[70] In a document drawn up for the Congregational Union in March 1896, Guinness Rogers still expressed the conviction that Britain's obligations to the Armenians could be fulfilled 'without having recourse to war'.[71] By the third phase of the agitation in the autumn of 1896, however, many Nonconformist pronouncements threw all restraint to the winds. W. J. Dawson, a Wesleyan turned Congregationalist, was reported as declaring at his London church that 'he should say "Thank God!" if he heard that the English guns were thundering in the Dardanelles'.[72] The congregation burst into frantic cheering. At a national Free Church demonstration on 5 October Hugh Price Hughes unreservedly demanded British intervention against the 'devilry' of Turkey. If the other powers united against us, he assured his excited audience, the struggle would not last long because the combination would be directed not so much against us as against God.[73] Anger born of frustration boiled over during the Armenian affair. It accomplished little for the Armenians, whose lot was virtually unchanged and who were to suffer far worse massacres, especially during the First World War. But it did have a major effect on the Nonconformists themselves. It was the intense humanitarian feeling of the Armenian agitation that did most to change the Nonconformist view of a moral foreign policy. Instead of believing that it was best to approximate to a policy of non-intervention they were beginning to endorse the use of force in righteous causes.

Two subsequent episodes confirm this analysis of the transformation that had taken place in Nonconformist attitudes. In 1897 the European powers acted together to halt a dangerous outbreak of fighting between Christian rebels and the Turkish authorities in Crete. Nonconformists deeply sympathised with the Cretans and the Greeks who were supporting their efforts, and expressed outrage when warships of the powers fired on a party of Greek–Cretan troops. The British government, they argued, was joining in a pro-Turkish strategy when it should be helping the Cretans and their Greek allies.[74] At the National Free Church Council meetings in March it was noticed that 'nothing seems to rouse them to such a pitch of excitement as any reference to Crete'.[75] There was a distinctly bellicose mood in Nonconformity. Far from hoping that Britain could share in relaxing the tension between Greece and Turkey that in fact led to war, Nonconformists wanted British support for one side against the other. The 'popular Nonconformist line', as the critical editor of the *Daily News* put it, was to 'encourage Greece to go to war'.[76] It is clear that the preparedness to sanction the use of force generated in the Armenian agitation was no passing vagary. And an incident two years later illustrates something of the chapel psychology that was responsible for the change of view. Joseph Parker, in preaching at the Free Church Council Cromwell Tercentenary celebrations, created a minor sensation by solemnly calling on God to damn the sultan in his capacity as 'the Great Assassin'.[77] At first his words seemed to paralyse the congregation, but then it broke out in frantic applause. The sultan had become a symbol of wickedness, as much a target for moral crusades as drunkenness or gambling. Nonconformists felt bound to resist his tyrannies, as they showed again when in the autumn of 1903 they protested against his suppression of another Christian revolt, this time in Macedonia.[78] Wrong had to be put down in any sphere, and force seemed the most effective method of dealing with an intrinsically wicked foreign ruler. Accordingly, Nonconformists concluded in the late 1890s that they must be prepared to agitate in favour of military intervention.

The changing Nonconformist stance inevitably affected organised efforts for peace. In 1894, at the invitation of the Society of Friends, representatives of most Protestant denominations had formed 'The Arbitration Alliance of British Christians'. A memorial signed by denominational leaders requesting the government to propose an international decrease of armaments was forwarded in August by Robert Perks, as treasurer, to Lord Rosebery, but the Prime Minister replied merely that the issue was constantly receiving government attention and declined to receive a deputation.[79] This dismissive attitude no doubt discouraged further action, but the subsequent disappearance of the Alliance must also be partly due to the distractions from the cause of peace offered by the Armenian agitation. The desire for peace did not entirely wither. When, at the end of 1895, war with the USA suddenly seemed likely as a result of President Cleveland's implied threat to use force in a boundary dispute between British Guiana and Venezuela, the chapels and their American counterparts led the way in the interests of a pacific settlement.[80] W. T. Stead tried to maintain the resulting momentum in favour of arbitration and in 1898 launched an International Crusade of Peace that drew support from Free Church councils.[81] Projects aiming for peace could still command enthusiastic support among the Nonconformists. Yet during the later 1890s there were problems for the Peace Society as some of its members were swept away by the tide of interventionism. At the pro-Armenian demonstration of 17 December 1895, for example, the society's treasurer, the Congregational MP Walter Hazell, announced that he could not believe in peace at any price and that the time was coming for the use of force.[82] Militarism was invading even the Peace Society. The tension in the society snapped during the Cretan crisis, when the editor of the *Daily News* suggested that its members were honourable exceptions to the belligerent tone of Nonconformity. Robertson Nicoll of the *British Weekly*, in the van of the popular Nonconformist pro-Greek feeling, demanded that the society's office-holders should explain themselves.[83] Some agreed with Nicoll in favouring the cause of the Cretan Christians: in spite of their peace principles, they were prepared to countenance Greek military intervention. Others, including the secretary, Dr Evans Darby, put up a defence of the society's traditional commitment to opposing all war. Nicoll would have no truck with this position. He called on his readers to take care that the Peace Society should no longer be permitted to use chapel buildings.[84] The bulk of Nonconformists undoubtedly agreed with Nicoll. They were rejecting the idea that Britain should always seek to avoid war.

The other side of the same coin was the emergence of an enthusiasm for the navy. Willing the end of intervention dictated willing the means of powerful armed forces. W. T. Stead, whose wish for peace was only one strand in a complex mind, had done a great deal during 1884 to foster popular interest in the navy by publicising its weaknesses and calling for higher defence spending.[85] During the 1890s Stead's point of view became conventional wisdom. The so-called 'blue water' school of maritime strategists argued that Britain's defence policy must be based not on any hopes of resisting invaders once they had landed but on using a strong navy to prevent their landing in the first place. This was held to be the natural course for an island power that lacked reliable allies and needed to ensure the security of her external trade.[86] Apart from Stead, few Nonconformists could muster sympathy for the increased spending on ships, sailors and equipment that such a policy entailed until the Armenian agitation began to remodel their whole view of foreign policy. The Wesleyans, with their existing streak of imperialism, became favourable at an earlier date than the other denominations. In January 1896 the Wesleyan *London Quarterly Review* carried an article dwelling on the past achievements of the navy in suppressing the slave trade and arguing that our capacity for doing good and even for spreading the gospel 'depend upon our naval supremacy'.[87] To justify the Royal Navy as an evangelistic tool was a sure sign of its popularity. The Cretan crisis crystallised similar feelings in Nonconformity as a whole. The fleet was shown to be a means by which Britain could intervene for moral purposes abroad, even if it was sometimes being used on the wrong side. The *Christian World* welcomed higher naval estimates in March 1897 and under the heading of 'The Empire of the Sea' gave a succinct synopsis of 'blue water' thinking.[88] Favourable references to brave British sailors began to pepper the pages of Nonconformist journals. The chapels were encouraged further along this line of thinking by the intervention of the USA in Cuba in April 1898 to end the attempts of the Spanish authorities to put down a rebellion against her colonial rule. Nonconformists endorsed the American action, even though it had no justification in treaty obligations. James Owen of Swansea declared at the Baptist Union assembly, 'America was doing for Cuba what England ought to have done, what Oliver Cromwell would have done, for Armenia'.[89] The *Christian World* responded to American successes against Spain in Cuba and the Philippines by indulging the hope that one day the British and American fleets might possess the whole ocean and so prevent war.[90] The army played little or no part in Nonconformist dreams, precisely because the 'blue water' school taught that all but token land forces suitable for imperial policing were superfluous. Before the outbreak of the Boer War, however, Nonconformists had ceased to regard armaments spending as a dangerous waste. The fleet, they held with more than a touch of paradox, should be available to impose peace by force.

The transition to the dominance of imperialism in Nonconformity was completed by a sharp upsurge of nationalism and racialism. For several decades the idea that ethnic traits qualify nations either for success or failure in the struggles of the world arena had been gaining ground among the intelligentsia, but only at the end of the century did it begin to fascinate the popular mind. Britain's distinctive racial qualities, it was felt, marked her out as destined to rule over the 'inferior' races. The increasing recognition that the USA had attained the status of a great power encouraged this way of thinking, for Americans came from the same stock. Stead had held this attitude for many years, but it appeared among other Nonconformists only from 1896 onwards. In the aftermath of the Venezuela crisis, Clifford began to urge that two nations united by blood, legal traditions and ideals should be consolidated as a single 'Anglo-Saxon people'.[91] Soon Hughes was to dream of 'a day when the British Parliament should steam across the Atlantic to join the Federated Imperial Assembly at Washington'.[92] The Spanish-American War of 1898 intensified such attitudes. The decadent Spaniards seemed to be receiving due punishment at the hands of the Americans for their oppressive rule in Cuba. The Americans were 'our kith and kin';[93] Spain, still stamped in Protestant minds with the brand of the Inquisition, was little different from the unspeakable Turk. A corollary of taking the American side was suspicion of France, which in May seemed likely to enter the war in defence of Spain. The spectre of a Franco-Spanish coalition fanned the flame of an anti-Catholic nationalism in the chapels. French ambitions were very much in mind during the summer of 1898. These developments explain why Nonconformity entered so fully into the chauvinistic outburst of the Fashoda crisis in September. Hard on the heels of the news of the Battle of Omdurman that sealed the reconquest of the Sudan, there came a report of French troops at Fashoda on the upper Nile who seemed bent on robbing Britain of the fruits of victory. At the height of the tension, when Rosebery had just made a firm anti-French pronouncement, Dr Albert Goodrich of Manchester was called upon during the Congregational Union autumn assembly to welcome international arbitration proposals put forward by the tsar. Goodrich found himself passing over his prepared pacific remarks, and instead announced his agreement with Rosebery's speech, demanding that France must retire. They were not Jingoes, but, he added, amid cheers, 'We are Englishmen'.[94] Guinness Rogers, in seconding the resolution, was at one with Goodrich. In the following January, John Morley drew attention to the incident as a sign of the deplorable war fever that had swept the country. Goodrich and Rogers, according to Morley, were no better than the fighting bishops of the Middle Ages. Yet there can be no doubt, as the *Christian World* commented, that they accurately represented the overwhelming feeling in the chapels.[95] The racially based nationalism of the time ensured that residual Nonconformist reluctance to use force in support of imperial claims evaporated. Nonconformists shared fully in the climax of the growth of popular imperialism marked by the Fashoda crisis.

This recently embraced imperialism determined the prevailing Nonconformist response to the Boer War. During the spring and summer of

1899, as Britain tried to compel the Transvaal to concede the franchise to British gold prospectors, the Nonconformist press, while sometimes critical of government policy, displayed a certain imperial hauteur. The *British Weekly*, in urging the Boers to submit gracefully, reflected on what 'an almost omnipotent empire like ours should do'.[96] After the outbreak of war in October, both the leading Nonconformist weeklies favoured Rosebery's brand of imperialism which was virtually indistinguishable from that of the Conservative government. A typical Nonconformist view was that of Alfred Rowland, the cultured and influential Congregational minister at Hornsey. He expounded his version of 'Christian Imperialism' in February 1900:

> I believe it is for the world's welfare that we should rule. Has not the extending rule of Britain been for the advantage of the human race? Our Empire is no sordid monopoly; it is a sacred trust. And it is because I believe that the British ideal for South Africa is nobler than the Boer and more for the advantage of the world at large that, while I deeply deplore the war now being waged, I can and do pray for the success of British arms.[97]

The bulk of Nonconformists who held, like Rowland, that the war was honourable though lamentable were neither Jingoes nor pro-Boers, but their favourable disposition to empire separated them far more sharply from opponents of the war than from those who gloried in it outright. Among the denominations, the Baptists were not (as has been suggested) solidly against the war.[98] The London Baptist Association avoided discussing the war in the autumn of 1901, apparently for fear of revealing its divided counsels;[99] Baptists leaders included J. G. Greenhough, president of the National Free Church Council in 1902, who was a firm imperialist;[100] and the *Baptist Magazine* in February 1900 put all the blame for the war squarely on the Transvaal.[101] It is nevertheless true that more Baptist ministers than Congregationalists expressed opposition to the war, especially in its earlier months.[102] At the Congregational Union assembly in October 1899 a statement that Britain had been forced to go to war by Boer insults was received with great cheering and only a tiny volume of hissing,[103] although two years later a Congregational anti-war rally drew nearly four hundred assembly delegates.[104] The Wesleyans had the smallest number of pro-Boers in their ranks. Hughes led the greater part of the progressives in the denomination into vigorous support for the war; both connexional newspapers were closed to its critics; and in the Commons the leading Methodist MP Robert Perks had become so much the organiser of Liberal imperialists that he was dubbed 'Imperial Perks'.[105] It was estimated that at least three-quarters of the Wesleyans were convinced supporters of the war.[106] More concretely, it is known that as late as July 1901, when war fever had abated, only four of the ninety-four Wesleyan ministers in the Liverpool area opposed it.[107] Nonconformity on the whole endorsed the imperial war.

Peace feeling had nevertheless been strong up to the outbreak of hostilities. At the beginning of October local Free Church councils held peace prayer meetings;[108] the National Council urged the government to further patience;[109] and the great majority of the peace resolutions reaching the Colonial Office up to the start of November were from Nonconformist bodies.[110] The war, after all, would be fought not against a pagan, Muslim or Catholic nation in the grip of the forces of degeneration, but against a people steeled by a firmer Protestantism than prevailed in many of the Free Churches. Once Britain was at war, however, much of the pacific sentiment melted away. The remaining hard core of Nonconformist opposition can be divided into two groups. The first consisted of older men like the MPs Halley Stewart and R. L. Everett and the ministers Urijah Thomas, a Bristol Congregationalist, and Alexander Mackennal, of Bowdon Downs, Manchester. Mackennal was so distressed by the Free Church Council's failure to condemn the war that he refused to attend its committees.[111] These men felt passionately because to them the peace movement was still a crusade against wrong. They were of the generation that had been stirred by John Bright and marshalled by Henry Richard, and they would not renounce their principles, however unfashionable they had become. The second group of those who courted the taunt of being 'pro-Boer' was younger. A few like Basil Martin (Congregational minister at Hereford) repudiated all wars as un-Christian;[112] more, like Charles Aked (Baptist minister at Liverpool), embraced the theory that the war was the result of capitalist machination.[113] Silvester Horne was typical of them in experiencing 'horror and shame' at the nation's policy and an intense loneliness in his convictions.[114] Another of them, Silas Hocking, who had recently resigned from the United Methodist ministry to concentrate on writing popular novels, contrived to circumvent a ban on discussion of the war at the Free Church Council meetings in 1900, imposed for fear of divisions, by censuring the word 'empire' during a speech on a different subject.[115] The younger men, who if anything were more committed to their convictions than the older group, were among the earliest of the pacifist idealists of the twentieth century. They were responsible for creating, in January 1900, a 'Stop the War Committee', with Hocking as chairman of the committee.[116] Its president was the most distinguished of the Free Church critics of the war, John Clifford, who had drawn back from the imperialist implications of some of his earlier declarations.[117] Unlike the more moderate South Africa Conciliation Committee, the Stop the War Committee insisted that since the war was unjust it must be stopped immediately. Here was the mark of Nonconformist moral absolutism. Branches of the committee often depended on members of the Social Democratic Federation for their rank and file,[118] but they also drew extensively on Quaker support, as at Scarborough, where the ex-MP Joshua Rowntree was branch patron.[119] W. T. Stead's journalistic talents ensured greater public attention than was justified by the organisation's strength and it soon became the target for Jingo mobs.[120] Blood was drawn in struggles between intruders and attendants at a London rally addressed by Hocking, Rowntree was hustled at Scarborough and Clifford's chapel was threatened by rowdies.[121] The impression went round that Nonconformity was far less devoted to winning the war than was in fact the case.

Such an impression was encouraged by further efforts towards bringing the conflict to an end in which Clifford was the prime mover. In April 1900 he promoted a memorial to Lord Salisbury, signed by over a hundred Free Churchmen, calling for a government statement that the independence of the Boer republics would be respected in the eventual settlement.[122] In July 1901 he put to a conference of ministers in the Memorial Hall a set of proposals for a peace manifesto that he hoped would unite Nonconformity, including the idea of a South African federation with internal self-government reserved to the states. Although Clifford had come to believe that annexation was inevitable, Hocking and a vocal body of adherents still insisted, as Hocking himself put it, 'that annexation was stealing, and stealing was wicked in nations as well as individuals'.[123] These men were pure pro-Boers who hoped that Britain would gain nothing from a war that was intrinsically unjust. They were few, but they felt passionately. After a week's adjournment, the amendment sponsored by Hocking's side was defeated amidst unruly scenes.[124] The resulting peace manifesto represented the central bloc of Nonconformist opinion, not the extremists. It had even been remodelled to make it more attractive to the stauncher imperialists. Five thousand, two hundred and seventy ministers signed the manifesto before it was published in the *Daily News* in December. Its terms were laughably vague, recommending the unity of the peoples of South Africa, security against the recurrence of war, compensation for destroyed homes and a general amnesty. Even Hughes, though his name was said to have been lost through a misunderstanding, gave the manifesto his benediction.[125] The manifesto does not suggest that condemnation of the Boer War was widespread in the Free Churches, even at this late stage in the conflict. Rather it confirms that peace principles had to be watered down before they were acceptable to the bulk of imperially minded Nonconformists.

Yet a concern for peace in the chapels did survive the Boer War. Probably most deeply felt, because grounded in racial empathy, was a wish for good relations with the USA. When President Taft appealed for an Anglo-American arbitration agreement in 1911, there was a flurry of resolutions by Nonconformist bodies, and F. B. Meyer, in conveying a congratulatory address from the Free Churches to the White House, found himself invited to Taft's silver wedding celebrations.[126] The *entente cordiale* with France was approved by the *Christian World* as 'one of the most distinctly Christian procedures that modern history records',[127] but Nonconformist spokesmen, wary of entanglements with a specific power, tended to argue that it should be made the prelude to an era of general peace among the civilised nations.[128] There was a widespread welcome among Free Church councils for the international peace conference that assembled in 1907 at The Hague.[129] Germany's opposition to arbitration proposals at the conference provoked one of the British delegates, the Quaker MP, J. Allen Baker, into conceiving the idea of fostering closer Anglo-German links through the churches.[130] He launched the scheme through the Metropolitan Free Church Council, of which he was president in 1907, and in the following year a delegation of German churchmen spent ten days on a goodwill visit to Britain.[131] In 1909 the Metropolitan Free Church Council organised a return visit by some 140 British church leaders to Germany.[132] Both trips were matters of display rather than solid achievement, with much sightseeing, eating and speechifying.[133] But they did have a significant effect on opinion in all the churches. Denominational organisations resolved in favour of peace with Germany, and 'The Associated Councils in the British and German Empires for fostering Friendly Relations between the Two Peoples' were set up in 1911.[134] The Nonconformist press swung towards a mildly pro-German stance. The people of Britain, according to the *British Weekly* at the time of the Agadir crisis in 1911, had no will to go to war for the sake of France.[135] There were individual Nonconformists, like P. W. Wilson, MP, a columnist of the *Daily News* and a member of the council of Silvester Horne's London congregation, who spoke out against the arms race with Germany,[136] but it was not until December 1913 that there was anything like a mass movement of opinion against the stockpiling of armaments.[137] Lloyd George, as part of a Cabinet battle against Winston Churchill's increased naval estimates, encouraged the public to denounce militarism. Ironically, the Free Churches as a result became more devoted to peace than for twenty years in the months immediately before the outbreak of the Great War. The Free Church Council organising committee urged the government to reduce its armaments;[138] at the Peace Society annual meeting Clifford declared that there must be renewed vigilance against war;[139] and the *British Weekly* ran a series of articles on 'War and Christianity' in which several writers called for Christians to be pacifists.[140] A number of Nonconformists including Allen Baker and Clifford were actually travelling to a Churches' Peace Congress at Constance when hostilities commenced.[141] At first a great number of Free Church councils called for neutrality so that Britain could mediate in the conflict.[142] But attitudes soon hardened, especially when the first reports came in of German atrocities. Immediately yearnings for peace were extinguished and stronger Nonconformist passions were stirred. The rulers of Germany assumed the role of the Sultan of Turkey in the demonology of the chapels. Robertson Nicoll called on 3 September 1914 for the crushing of the Prussian military system. 'There is not', he concluded, 'a more flagrant iniquity on earth.'[143] The Great War became a crusade.

By the opening of the twentieth century Nonconformity had embraced a new set of attitudes to foreign affairs. At the centenary of Cobden's birth in 1904 the *Christian World* declared confidently that while its readers still adhered to Cobden's principle of free trade, they no longer believed that political separation from the colonies was desirable.[144] The Free Churches had started to take pride in the expanding empire and did not shrink from the implication that Britain would have to defend her world-wide interests by force of arms. R. F. Horton was right when he said of the Boer War in 1901 that 'Free Churchmen as a body are in line with the general national sentiment on this question'.[145] Their views had ceased to be distinctive. There were, of course, exceptions, chiefly among those of an older generation who harked back to resistance to imperialism in the 1870s and among some in a younger generation who inclined to pacifism. By the time of the Great War the first of these groups had virtually disappeared, and so in 1914 only a handful of younger men like Leyton Richards, minister of the Bowdon Downs Congregational Church, swam against the tide of patriotic militarism that swept away most Nonconformists.[146] The great change of view was not an entire about-turn, for Nonconformists as a whole had never been committed to the great radical rallying cry of non-intervention. Wesleyans, in particular, were at all times in the nineteenth century favourably disposed to the spread of British political influence as a counterpart to British missionary influence. Other Nonconformists, however, had shown far greater sympathy for the principles of Cobden and Bright. They remained opposed to the growth of empire and suspicious of the armed forces into the last decade of the nineteenth century. Humanitarian concern for the Third World had not sapped their resistance to imperialism, even though it did affect their missionaries in the field. The transformation of their views was achieved partly by the ideas of racial superiority current in the 1890s, but far more important was their intense sympathy for the Christian victims of Turkish oppression. The Armenian agitation of 1894–6 was primarily responsible for the shift in Nonconformist attitudes. In the midst of a heady crusade old convictions could be cast aside when they conflicted with an apparent moral imperative. The wickedness of the sultan was sufficient to justify British intervention. The Nonconformist passion for righteousness had enormous political repercussions. It made a great impact in the field of education also.

7 The Education of the People

They had no doubt that they were on the side of God, of truth, and of the children. (C. H. Kelly, an ex-president of the Wesleyans, to the Free Church Council National Conference against the Education Act, April 1902)[1]

Education was the issue that brought Nonconformity most prominently into the political arena in the late nineteenth and early twentieth centuries. This was the period of the creation and consolidation of a national system of elementary education in England and Wales. In 1870 W. E. Forster's Education Act provided for the establishment of the first schools under public control, the board schools; and in 1902 Balfour's Act decreed that local authorities should assume responsibility for elementary education. Although the state was taking over as schoolmaster to the nation, the churches, which had traditionally filled this role, still expected a large share in the determination of public policy in this field. There was some scope for tension between Church and state, but the division of the religious life of England determined that the chief controversies should be between the Church of England and the chapels. As over four-fifths of the publicly inspected elementary schools in the middle years of the century had been set up under the auspices of the Church of England, and as they continued to be Anglican-controlled after the Act of 1870, the great aim of the Church of England was to defend its existing stake in education. Nonconformity possessed few schools to defend. Dissenters had often been the mainstay of the undenominational British and Foreign Schools Society, and following the passing of Forster's Act many British schools were transferred to newly created school boards. Nonconformist elementary schools belonging to particular denominations had been relatively few before 1870 and only the Wesleyans retained an appreciable number during the school board era. Consequently, the major aim of Nonconformity was not to preserve its interests against the state but to roll back the educational hegemony of the Church of England. Although this was a persistent object throughout the period, the campaign varied in intensity over time. Educational grievances were most strongly felt in the wake of the two great Acts of 1870 and 1902. There was a period of relative calm from the mid-1870s to the early 1890s, but even before the passing of the 1902 Act there was a quickening of the tempo of the controversy. At the start of the period and for a longer span of years later on, education was a crusading issue.

Around 1870 the education battle was treated as a branch of the broader crusade for religious equality. There must be no public recognition of a favoured position for the Church of England in the schools, it was argued, just as ecclesiastical privilege must not be tolerated anywhere. This stance went back to 1843, the year of the previous attempt by the state to set up the rudiments of a national system of education. The education clauses of Sir James Graham's Factory Bill provided that schools maintained at public expense should be run by the Church of England, but an outburst of Nonconformist protest induced the government to abandon the scheme. In the course of the controversy Nonconformists began to contend that the state should never venture into educating the nation's children at all. Edward Baines, the proprietor of the *Leeds Mercury* and a leading Congregationalist, became the champion of this view. Nonconformity, he pointed out, had concluded that Church and state should be separate. If that was true in general, it was specially true of education. State help to the Church of England would enable it to indoctrinate children with its distinctive denominational teaching. That would be a serious infringement of religious liberty. Furthermore, it would be for the state to go beyond its proper secular bounds. Instruction of the young, according to Baines and his friends, necessarily included the imparting of religious knowledge which should be left to voluntary agencies formed by the churches.[2] Such educational voluntaryism was the normal ground taken by Congregationalists and Baptists in the 1850s and 1860s. Wesleyans, who were grateful for government grants to their schools, never toyed with this view, but, as Edward Miall frequently argued in *The Nonconformist*, it was a natural position for disestablishers to adopt. Only at the end of the 1860s did doubts begin to creep into the minds of the younger men. Population growth was hopelessly outstripping funds given voluntarily for popular education. Perhaps, after all, the state should be entrusted with responsibility for schools. After the Reform Act of 1867 there was both a need for electors to be educated and a check at the polls on government manipulation of education in the interests of the established order. Such thoughts promoted R. W. Dale of Birmingham to urge on his fellow Nonconformists the need for a national system of education, publicly funded and publicly enforced. The realities of the situation ensured him a rapid success. By the beginning of 1870 he was able to win over even a majority of Nonconformist ministers in Leeds, the stronghold of Edward Baines.[3] Dale, together with Miall and the Liberation Society leadership, had come to accept that the state alone had the power to bring instruction to the mass of the nation's children. But neither Dale nor those who agreed with him wished to abandon Baines's insistence that education must not be an instrument for the aggrandisement of the Established Church.

Nonconformity therefore welcomed the Liberal government's introduction in 1870 of a measure designed to make elementary education available to all. There was soon dismay, however, over some of the advantages assured by the Bill to the Church of England. In particular, it did not prohibit Anglican denominational instruction in the new schools which were to be created. Nonconformists would have to pay for the teaching of doctrines they believed to be false. They felt betrayed by a government that they had done a great deal to elect. Their cause was taken up by the National Education League, founded at Birmingham in the previous year by a group including Joseph Chamberlain to press for a free system of unsectarian national education.[4] The league's chief parliamentary spokesman, George Dixon, was an Anglican, but much of its support was Nonconformist. A Central Nonconformist Committee, with Dale as one of its secretaries, also sprang up at Birmingham to concert protests against the Bill. The committee engineered a telling demonstration of the volume of opposition. Every Nonconformist minister was requested to sign a petition to the House of Commons and a protest to Gladstone. Of 7,300 canvassed, 5,173 returned their signatures within four days. Even a majority of Wesleyan ministers, in defiance of the conventional 'no politics' rule, responded favourably. Gladstone was impressed. As the Bill was entering its committee stage in June, he announced that the government would accept an amendment proposed by William Cowper-Temple excluding from the new schools any 'catechism or religious formulary' distinctive of a particular denomination. The concession did something to dampen the fires of resentment among Nonconformists. Yet their grumbling persisted, as even if distinctive formularies were banned, distinctive teachings might creep in; and they were irritated by Gladstone's simultaneous statement that exchequer grants to Church schools would be increased by one half. Persistent opposition by Nonconformists and their sympathisers in the Commons, the so-called 'Irreconcilables', could not prevent the carrying of the Bill by the government, which was able to draw on Conservative support. The parliamentary battle, however, was merely the overture to a more sustained campaign against the final form of the Act, the 'Nonconformist revolt'. Early in 1871 attention turned to the twenty-fifth clause, which provided that children in poor law institutions should be sent to school as a charge on the rates. The school might be a denominational school. There was deep annoyance that, despite the modifications made to the Bill, the public might still be compelled to pay for denominational instruction.[5] It was a problem of tiny proportions: in 1872 only forty-three school boards chose to send any very poor children to Church schools.[6] Yet Dale led the way in declaring that it was sufficient ground for the severance of Nonconformist support for Liberalism; official Liberal candidates were opposed;[7] and in 1872 and 1873 at a few places like Sheffield rates were refused.[8] The explanation of the intensity of feeling among Nonconformists is not that they calculated that this would be a favourable opportunity for exerting their political influence. On the contrary, the effect of their revolt, as Dale foresaw, was a weakening of support for Gladstone's ministry that contributed to its defeat at the polls in 1874 and a consequent nullification of Nonconformist influence. They reacted so sharply because they believed that it was intrinsically wrong for the Church of England to receive assistance from public moneys. 'The School rate', as the *Baptist Magazine* put it, 'becomes the successor of the church rate'.[9] The principle of religious equality, still generally a matter of religious conviction in the early 1870s, was at stake.

In the heat of the reaction against the 1870 Education Act a new Nonconformist attitude was forged. It was unanimously felt that the provisions of the measure were obnoxious, but at first there was disagreement over the alternative to be proposed. What form of religious education could safely be entrusted to the agents of the state? Because until very recently Nonconformity had contended that the state should not meddle with education at all, the question had not previously arisen. But when in June 1870 it became necessary to put forward a Commons amendment, a decision had to be taken. There were long consultations between Dale, Miall, Henry Richard and a knot of other leading men and it became clear that there were two alternatives: either schools should be restricted to Bible reading or else their teaching should be purely secular, with religious instruction left to the churches. The first seemed unsatisfactory both because it presented a version of Christianity shorn of its doctrinal basis and because it was offensive to Roman Catholics who believed that the Bible and church teaching must go hand in hand. The second seemed more logical to Liberationists and was known to be less unacceptable to Gladstone. Accordingly, Henry Richard moved an amendment to the Bill on going into committee urging that 'religious instruction should be supplied by voluntary effort, and not out of public funds'.[10] Dale soon earned a measure of popular notoriety as the man who wanted to abolish the Bible in the schools of England. 'Let the school be secular', he would argue; 'Let the churches find how to draw the children to Christ . . . '[11] It was entirely novel and rather strange for men who prided themselves on their biblicism to adopt a policy of excluding the Bible from schools. Inevitably there was opposition. Four hundred ministers and laymen, many of them distinguished figures like Eustace Conder, John Stoughton and Newman Hall, issued a round robin protesting against the secular theory as inconsistent with Christian responsibility for educating the nation's youth.[12] But the view steadily gained ground until, for instance, the *Baptist Magazine* noted in February 1873 that a 'large majority' of the denomination accepted the secular platform.[13] Similarly the 1872 Congregational Union assembly voted overwhelmingly in favour of eliminating religious instruction from the national education system.[14] The crucial break-through had come in January 1872 at a conference of nearly 1,900 Nonconformist delegates summoned to Manchester to consider their attitude on the education question. One decision was to withold support from parliamentary candidates unless they pledged themselves to modify the Education Act. The other was to insist that the only satisfactory solution to the education problem lay in excluding the Bible from state-provided schools.[15] Militant Nonconformity took this axiom as its battle-cry. It was a sign that enthusiasm for the separation of Church and state remained the chief determinant of Nonconformist convictions about education.

After 1874 there was a period of quiescence in the national debate over education that lasted for twenty years. Local controversy was often fierce as Church and chapel contended for control of the school boards set up under the terms of the 1870 Act, but no more than echoes of the battles of 1870–4 were heard at Westminster and in the national press. Nonconformist passions subsided. Part of the explanation lies in political circumstances. The twenty-fifth clause of the 1870 Act was re-pealed by Lord Sandon's Education Act of 1876 so that the main target of the Nonconformist resentment disappeared. No longer was there a standing educational irritant. From 1876, also, attention was diverted elsewhere. The rank and file in the chapels became more concerned with foreign affairs. Even the leaders turned to other matters – Dale to academic and denominational issues, Guinness Rogers to encouraging Nonconformist permeation of the Liberal Party, and Henry Richard, though still concerned with the world of learning, to the task of promoting secondary and higher education in Wales. The Liberation Society leadership paid very little attention to the elementary schools. When in 1881 it considered pressing a number of issues, for instance, the only educational items discussed were ensuring religious equality in the college statutes of Oxford and Cambridge and campaigning against ecclesiastical tests in teacher training colleges.[16] The national education system was ignored. Furthermore, the whole question of elementary schooling was a sensitive area for the Liberal Party. It risked losing the support of Churchmen if it veered towards criticising denominational schools or adopting a Nonconformist position about the curriculum of board schools. After 1886 the problem was aggravated by the need to accommodate the wishes of the party's Irish allies in the Home Rule campaign. Catholic voters were as committed to the welfare of their own denominational schools as to the cause of Ireland and might defect from their Liberal allegiance if they noticed any hostility towards them.

Nonconformists with one eye for the electoral position of the party could not afford to push forward the education issue. Political circumstances conspired to weaken the cause.

A more fundamental reason for Nonconformist acceptance of a national truce over elementary education was the decline of the principle of religious equality among them. The process analysed in Chapter 2 affected attitudes to education as much as to the other questions within the ambit of the Liberation Society. A good gauge of the decline is the decreasing popularity of the secular solution. In 1891 J. A. Picton, once a Congregational minister and then a staunch Liberationist MP, lamented that since 1870 'we have almost completely abandoned our objections to the endowment of religion so long as it is only endowed in the schools'.[17] Similarly in 1887 Charles Williams admitted that although Baptists might in theory prefer a secular system, there was in practice a general acceptance of the unsectarian teaching actually given in the board schools.[18] The theological acceptability of board school religion to almost all Nonconformists except Unitarians helps explain the rapid decay of the secular policy after the early 1870s. Most boards had given religious instruction according to a formula first adopted in London on the proposal of Joseph Angus, principal of the Baptist Regent's Park College and one of the leading Nonconformist defenders of the place of the Bible in state schools. Teachers were to read the Bible 'with such explanations and such instruction therefrom in the principles of Morality and Religion as are suited to the capacities of the children'.[19] Evangelical Nonconformists could hardly cavil at a presentation of Christianity at once so biblical, definite and educationally respectable. It was virtually identical with what they would have taught in their own Sunday Schools. In the regular three-yearly school board elections, Nonconformists became accustomed to championing this undenominational religion against the criticisms of the Church of England. Their candidates would be called 'The Undenominational Eight' or 'The Unsectarian Six'. As they came to identify themselves with undenominational religion so they gradually shed their belief that ideally schools should be rid of it. By 1888 the Hampshire Congregational Union, when passing a resolution on education policy, said nothing of the secular goal, but merely condemned any tampering with the 1870 prohibition of denominational formularies.[20] The mass of Nonconformists had abandoned the principle of secular education that had been their rallying call in 1872. They were content with the existing state of affairs.

If Nonconformists had little desire to change the elementary education system in these years, both the Church of England and the Conservatives took care to avoid provocative action. There were only three occasions when Nonconformists felt that their interests were threatened. Each time their protests were muted because the proposals were hard to oppose outright. The first occasion was in 1876, when the

Conservative government made elementary education compulsory in many parts of the country. Nonconformists would therefore be forced to send their children to an Anglican school if there was none other in the area. Henry Richard vainly proposed a Commons amendment urging that compulsory education should be accompanied by a transfer of denominational schools to public management so that the children of Nonconformists should be safeguarded.[21] But there was no popular agitation. The leaders of the National Education League at Birmingham had announced their view that, since Nonconformists in practice already sent their children to nearby Anglican schools rather than leave them uneducated, the Bill would do little to aggravate the injustice they suffered. Dale and Guinness Rogers concurred, and the Bill was generally accepted.[22] The second occasion was in 1888, when the Royal Commission on elementary education under Viscount Cross published its reports. Although the Royal Commission included Dale, Richard and other friends of religious equality, most of its members had been selected by a Conservative administration with a view to ensuring recommendations favourable to Church schools. The Majority Report, issued in August, duly proposed increased government financial support for denominational schools and, most alarmingly to Nonconformists, rate aid for them as well. Guinness Rogers had already given warning that Nonconformists would refuse rates for schools 'managed by the priesthood' and vehemently attacked the Majority Report at the Congregational Union autumn assembly.[23] The Liberation Society summoned a conference which, at the end of November, gave birth to a new body, the National Education Association, that was designed to demand that denominational schools should receive no rate aid unless they came under effective popular control.[24] Battle seemed about to be joined. The National Society of the Church of England, however, decided at the beginning of November against pressing for rate aid for the schools under its care since it feared that its opponents' call for popular control might be successful. The government also cried off. The Conservative leaders were afraid to introduce legislation lest they should lose the support of board school defenders among the Liberal Unionists, upon whom they depended for a majority.[25] Proposals never assumed concrete form and so, as in 1876, there was no outburst of Nonconformist passion.

The third occasion when policies unwelcome to Nonconformity were put forward was in 1891. The Conservatives carried a Bill providing an extra grant to enable elementary schools to give their education free. Most, though not all, schools seized the opportunity to abolish fees. Salisbury knew that this measure would prove popular with agricultural labourers,[26] but he had other political objectives as well. He wanted to eliminate the risk that a future Liberal administration would couple popular control with free education; and he was eager to sow confusion in the Liberal ranks, knowing that they were divided over whether to accept free education without popular control.[27] The more extreme Nonconformists like Alfred Illingworth were unwilling to see the clerical ascendancy in Church schools buttressed by permitting them extra financial support from the state. In 1885, for instance, Illingworth had resisted an attempt by Chamberlain to make free education alone the immediate policy of the Liberals. At the National Liberal Federation, Illingworth had carried an amendment affirming that the abolition of fees must take second place behind full popular control.[28] Illingworth had not changed his position in 1891. At a meeting held at the National Liberal Club in May to discuss the party's attitude to free education, Illingworth, with typical doggedness, insisted that they should demand public management at the same time.[29] He maintained his personal campaign by inveighing in the Commons against the Bill as conceived in the interests of the national Church.[30] There can be no doubt that Illingworth's stand enjoyed widespread sympathy among Nonconformists, but there was no mass agitation against the government measure. Free education, after all, was believed to be desirable in itself. Furthermore, Guinness Rogers, at this time at the height of his influence over Nonconformist politics, had set himself to deprecate any movement against the measure. Devoted as usual to the interests of Liberalism, he wanted to avoid playing Salisbury's game by causing embarrassment to the party leaders.[31] Following Rogers's lead, the Liberation Society criticised the Bill for increasing the endowment of denominational schools, but urged only amendment, not unequivocal opposition.[32] 'Why do not Nonconformist ministers speak out?', asked an editorial in the *Christian World* probably written by Picton, who shared Illingworth's intransigence.[33] The answer was both that Salisbury had deliberately chosen favourable ground for an engagement and that by 1891 too few Nonconformists felt passionately about the need to curb Church control in the schools.

Over the next few years, however, there was a quickening of Nonconformist interest in the education debate. The period of quiescence did not last beyond 1894. The change was not a consequence of any revival of convictions about religious equality. On the contrary, as Chapter 2 showed, they continued to decay. The primary explanation is that the Church of England moved on to the offensive in the field of education. This was part and parcel of the Anglican resurgence at the end of the nineteenth century. By the 1890s the proportion of the population taking communion on Easter Day in the Church of England was certainly on the increase. Underlying the growth in the number of worshippers was a confident spirit that was specially marked in the clergy. Clerical recruitment was at an all-time peak in the 1880s.[34] Consequently there was at work an army of young clergymen, many of them Oxford and Cambridge graduates, zealous for the advance of the

National Church. The prevailing tone among them was a High Churchmanship that looked back to the Oxford Movement of the 1830s for its inspiration. What Nonconformists usually stigmatised as 'ritualism' was to them the norm. By 1894 in over 5,000 churches the clergyman had adopted the eastward position at the eucharist with its implication that he was a priest offering sacrifice to God on behalf of the people.[35] There was a growing fringe of extremists eager to experiment with vestments, incense and processional lights. Some hoped for early reunion with the Roman Catholic Church; a few acknowledged in private the legitimacy of papal authority. Church schools were important to them all. Education was the key to inculcating a devoted churchmanship in the rising generation. There was, therefore, no question of surrendering Church schools to the control of the state or a godless public authority of any kind. Churchmen nevertheless argued that it was the duty of the state to assist the Established Church in its educational responsibilities. By the 1890s the denominational schools – or, as they were now usually called, the voluntary schools – were in acute need of financial support. Their buildings, mostly built before 1870, were in constant need of repair; ordinary expenditure on salaries and facilities had to be increased in order to compete with the board schools; and income from voluntary subscriptions was not keeping pace. After 1890 the number of voluntary schools, which had increased steadily since the beginning of the century, began to fall.[36] There was a rising tide of opinion that the state must bale out the Church schools. Nonconformity was confronted by a Church militant.

Hostilities reopened as a result of events surrounding the London School Board. A group of energetic High Churchmen on the board led by a layman, Athelstan Riley, determined to ensure that the teaching given in its schools was thoroughly dogmatic. One of Riley's group, the Rev. J. J. Coxhead, while attending religious instruction at an infants' school in November 1892, noticed that a child who was asked the name of the father of Jesus answered 'Joseph' and was not corrected.[37] Coxhead believed that failure to insist that God was the father of Jesus amounted to a denial of the doctrine of the incarnation. He and his friends used the incident to illustrate their view that board school instruction could degenerate into practical Unitarianism. As a remedy, they brought forward and eventually carried in January 1894 a contentious proposal to strengthen the board's definition of the type of explanation of the Bible to be given in the schools. The compromise phrase of 1871 about 'Morality and Religion' was replaced by 'the Christian religion and morality'. They then wished to issue a circular imposing a Trinitarian understanding of the term 'Christian' on their teachers. There was vigorous opposition on the board from those, including Nonconformists, who did not want teachers in publicly managed schools to be subject to tests of religious orthodoxy, and resistance by the teachers' union soon compelled the withdrawal of the circular.[38] Nonconformists, together with teachers' bodies and labour organisations, were provoked by the episode into launching a campaign to replace the Moderate and 'clericalist' majority with Progressives at the next school board election in November 1894. Leading Nonconformists held a meeting to plan their strategy over a year beforehand.[39] In the event, the Moderates retained control, though with a reduced majority. But in the course of the protracted controversy the chapels of the capital were deeply stirred: all the Nonconformist ministers of the St Pancras division, for instance, urged support for the Progressives from their pulpits on a Sunday evening in July.[40] The struggle also drew national attention. Both the Congregational and Baptist Unions endorsed the Progressive policy[41] and the *Christian World* commenced a weekly column headed 'The Church and the Schools' to publicise clerical machinations throughout the country. Nonconformity began to feel strongly about education again. Although the battle was partly occasioned by the issue of religious tests, favourite ground for advocates of religious equality, this aspect was not what roused the chapels. Silvester Horne, a Congregational minister in the thick of the fray, noted in his diary that 'it was curious to see how we fought on the old Catholic and Protestant lines. Our side urged that the Bible should be trusted to tell its own story and teach its own doctrines. Their side said, No, it needs to be explained by a circular . . .'[42] Nonconformist anti-Catholicism, already stirred up by debate over Ireland, was turned against Anglican High Churchmen. The false and wicked teaching insinuated into the National Church, they felt, had to be resisted at all costs. According to John Clifford, Athelstan Riley was 'attempting to capture the schools of the nation for Roman Catholicism'.[43] Perhaps the chief effect of the London School Board election of 1894 was to inject anti-Catholicism into Nonconformist attitudes to the schools and so to reinvigorate their willingness to do battle over education.

The other side of the coin was that the 1894 controversy rallied Nonconformity as a whole to the defence of Bible teaching in the elementary schools. Even Guinness Rogers, who had wholeheartedly backed Dale's secular policy in the past, acquiesced in Bible teaching.[44] One reason was that, since the High Church party presented the issue as one between Christianity and secularism, Nonconformists were eager to repudiate the charge by emphasising that they wanted definite religious instruction based on the Bible to be given in the schools. The Progressive candidates were even pledged to accept the insertion of 'Christian' in the 1871 compromise formula.[45] Those Nonconformists who entertained lingering doubts about the wisdom of keeping Bible teaching were swayed by their allies as much as by their foes. In particular, the Wesleyan contingent had no time for any suggestion that their ultimate aim was the elimination of religious instruction from state schools. The

Wesleyans had remained untouched by the theory of religious equality and so had no sympathy for the secular solution. In 1870 they had sent a deputation to Gladstone urging that no school board by-law should prohibit scriptural instruction.[46] On this issue the more advanced members of the connexion led by Hughes were at one with the defenders of tradition like Dr Rigg, principal of the Wesleyan Teacher Training College, who often announced his antipathy to 'the complete secularization of all public day schools'.[47] Wesleyan participation in the election campaign of 1894 was therefore a powerful inducement for Nonconformity to avoid breaking ranks on the question of the Bible. But the chief explanation for the dropping of the secular policy was that the prevailing Nonconformist attitude was beginning to be determined not by cold theory but by the warm emotions of popular Protestantism. Fairness to all religious groups must bow before the imperative to teach children the way of salvation. The exclusion of the Bible from the schools became almost as unthinkable as the inclusion of Anglican teaching. Either policy would be an assault on Evangelical religion. Very few apart from the Unitarians, untouched as they were by Evangelicalism, remained wedded to the secular position. In February 1894, at the height of the battle against Rileyism, John Clifford was actually prepared to enter public controversy against a leading Unitarian opponent of Bible teaching.[48] In June, Clifford and other prominent Nonconformists began to co-operate with a group of Anglicans, chiefly Evangelicals, who preferred simple Bible teaching to denominational instruction with an Anglo-Catholic slant.[49] The joint Bible Education Council that emerged drew up its own list of candidates who would support what they held to be a distinctly Christian curriculum.[50] Nonconformist leaders, as well as the rank and file, were beginning to see themselves as champions of the Bible. Contentment with the Bible in the board schools had previously bred passivity in the chapels over education, but when its place was attacked by either High Churchmen or Unitarians the biblicism of Evangelical Nonconformity was a powerful spur to action.

A second Anglican initiative, launched within a year of the London School Board controversy, gave fresh impetus to Nonconformist concern with education. Before the general election of 1895 the National Society put forward, with Lord Salisbury's blessing, proposals for reorganising the elementary education system. The Conservative Party was committed to helping Church schools. Consequently the primary issue at the election, according to the *Christian World*, was 'the fate of our schools'.[51] Following the Conservative victory, the government introduced in the 1896 session a Bill designed to give greater financial support to voluntary schools and (even more seriously in Nonconformist eyes) to permit the entry of clergymen into board schools to give denominational instruction. Not least because of the volume of

Nonconformist denunciation, the Bill encountered serious parliamentary difficulties and was eventually withdrawn. Its successor in the 1897 session was far narrower in scope. It provided that there should be state aid of 5s per child to voluntary schools, but did not tamper with board schools. Although Lloyd George led a campaign of harassment in the Commons, there was little mass opposition and the Bill passed with relative ease. In 1895–6, however, there had been a remarkable upsurge of Nonconformist agitation. The basis of the nationwide movement, as in the 1894 campaign in London, was a stirring of popular Protestantism. At the June meeting which formed the climax of the protests in 1896, the loudest cheering was reserved for speakers who declared that they were the champions of Protestantism against the crypto-Catholicism of the Church of England.[52] One or two new organisations sprang up, it is true, to argue the case chiefly on religious equality lines. A Birmingham and Midland Education League, a conscious revival of the National Education League of 1869, and a Lancashire and Cheshire Unsectarian Education Committee were created with largely Nonconformist support. Before the end of 1896 the Lancashire body had fused with a Yorkshire Committee of Civil Rights to become the Northern Counties Education League, which, under Alfred Illingworth, was for many years to maintain a vigorous propaganda in favour of universal school boards.[53] These organisations, however, were less representative of rank-and-file chapel opinion than the Free Church councils, which for the first time played a significant part in national politics by fighting the government proposals. During the autumn of 1895 council after council passed a resolution condemning increased grants to denominational schools. Policy statements reflected the overwhelming current of opinion in favour of keeping Bible teaching. The Free Church Congress in March 1896 endorsed existing religious instruction under the Cowper-Temple clause without any attempt by the remaining advocates of the secular solution to move an amendment.[54] The Free Church council movement responded to the Anglican initiative of 1895–6 by voicing the popular Protestantism of ordinary chapel-goers.

The quickened tempo of the education debate in the 1890s meant that Nonconformists became more sensitive about their existing grievances. The chief problem was the state of affairs in many rural elementary schools. As it became more widely assumed that the day would soon dawn when a publicly administered school would be available in every locality, it seemed anomalous that so many villages had only a Church school. In the 1890s there were some eight thousand such 'single-school areas'. Nonconformist parents suffered the standing grievance of having no choice but to send their children to a school where denominational instruction was given. There was, in theory, the conscience clause that allowed parents to withdraw their children from religious instruction. Most incidents involving pressure on the children of Nonconformist parents, however, took place outside periods of religious instruction. It is hardly surprising that those responsible for Church schools should sometimes try to persuade the pupils to attend church rather than chapel. 'One day', the 1891 Congregational Union assembly was told of a village school near Dudley, 'the curate asked the children who attended the Nonconformist Sunday-school to put up their hands, and he said, "I am sorry there are so many children not going to heaven!" and told them that Jesus never went to a chapel, and that chapels were not mentioned in the Bible.'[55] Such tales were no doubt elaborated in the telling, and Dale found it difficult to obtain details of authentic cases for presentation to the Cross Commission.[56] Yet it was inevitable that in the minority of schools under close supervision by the parson and the squire's lady the whole tenor of school life should encourage Anglican loyalties. Furthermore, Nonconformist parents were normally reluctant to request the withdrawal of their children from denominational instruction. Of some two million children attending National Society schools in the mid-1880s, only 2,200 children were wholly withdrawn and 5,960 partly withdrawn.[57] The failure to take advantage of the conscience clause was partly because the denominational content of the religious teaching was often in practice low, and partly because the alternative was no religious teaching at all. Some parents were deterred from exercising their rights, however, because they hesitated to incur the odium of breaking the customs of a tight-knit community, and others because they were unwilling to mark out children among their fellows. For these reasons the conscience clause itself became a grievance. Robert Perks frequently referred to the sad lot of the pupil who was excluded from the early morning session of religious instruction. 'The picture of a little child', ran the report of his speech to the first Free Church Congress, 'shivering outside a schoolhouse door on a winter's day, waiting to get in and get warm, and having the finger of scorn pointed at it because it took advantage of the conscience clause, brought ringing cheers.'[58] There was resentment of the stigma of appealing to the clause. Although most Nonconformists carrying political weight lived in the cities, sympathy for their rural brethren significantly reinforced their determination to resist 'clerical aggression' in the schools.

A second educational grievance, though less widely canvassed than the problem of single-school areas, affected Nonconformists in the cities as much as in the countryside. This was the problem of entry to the teaching profession. In 1886, two-thirds of the places for students in teacher training colleges were at Anglican institutions. Only one-fifth of the places were available at institutions where Nonconformists could enter open competition with other applicants.[59] Wesleyans had their own training college, and so seldom suffered, but in some parts of the country other Nonconformists were effectively debarred from becoming teachers. George Hay Morgan, for instance, a Baptist barrister who was to sit in the Commons from 1906 and act as secretary to the Nonconformist group of MPs engaged in the education controversy, had become a pupil teacher in a Church school in the 1880s, but abandoned a career in teaching when he was told that he must become a Churchman if he were to receive a public grant for entering training college.[60] The grievance was particularly acute since few could follow Morgan's steps into an alternative profession. Teaching was commonly, especially for women, the only potential avenue to social advancement. Various remedies were proposed to the Cross Commission. It was suggested that denominational tests should be abolished in training colleges, as they had been in the universities, or that the government should found new unsectarian colleges.[61] Nothing, however, was done during the 1890s. In 1901 thirty-five of the forty-four training colleges still maintained a religious test.[62] The problem was specially galling in that the state paid some 95 per cent of the expenses of the colleges.[63] The Liberal administration eventually grappled with the problem in the wake of the 1906 victory. In 1907 it issued regulations imposing conscience clauses on teacher training colleges.[64] After two years of haggling, a compromise was reached whereby candidates would train for the profession without making a statement of denominational allegiance and without having to receive instruction about giving religious education.[65] Up till then, however, the sense of the injustice of arrangements for entering the teaching profession aggravated Nonconformist resentment about their broader educational grievances.

Another education issue inflamed Nonconformist feelings intermittently during the period, and more especially in the late 1890s. The Roman Catholics of Ireland repeatedly called for the creation of a publicly endowed degree-giving university that would give definite Catholic teaching to laymen. From time to time governments wishing to conciliate Ireland tried to devise arrangements that would satisfy them and yet not trigger off an outburst of Protestant objections. Gladstone's Bill of 1873, designed to set up an examining university body to which Irish colleges of any denomination could affiliate, was a signal failure, for the reaction was so strong as to cause the Bill's defeat and the temporary resignation of the government. There were grumbles of Nonconformist discontent over Beaconsfield's Act of 1879 that founded a degree-giving Royal University of Ireland and again over Balfour's suggestions, as Chief Secretary for Ireland, for a more full-blooded Catholic university in 1887 and 1889. The sharpest Nonconformist reaction came in the few years after 1897, when Balfour again raised the Irish university question by accepting an amendment to the Queen's Speech moved by Nationalists. His proposals, which emerged two years later, were for two new universities at Dublin and Belfast, both technically undenominational but intended for Catholics and Protestants respectively.[66] The leading campaigner against any concession to

Catholic claims for a university was Robert Perks, who used to attribute the intensity of his views on this question to the old Methodist nurse who looked after him in his earliest years.[67] Early in 1898 the Metropolitan Free Church Federation, on which Perks was a dominant figure, condemned the idea of a Catholic university; a large number of Free Church councils took the cue; and the National Free Church Council meetings passed a similar resolution, seconded by Perks.[68] When in August 1899 Dillon raised the proposal in the Commons, Perks declared that Nonconformists would never allow a Liberal government to consent to it.[69] At the 1900 general election, the only action of the National Free Church Council was to request all candidates to state their position on the Irish university question for the guidance of Free Church voters.[70] It was a time when Protestant feeling in the nation was high owing to attempts to curb ritualism in the Church of England. There can be no doubt that the issue of an Irish university helped significantly to buttress Nonconformist fears of Catholic ambitions in education. Yet when in 1908 Birrell steered through Parliament a settlement based partly on Balfour's proposals, Nonconformists exhibited, as Clifford pointed out to Asquith, 'a reticence of speech and a restraint of action' that were remarkable.[71] The Bill was sensible, according to the *Christian World*, and welcome to all but Ulster Unionists.[72] By 1908 Nonconformists were so preoccupied with obtaining a reversal of the 1902 Elementary Education Act that other matters paled into insignificance. If Nonconformist concern with educational issues increased during the 1890s, it reached new peaks in the elementary schools controversy of the following decade.

The Education Act of 1902 was an attempt to rationalise the elementary school system. School boards were swept away and local authorities, acting through education committees, were put in charge of the nation's education. Denominational schools were integrated into the system. They were given rate aid to alleviate their financial problems and it was provided that the public should be represented by one-third of their managers. This, however, stopped short of the public control that Nonconformists had long been seeking, and, in order to ward off their criticism, the government offered the right to erect a school giving a particular form of religious education wherever it was requested for at least thirty children. Nonconformists spurned this remedy for the problem of single-school areas and, from the time of the Bill's introduction in March, subjected it to heavy criticism. There were three reasons for the strength of their reaction. First, they were expecting to find the Bill objectionable. There had been attempts by the government in 1900 and again in 1901 to reorganise education, but both had been dropped. The proposal in the 1901 Bill to abolish school boards without giving public control of denominational schools had antagonised Nonconformists, and on its withdrawal the National Free Church

Council had recommended local councils to mould public opinion in favour of universal school boards ready for the introduction of a new Bill in the following session.[73] Nonconformists were on the alert. Secondly, they were delighted to have an opportunity for united action. They were divided over the continuing Boer War and the associated question of whether Rosebery the imperialist or Campbell-Bannerman, with his reservations about the war, should lead the Liberal Party. Earlier in the month when the Bill was published there had been a meeting between Campbell-Bannerman and leading Nonconformists that served only to accentuate their divisions and, according to Silvester Horne, 'ended with a feeling on the part of most of utter hopelessness'.[74] What Nonconformists most wanted was a cause to lift their drooping spirits. The education issue supplied an ideal excuse for closing ranks against a common enemy. Thirdly (and most importantly), they took deep offence that denominational teaching was to be paid for out of the rates. Ever since Frederick Temple had been designated Archbishop of Canterbury in 1896, the Church of England had been asking for rate aid, but Nonconformists had supposed that, as in 1897, the Conservative leadership would reject the idea as too contentious. The 1902 Bill, however, proposed to make all citizens pay an equivalent of the church rate that Nonconformists had thought to be a thing of the less enlightened past. In fact, it was worse than an equivalent, as Robertson Nicoll pointed out.

> Our objection as to the new Church rate is much more serious than that of our fathers of old. If the new Church rate were imposed, we would not only be asked to pay for the support of a religion we do not believe in, but we should be compelled to hand over our children to its teachers in order that they might be perverted. In other words, we should have to pay for the destruction of Nonconformity.[75]

The Bill seemed to be a throwing down of the gauntlet by the Conservative government, its Anglican backers and their Catholic allies.

Nonconformity had no hesitation in picking up the gauntlet. Its response was a classic crusade of unprecedented proportions. The National Free Church Council summoned a national conference of representatives of local councils which met in London on 15 April. At a preliminary luncheon, in proposing a toast to the National Council of the Evangelical Free Churches, Silvester Horne declared that Nonconformists had assembled to make a united protest. 'If the government', he went on, 'had designed the Bill with the distinct intention of inducing the Free Churches to show to the country an impressive demonstration of their strength they could not have done it more effectually than they had done.' The president of the National Council, the Rev. W. J. Townsend of the Methodist New Connexion, denounced the 'new church rate' and demanded its withdrawal 'in the name of national righteousness'. A disinterested observer might have questioned how the dropping of the Bill would further national righteousness, but it was natural for Townsend to employ the conventional rhetoric of indignation meetings. The whole assembly, which contained no disinterested observers, believed that it was struggling against an outright wrong – what Townsend described as 'the lust for power, native to the clerical breast'. Clifford, in moving the first resolution, spoke eloquently of the threat to the principle of civic control. He was soon followed by Perks, who in a characteristic speech warned of 'that ominous and dangerous alliance between the Protestant Churchmen . . . in England, and the puppets of the Church of Rome'. Guinness Rogers and Alfred Illingworth spoke, there was a collection for the education campaign and someone spontaneously launched the singing of 'O God, our help in ages past'. After a further series of ringing speeches, a Mr Upson, from Maidenhead, vainly tried to propose a resolution to the effect that the Bill was capable of amendment. Nobody offered to second the resolution. The meeting believed that the Bill was far too bad to amend.[76] Although on a grand scale, this gathering was a fair sample of thousands of rallies directed against the Education Act held during 1902 and the following years. Up to September 1903, when the troubles of the Macedonians seized their attention, Nonconformists concentrated all their powers on demonstrating their fury. The long passage of the Bill through the Commons, harried by Lloyd George and other Liberals all the way, offered a protracted season for agitation; and the pressure was kept up during the 1903 session, when a sister measure for London was receiving Parliament's time. Intermittent meetings continued to keep feelings seething between the autumn of 1903 and the general election of 1906. Nonconformity was stirred more deeply and more unanimously on a public issue than ever before or since.

One symptom of the depth of feeling was the emergence of the passive resistance movement. The refusal of the part of the rates going towards the maintenance of denominational schools had been mooted a number of times over recent years. It had been held in reserve as the ultimate sanction against any government introduction of rate aid. When in 1902 rate aid was actually proposed, George White, the Baptist MP for North-West Norfolk, gave warning that Free Churchmen might bind themselves to refuse payment of school rates.[77] Robertson Nicoll publicised the call for what he labelled 'passive resistance' in the *British Weekly*[78] and in the autumn both the Congregational and Baptist Unions recommended this course of action with only a handful of dissentients.[79] Principal Fairbairn of Mansfield College, Oxford, supplied a text for the movement when at a Free Church Council deputation to Balfour over the Bill in June he announced, 'We will not submit',[80] but he, like a number of others, expressed dismay about any attempt to give central direction to rate refusal. Conscience, he argued, should not be organised.[81] Others had more serious misgivings. Passive resistance, urged G. H. R. Garcia, the minister of Union Church, Sunderland, approximates to a revolutionary act. Democracy, he continued, entails acquiescing in legislation that is conscientiously opposed, as there is a chance to reverse it through agitation and the ballot box.[82] Reservations were at their strongest among the Wesleyans, a few of whom actually applauded the Act for coming to the rescue of their own denominational schools. The Wesleyan Conference in July 1903 would go no further than expressing sympathy for passive resisters but explicitly refusing to offer an opinion on passive resistance itself.[83] Divided counsels meant that the National Free Church Council pursued a highly erratic course over the issue. In May the organising committee declined to take up a suggestion by Robertson Nicoll that it should sponsor a conference to lay plans for rate refusal.[84] In July the general committee decided to sound the opinion of local councils and in October it was reported that 412 favoured taking the names of those who would pledge themselves to resist the education rate, 29 opposed such a course and 48 were non-committal.[85] Mass feeling so clearly backed the proposed action that enrolment was begun, but at this point Scott Lidgett, who was emerging as the leading Wesleyan educationalist, insisted that many Wesleyans and Presbyterians could not tolerate the council organising civil disobedience.[86] The council withdrew its request for names, causing immense confusion, but then agreed to receive them again.[87] Eventually, in December, it was decided to hand over the names to a separate National Passive Resistance Committee chaired by John Clifford and the movement took shape outside the auspices of the Free Church Council.[88] Already local passive resistance groups, often called Citizens' Leagues, had begun to meet and a magazine, *The Crusader*, had started publication. Rate refusals began in the spring of 1903. What normally happened was that offenders were summoned to court, which amounted to an opportunity of securing publicity for their principles, and it was ordered that sufficient of their goods should be distrained and auctioned to defray the rate. It was usually arranged that a friend of the refuser should be on hand to buy back the goods for him. Court appearances could be frequent: Clifford went forty-one times before the outbreak of the First World War.[89] The process soon became a regular ritual of removing the same items, in Clifford's case two silver trowels presented to him at chapel foundation stone layings.[90] If, however, the offender refused to allow his goods to be distrained, he might be imprisoned. By November 1904 there had been 33,678 summonses, 1,392 auctions and 54 resisters imprisoned;[91] by March 1906 there had been 70,880 summonses, 2,568 auctions and 176 persons had been to goal.[92] After the general election of 1906, despite persistence by a hard core of militants, enthusiasm drained from the movement as the prospect of a remedy from the Liberals seemed near at hand. At least up to then the movement did succeed in keeping the issue before the public.

Its impact, and much of the impact of the Nonconformist campaign against the Education Act as a whole, stemmed from the leadership given by John Clifford. His ascendancy in Nonconformist politics dated from before the education controversy – he had been the leading Nonconformist spokesman in the Boer War – but it was in the battle over the schools that his personality was stamped on a phase of English history. He was already fairly advanced in years, having been born in 1836, but contemporaries were unanimous in commenting on his youthful manner.[93] He himself used to attribute his continuing vigour to efforts to keep his mind lively. Clifford retained the reverence for learning of a mid-century self-taught man,[94] even though, after coming to Paddington as the minister of the chief metropolitan General Baptist cause in 1858, he had studied at University College for the BA, B.Sc., MA and LL.B. in succession.[95] There was an intellectual tone to his church at Westbourne Park almost unique among London Baptists. A passive resister who visited an ordinary service there in 1907 recorded that the Bible reading was from the recent Weymouth edition of the New Testament, a telegram was read about the progress of the Hague Peace Conference and the sermon, which had no text, was about 'Sabatier on the present condition of Roman Catholicism'. Yet conviction and emotion were present too. Clifford sang heartily, the climax of the sermon was an evangelistic appeal based on the marks of true religion and the hymn after the sermon had to be omitted because the preacher was carried away by his theme.[96] Silvester Horne noted the impression he made in 1902. 'Clifford is somewhat below medium height, and his naturally red hair – beard and moustache – has turned very grey. He has one of the most childlike smiles I ever saw, and indeed is as simple as a child and as guileless.'[97] The better he was known, the more he was respected. He steadfastly refused to draw a salary of more than £600 although an increase was repeatedly urged on him by his deacons.[98] From the 1880s on he laid special stress on the political responsibilities of Christians. 'He could not', he told a conference on Christian legislation in 1892, 'shut off his Christianity from any department of his life.'[99] He was strongly conscious of the historic role of Nonconformity and would frequently appeal, as he did at the rally of 15 April 1902, to the inspiring example of Cromwell.[100] The duty of the Free Churches in the twentieth century, he believed, was to occupy the vanguard of a grand campaign to give the people control of their own destinies. The chief foe was priestcraft. The same battle, he often declared, was being fought against clericalism throughout the world.[101] Such a vision gave dynamic to Clifford's leadership in the education struggle. He brought the power of a rousing orator whose denunciations of 'Rome on the rates' evoked mass enthusiasm. He exercised more subtle skills, especially in harmonising the wings of his movement, those who wanted full biblical instruction and those aiming for the secular solution, by means of his own compromise formula of explaining the Bible in literary and spiritual terms but without dogma.[102] Although he was a thorn in their flesh, he had earned the grudging esteem of the Liberal leaders as a committed and popular party man who gained the highest vote for the National Liberal Federation executive in 1903.[103] Most of all, Clifford, a man of the people, was responsive to the rank and file of his followers, well aware of how little compromise they would tolerate in the heat of an agitation. He knew provincial feeling intimately through regular travel and an immense correspondence. He enjoyed the full confidence of the movement he led.

The campaign against the Education Act drew particular support from three groups within Nonconformity. First, there was specially intense opposition to the Act in the West Riding. Illingworth's Northern Counties Education League, with the prolific Congregational minister J. H. Hollowell as its secretary, had prepared the way for six years by vigorous campaigning in favour of universal school boards. It so happened that a by-election took place in the North Leeds division at the end of July. The Liberal candidate, Rowland Barran, though not a practising chapel-goer, was the grandson of Sir John Barran, a doughty Baptist MP up to 1895, and his campaign concentrated on the iniquity of the Education Bill.[104] The Free Church council threw itself into the fray, Clifford spent three days in the constituency and, as Perks told Rosebery, 'It is the first time for 35 years that the chapel bell has rung . . .'[105] A Conservative majority of over 2,500 was turned into a Liberal majority of 758. The campaign stimulated Nonconformists in the area into decisive action. The Leeds Free Church Council led the way in declaring in favour of passive resistance – by eighty to one, with eight abstentions.[106] On 20 September there was a mass demonstration against the Bill on Woodhouse Moor above the city, preceded by a lunch for local notables given by Illingworth.[107] Leeds set the example of determined agitation against the Act. Secondly, Wales steered a separate course of opposition, very much as a result of prodding by Lloyd George. Welsh Nonconformity wielded a unique degree of local power that could be used to obstruct the administration of the Act. In August 1902 the County Council in Caernarvonshire, Lloyd George's home county, announced its intention of refusing to grant rate aid to denominational schools unless stringent conditions were met,[108] and in January 1903 Lloyd George persuaded a conference of Welsh local authorities to follow suit.[109] The schools were to agree to appoint half their committees of management from local authority nominees, to abolish religious tests for teachers and to grant facilities for undenominational religious instruction when required. By no means all the authorities enforced these conditions, which amounted to no more than sensible arrangements in a country with the religious balance of Wales.

It was, in fact, very much a propaganda exercise by Lloyd George, who had the press give the impression that 'the Welsh Revolt' was a matter of categorically refusing to pass on rates to any Church schools.[110] He frightened the government into passing legislation in 1904 to deal with defaulting local authorities and achieved his primary goal of enhancing his national reputation. But the apparent strength of Welsh opposition also helped to steel Nonconformist fibre in England. Thirdly, the campaign secured the wholehearted commitment of the Primitive Methodists, who remained the most rural of the major Nonconformist denominations and so most liable to discrimination in single-school areas. The connexional education committee gave official endorsement to passive resistance,[111] the first summons for rate refusal went to a Primitive Methodist farmer, Thomas Smith of Ashleyhay in Derbyshire,[112] and more Primitives went to prison than members of any other denomination – despite their being much smaller than the three biggest denominations. The figures for imprisonment up to February 1907 were 60 Primitives, 48 Baptists, 40 Congregationalists, 15 Wesleyans and 27 others.[113] It was the Primitives, therefore, who were most restive when Nonconformists began to feel irritation that the Liberal government elected in 1906 was failing to deal with their educational grievances.

The first Liberal attempt to reorganise elementary education was put forward by Augustine Birrell in the 1906 parliamentary session. Nonconformist hopes were raised by Birrell's appointment for, although never a convinced Christian, he was the son of a distinguished Liverpool Baptist minister, had attended Free Church Council demonstrations and gloried in the Nonconformist tradition.[114] Furthermore, the Free Church Council was consulted before the Bill was introduced.[115] All seemed to be moving smoothly towards the reversal of the 1902 Act. Disappointment was therefore all the greater when Birrell's Bill turned out to admit denominationalism into the new state elementary education system. Clause four provided that in areas with a minimum population of 5,000, if four-fifths of the parents were of one religious conviction, they could petition that a school should be allowed to give daily denominational instruction. The Free Church Council resolved on 14 May to demand the withdrawal of clause four[116] and a month later it was able to send a deputation to Birrell carrying protests against the clause from 1,000 local councils.[117] The disaffection was also expressed by a committee of Nonconformist MPs that had been formed after the election on the initiative of Robert Perks. In theory it numbered in its ranks the whole body of 180 or so Nonconformists in the Commons, but only about 50 attended its rare general meetings and most of its affairs were conducted by an executive of 20. Herbert Gladstone, the Liberal Chief Whip, knowing Perks's wonted truculence, had tried to engineer his exclusion from the chair, but Perks had successfully resisted the attempt and so shaped the committee's policy.[118] On 14 May he led the executive to visit Birrell. 'I told him', Perks reported, 'that the tide of hostile feeling was rising fast & that if the Government had to choose between their friends, the Noncons, & their foes, the Catholics, we hoped he would choose the former.'[119] Perks gave no thought to the need of the government to achieve some accommodation of the wishes of his arch-foes the Catholics and simply ignored the Church of England. He made speeches encouraging Nonconformist opposition to clause four and, descending on the Wesleyan Conference, ensured that it did not endorse the Bill.[120] Resentment in the country was only seething rather than boiling, but when in the autumn the Lords began making drastic amendments in favour of denominational teaching agitation burst out. A national Free Church Council delegates' conference called on the government to stand firm[121] and it was echoed by a special assembly of the Congregational Union. 'The Assembly had come', declared John Massie, a staunch Liberationist and a newly elected MP, 'not to parley, but to fight.'[122] The militant tone was sustained when a deputation of Nonconformist MPs presented a request to the Prime Minister, Campbell-Bannerman, that the Lords' amendments should be rejected *en bloc* rather than considered individually.[123] The Cabinet, Perks later heard, was swayed by this appeal. It had previously determined to let the Commons discuss the amendments individually, but now Campbell-Bannerman declared that he was not going to risk a Nonconformist revolt like that of 1870: the Commons would mark its intense displeasure by refusing to consider the views of a non-elected chamber.[124] It was this Cabinet decision, precipitated by Nonconformist pressure, that led directly to the breakdown of the Bill. Conservative and Anglican leaders, many of whom wanted to reach a compromise, treated this rebuff as an insult, and, despite the intervention of the king, the Bill foundered before Christmas. Nonconformists generally were more relieved than dismayed.[125] No further concessions to the denominationalists had been made and, they hoped, the government would be able to solve the problem in the next session.[126] The parliamentary leadership, as well as the rank and file of Nonconformity, had adopted a characteristic stance during 1906. They protested vigorously against arrangements they disliked, causing the government considerable embarrassment and contributing to the eventual demise of the Bill, but they set out no alternative strategy. They demonstrated the futility of the crusading style of politics for dealing with a complex issue that called out for settlement.

In the following year the parliamentary leadership learned to be more constructive. Reginald McKenna, who had succeeded Birrell as President of the Board of Education, introduced two short Bills, one to enact the non-controversial sections of the 1906 Bill, the other to allow local authorities to refuse rate aid to denominational schools. Nonconformists showed little enthusiasm, and when Lords threats made the government consider abandoning the controversial Bill they reacted angrily. There were ominous rumblings against the government among the Primitives and at the Yorkshire Baptist Association meetings a speaker commented that 'Conscience and justice were greater than Liberalism'.[127] The Free Church Council called for efforts to pass the Bill to be redoubled. But at this stage there was a palace revolution in the committee of Nonconformist MPs that made a compromise solution much more likely. Perks had set off across the Atlantic on a long business trip and so the chair of the committee devolved on George White[128] who, though he had launched passive resistance, was moderate by temperament and thought it essential to find a way through the impasse. White's attitudes were shared by Joseph Compton Rickett, a Congregational coal-owner, who was eager to secure a government post by pleasing the Prime Minister and so wanted to abandon the intransigent posture adopted by Perks.[129] His absence was their opportunity. The government asked whether the Nonconformist MPs would prefer McKenna's Bill that session or a more comprehensive measure the next. They opted for the promise of a better Bill next year and McKenna's was dropped.[130] White was subjected to a spate of popular criticism but, while admitting that he would have preferred to continue with the existing Bill, he insisted that they must now concentrate on making a new Bill effective.[131] The Nonconformist MPs therefore set about producing a draft of what they would like to see in the legislation of the following session. After much debate they decided to ask for Bible instruction to be given by official teachers in school hours, thereby rejecting the elimination of religious education that was being canvassed as the logical solution by Robertson Nicoll and J. H. Yoxall, the Wesleyan secretary of the National Union of Teachers. They knew that public opinion wanted the Bible. The committee was prepared to pick up two other hot potatoes in order to help the framers of the next Bill. They would be prepared to let a certain number of denominational schools contract out of the state system, so long as they were not in single-school areas; and they would even permit facilities for denominational instruction in state schools, on condition that they were out of school hours and the lessons were not given by the official teacher.[132] A chorus of disapproval was put up by extremists like Hollowell of the Northern Counties League[133] and, on his return, by Perks. The committee, he said, should have insisted on no concessions to denominationalism.[134] When in February 1908 McKenna introduced a Bill transferring most Church schools to local authority control but permitting 'contracting out', Perks was alone among the Nonconformist MPs in denouncing it outright.[135] Perks's view that the committee had become a weak-kneed organisation was widely shared in the provincial chapels. But experience of the wearisome controversy in the Commons was driving MPs towards a compromise settlement.

The desire for educational peace spread. Clifford considered 'contracting out' unjust, but believed that it could not be avoided in a settlement.[136] At a meeting of the Free Church Council education committee in March, even Perks reluctantly endorsed McKenna's Bill.[137] Lloyd George was trying to resolve the educational difficulties of the government of which he was a member by conferring with the Bishop of St Asaph, the leading Welsh Churchman. With Lloyd George's encouragement, the bishop introduced in the House of Lords a Bill embodying an alternative solution that included provision for denominational instruction in ex-voluntary schools during school hours.[138] A conference of northern church leaders – Anglican, Catholic and Nonconformist – published in June another compromise scheme that conceded the right of entry by outside teachers to give denominational instruction.[139] There were rumours that a wider conference might be held to resolve the whole problem. The atmosphere of the education issue, as the *Christian World* commented, had changed.[140] Churchmen and Nonconformists were co-operating in demonstrating their support for the government's Licensing Bill and beginning to feel that their antagonism over education was folly. The Christian churches should unite to act firmly over the moral and social questions of the hour, not spend their time squabbling with each other. It seemed likely that there would soon be fresh initiatives and so McKenna's Bill ground to a halt. There was another new development. In the government reshuffle following Asquith's succession to the premiership, McKenna was replaced at the Board of Education by Walter Runciman, a loyal Wesleyan who in the following year was to become society steward of the West London Mission. While Runciman made exploratory consultations over the next step during the summer, Nonconformity in the country, as Clifford warned Asquith, became restive once more.[141] But the leadership was drawn further towards a compromise. Runciman told a select group of Free Churchmen – Clifford, Horne, White, Rickett, Scott Lidgett and J. H. Shakespeare, secretary of the Baptist Union – how far the Archbishop of Canterbury was prepared to move. Horne, with Shakespeare and Lidgett, set out a Nonconformist response in a memorandum that refused to concede the right of entry, but Runciman persuaded Horne that this must be the price of a solution.[142] Horne and Shakespeare secured Clifford's unenthusiastic acquiescence, Runciman put the proposal to the Nonconformist MPs on 9 November and after a meeting lasting four and a half hours they agreed, with half a dozen dissentients, to accept the terms.[143] When a final point raised by the Archbishop of Canterbury over the rights of existing heads of Church schools to give denominational teaching had been cleared up, the way was open for a settlement. The Prime Minister announced in the Commons on 19 November that a concordat had been reached and a new Bill was introduced shortly afterwards. The problems that now arose were wholly on the side of the Church of England. The archbishop became worried about financial arrangements and the High Church extremists determined to avert the loss of the Church's schools. Athelstan Riley led a request for a meeting of the Representative Church Council, at which both clergy and laity, though not the bishops, rejected the concordat.[144] The Church leadership, like that of Nonconformity, had moved much further towards a settlement than the rank and file. The Bill was no longer an agreed measure and so was withdrawn. The chance of ending the education controversy passed. But the latter stages of the negotiations had witnessed the emergence of a more moderate temper within Nonconformity. A sense of realism had triumphed. It had become clear that crusading did not solve all the problems of practical politics.

A preparedness to compromise outlasted the débâcle of 1908. A group set up on Runciman's initiative when a solution seemed near decided to carry on as an Education Settlement Committee. Its Non-conformist representatives were prepared to accept terms that went further towards the Anglican position than those agreed in 1908. Their proposals, published as *Towards Educational Peace* in May 1910, were criticised by Clifford for perpetuating denominational teaching on the rates and religious tests for schoolteachers, yet the *Christian World* thought they might prove acceptable to moderate opinion.[145] The temperature of feeling on education had lowered as the constitutional crisis of 1910 engrossed attention. There were nevertheless repeated attempts by the Free Church Council and the Nonconformist MPs to prod Asquith into committing the government to legislation. By early 1912 frustration was mounting. White expected that many Free Churchmen, and especially Primitives, would be neutral at the next election unless some remedy were found for grievances that had now lasted a whole decade.[146] F. B. Meyer, now secretary of the Free Church Council, feared an outburst of hostility to the government at the annual meetings in March and so managed to elicit from Asquith a declaration that the government intended to proceed with an Education Bill in the 1913 session.[147] Clifford was dissatisfied and moved a successful resolution, seconded by A. T. Guttery, the leading Primitive Methodist, that education should come first on the legislative agenda for the following year.[148] Early in 1913 Clifford and Guttery launched a series of demonstrations urging that a Bill should be introduced forthwith.[149] At the end of April the Free Church Council education committee and the Nonconformist MPs jointly urged the government to redress their grievances,[150] but the only Education Bill of the session was a minor one increasing grants in aid of building, and it was dropped in August. Clifford was indignant. The opportunity of forcing a solution of the pressing problem of the Church's widespread monopoly of rural education had gone. Letters threatening refusal to work for a Liberal government, he warned, were reaching him in abundance.[151] Asquith was sufficiently worried to announce a Bill confined to dealing with single-school areas for 1914. Consultations between the government and prominent Free Churchmen were opened and by June 1914 Jack Pease, now the minister in charge of education, was able to show them a draft Bill. When they raised objections to the right of entry, Asquith, indignant in his turn, announced that the government would not proceed with an Education Bill.[152] The intermittent efforts to seek a solution to Nonconformist grievances after 1908 came to absolutely nothing. There were to be local agreements between Anglicans and Churchmen on the syllabus of religious instruction in the interwar period, but the 1902 Act was to remain substantially in force until the Butler Education Act of 1944.

In 1870, for Nonconformists, education seemed to be bound up with questions of religious equality. If the state was to provide schooling, it should do so without discriminating against any particular religious groups. The twenty-fifth clause of the 1870 Act was so much of an issue because it breached that deeply cherished principle. The slackening of attention to education after 1874 was not because Nonconformist grievances disappeared, although in the towns little troubled them. In much of the countryside, however, the children of Nonconformists could still be victimised. Until the mid-1890s this state of affairs was suffered in silence. It was not sufficient of a spur to action because the power of religious equality slogans generally was decaying. When Nonconformists first became vigorously partisan over control of the schools again, in 1894, it was because of an initiative by High Church Anglicans to assert the claims of the Church of England in the elementary schools. Nonconformists launched a crusade against what they regarded as crypto-Catholic designs on the nation's children. It was anti-Catholicism, as much as a renewed sense of not receiving their due from the state, that fuelled the Free Church campaign against the 1902 Education Act. But the intense feeling over education could not secure a favourable settlement. The technique of mass indignation was totally unsuited to the delicate adjustments of negotiation at Westminster. The more realistic Nonconformist leaders realised this in the wake of the failure of the 1906 Bill. A black-and-white world view was subverted by careful consideration of the claims of opponents with a view to finding a solution. A gulf began to open between the militants in the country and the leaders at the centre of affairs. The new moderation almost achieved a settlement in 1908, but in the end Nonconformists gained nothing, except a minor concession over admissions to training colleges, from the whole controversy that started in 1902. The episode well illustrates the weakness of Nonconformist political campaigns. They could ensure that attention was drawn to certain issues, but they could not secure desired goals against determined opposition.

8 *The End of the Conscience*

*Nonconformity, in making corporate political action bulk
so largely upon its programmes, is forsaking its first ideals.*
(A Nonconformist minister in 1909)[1]

During the forty or so years before the First World War Nonconformists exerted themselves to wield an influence in political life.
Guinness Rogers was probably right when he claimed in 1884 that
Nonconformity had never been so powerful since the days of the Long
Parliament. The leading men in the chapels were commonly leading men
in the affairs of their localities too. They were often to be found as school
board members, as councillors, as mayors, and they often ran the
constituency Liberal organisations. They could affect the policy pronouncements of the Liberal Party through involvement in the National
Liberal Federation. From the 1890s they were organised to exert
separate political pressure, both locally and nationally, through the Free
Church council movement. The number of Nonconformists in Parliament climbed upwards at each Liberal general election victory, though
falling back some way at each Liberal defeat. In 1868 there were some 53
Nonconformist MPs, 90 in 1880 and 181 in 1906, the climax of the
process. The House of Commons had been stormed by what Silvester
Horne called 'an organised army of Puritans'.[2] The Cabinet itself had
been penetrated as early as 1868, when John Bright was appointed to the
Board of Trade. The statements of Nonconformist leaders on public
issues were given widespread attention in the press and agitations of
which Nonconformists formed the core could, on occasions, affect
national policy. The success of the struggle against the Contagious
Diseases Acts in 1883 is a case in point. The views of Nonconformists
were more often taken into consideration by the framers of public policy
than at any time since the mid-seventeenth century.

Yet it does not follow that views peculiar to Nonconformists could
prevail against entrenched opposition. In the instance of the repeal of
the Contagious Diseases Acts, the assault was guided by leaders outside
Nonconformity and directed against a policy for which support was
steadily being eroded. When Nonconformists turned their fire against

the privileges of the Church of England, or its position within the education system, they stood almost alone against the interests of the established order in Church and state. Power remained stubbornly beyond their grasp. The House of Commons, even in 1906, was still dominated by the landed and professional classes whose allegiance was overwhelmingly to the Church of England. The 1905 administration included only two practising chapel-goers, Lloyd George and the Wesleyan Sir Henry Fowler, at Cabinet level. Asquith, himself of Nonconformist parentage, brought in a few more: Walter Runciman in 1908, Jack Pease, of the Darlington Quaker family, in 1910 and McKinnon Wood, a Congregationalist, in 1912. That made a total of only four (Fowler, by then Lord Wolverhampton, died in 1911) out of twenty Cabinet members. Nonconformists liked to claim the Liberal Party as their own, but the fact was that they lacked influence at the top. Only Lloyd George at the end of the period was in a position to sway policy in their favour – as he did, for instance, in proposing a Royal Commission to document the numerical preponderance of Nonconformists in Wales with a view to securing disestablishment there. Consequently, Nonconformists had to press their demands from outside the centres of power. The essential strategic problem confronting them was that they had no alternative but to seek their goals through the Liberal Party. They could hope for little from the Conservatives, and Liberal Unionism soon ceased to offer a credible third way. There was the option of withdrawing support from the Liberals in order to make them more pliable, but the redundancy of such a policy was made plain when in 1874 Nonconformist lukewarmness helped to bring in the Tories. Thereafter conspicuous loyalty to Liberalism, the policy firmly maintained by Guinness Rogers, seemed the only rational course of action. But Liberal leaders knew that Nonconformists, by inclination as well as necessity, were their most loyal supporters. For that reason, unless concessions were convenient, their claims could be passed over. That is why it was possible for the greatest Nonconformist campaign of the period, the uprising against the 1902 Education Act, with all its rhetoric, central organisation and local enthusiasm, to achieve virtually nothing. Nonconformists were in a fundamentally weak position in national politics.

Their characteristic technique of agitation, what a young minister criticised in 1908 as 'the modern Free Church craze for monster demonstrations',[3] was therefore essential if they were to make an impression on the seats of power. They aimed to gain a maximum of publicity and in this they frequently achieved considerable success – as in the outcry against the Bulgarian horrors or the campaign for Home Rule in Ireland. But this method carried with it acute disadvantages. Seasoned politicians were inclined to dismiss noisy campaigns as unrepresentative of public opinion. The greater their intensity, the more contrived they appeared. Their loudly critical spirit alienated the sympathies of men who were used to more delicate modes of self-expression. Rosebery, in particular, found the task of leading a party whose rank and file so frequently broke out into censorious fits of morality too much for him. An Anglican critic of such crusades, Archdeacon Cunningham, writing in 1910, pointed out that there was a constant danger of using exaggerated language. 'The exaggeration is imprudent as a matter of policy', he continued; 'it discredits the agitation with which it is associated. But it is difficult even to make unexaggerated and truthful accusations in a Christian fashion . . .'[4] The whole approach to public life embodied in a man like Hugh Price Hughes seemed profoundly distasteful to outsiders. Furthermore, it was easy to level charges of inconsistency against Nonconformity. There were glaring cases of reversal of policy. Up to 1895, for example, Home Rule was claimed to be the only righteous way of settling the problems of Ireland; but in 1896 it was repudiated as an unwarranted concession to Catholics. The chief explanation of such shifts is that, in the excitement of an agitation, Nonconformist opinion was especially liable to be blown into a new course by gusts of emotion. Thus men who had stood for peace principles only a couple of years before became outspoken champions of war by Greece against Turkey in 1897 and war by Britain against France in 1898. Nonconformist attitudes, especially in the 1890s, were so volatile as to carry very little weight. And the method of agitation suffered from another serious weakness. It was impossible to mount a campaign marked by white-hot fervour on more than one issue at any one time. The chapel mentality seemed incapable of entertaining two passions sufficiently deeply, and the sheer logistic problems of simultaneously organising two categories of rally were too great, even for the Free Church Council. A good example of the resulting ebb and flow of feeling is the fate of the Armenian question during 1896. Sympathy for the Armenians, strong at the start of the year, gave way during the parliamentary session to the education controversy, revived again in September following fresh news from Turkey, but subsided in November when more education proposals were put forward by the Church of England. Politicians could afford to ride out the storm of Nonconformist displeasure, confident that it would die away as soon as a new obsession arose. Consequently the agitations, for all their fury, frequently made very little mark on national policy.

The target of the Nonconformist campaigns also had implications for their effectiveness. Because the chapels trained their adherents in a well-defined ethic, their crusades were consistently mounted against breaches of that code – whether persecution by the cruel sultan or horse-racing by the profligate premier. They were roused by indignation at the guilt of policy-makers and shame at being part of a nation that tolerated wrong. The volume of their protest depended on the degree of their sensitivity to wickedness. That is why religious excitement, bringing home an awareness of sin, could fuel political campaigns. As Meyer put it, 'every great revival would culminate in reform'.[5] Moralistic agitations prospered at a time when the spirit of revivalism was very much abroad in Nonconformity. Most strikingly the great Welsh revival of 1904–5, which invigorated the chapels of the principality and spilled over into England, added momentum to the electioneering of 1906. The religious vitality of the chapels made it easy to generate agitations. No section of the British electorate could more readily be mobilised for political protest. Nonconformist leaders like John Clifford knew this well; so did two eminent politicians. Lloyd George early learned to rouse the chapels of his native Wales by preaching a crusade and at the January 1910 election summoned the English Free Churches to battle against the Lords by denouncing them as the obstacle in the path to educational and social reforms. But the master of the technique during the period was Gladstone. The intensity with which Nonconformists denounced Turkish brutality in 1876 and the subsequent persistence which they displayed in opposing the Conservative pro-Turkish policy greatly impressed him. He recognised their enormous potential for taking up what he called 'the Christian side of political controversies',[6] and so for raising the morale of the Liberal Party. Between 1886 and 1892, in a series of carefully calculated speeches, he set himself to draw out a similar passion on the Irish question. So central were Nonconformists to his strategy that Gladstone preferred to cashier Parnell rather than allow their enthusiasm for the Irish cause to cool. These years form the high point of Nonconformist standing in the party. From the retirement of Gladstone in 1894, or even from the beginning of his fourth administration in 1892, when they were no longer needed to rouse the electorate in favour of Home Rule, Nonconformists ceased to occupy a strategic political position. Their fervour was thereafter an embarrassment rather than an asset to the Liberal leadership. They could look for boons only from a statesman familiar with the social dynamic of the chapels and capable of directing it to chosen ends. Nonconformist influence was possible because of the ascendancy of Gladstone.

Because they concentrated on denouncing wrongs, Nonconformists were typically the advocates of a negative policy. Mass protest movements could hardly be expected to formulate constructive proposals, but their forte was criticism. The Nonconformist political style was therefore better suited to times when their friends were in opposition than to times when they were in government. The Nonconformist conscience flourishing during a period, from 1874 to 1905, when the Conservatives were in power for twenty-two out of thirty years. The greatest campaigns – over the Bulgarians, Home Rule, the Armenians and education – all took place during Conservative administrations. Remarkably enough, at such times they could occasionally exert considerable influence over the course of events – although only negatively. Conservative leaders were reluctant to incur the displeasure of chapel-goers unnecessarily and after 1886 there was pressure on them from Chamberlain to do nothing that would antagonise the Nonconformists among his Liberal Unionist supporters. During the late 1880s and the 1890s, therefore, the Conservatives repeatedly postponed grasping the nettle of education for fear of the Nonconformist reaction. Salisbury, as he showed by addressing the Nonconformist Unionist Association on the Armenian issue, also desired to stave off criticism of his foreign policy in the chapels by humanitarian efforts abroad. Their potential for protest could exercise a deterrent effect on the Conservatives. On the other hand, it ill qualified them for wringing concessions from the Liberals. As soon as protest against Liberal failure to deliver the goods was mooted, powerful voices like that of Guinness Rogers were raised urging patience and confidence in the good intentions of the party leaders. The only remaining avenue open to them was negotiation with the Liberal leadership. But whenever it became necessary to turn from agitation to discussion, the strength of the Nonconformist position disintegrated. Either rank-and-file enthusiasm subsided or stalwarts in the country lost confidence in the negotiators at Westminster. The first danger is illustrated by the long-term evolution of the Liberation Society. The decision of its leaders to concentrate on behind-the-scenes requests meant that it lost its capacity to rouse the mass of Nonconformists on a point of principle. The second danger is apparent in the shorter-term process of seeking a reversal of the Balfour Education Act in the years 1906 to 1908. The preparedness of realist Nonconformist leaders to accept terms was denounced as treachery by many of their followers in the country. Compromise was essential if Nonconformists were to gain the substance of their aims, but the whole inspiration for Nonconformist political effort was the belief that with unrighteous policies there could be no compromise. The resulting tension was a fatal flaw in the politics of the chapels.

Nonconformists began to face the problems of their political position in the wake of the failure of the education settlement in 1908. If a Parliament containing so large a Liberal majority was incapable of doing justice on behalf of Nonconformity, the high hopes that had previously been pinned on political endeavour had evidently been misplaced. There was a new mood of disillusionment that ensured a ready hearing for an anonymous work published early in 1909 called *Nonconformity and Politics*. Its author was a Congregational minister, probably H. W. Clark of Harpenden, and its message was that Nonconformity was becoming altogether too political. The book did not set out to call in question the responsibility of individual Nonconformists to participate in politics; nor did it take up the cudgels against the Liberal Party. Its burden was that political activity was secularising the Free Churches. The casual visitor, the author suggested, could hardly distinguish a typical Free Church Council public meeting from a Liberal rally; Nonconformist ministers had often been so absorbed in politics as to lose their spiritual power; and while Nonconformity 'has been making numerous and ardent politicians, it has made scarce any saints'.[7] The book applauded George Cadbury's statement in the previous year that Free Church councils should not hold meetings in support of the government's Licensing Bill lest they should be diverted from more direct Christian work.[8] It also referred to the views of R. W. Dale, who had refused to participate in the early days of the Free Church council movement.[9] This appeal to Dale was entirely just, for he had argued that when the church seeks to grasp power in society it dissipates its powers. He feared that the chapels would be drawn after the Free Church councils into secular affairs and so lose their religious vitality.[10] Dale's warning had gone unheeded, so that by 1909 secularisation had clearly made deep and unnecessary inroads into the life of the chapels. In 1907, as was well known, membership of all the main denominations had begun to fall. It was hard to deny the validity of the thesis presented in *Nonconformity and Politics* that overconcentration on politics was partly responsible, and the book created a great stir. The Free Church Council annual meetings spent a session considering it[11] and the subject became a staple theme at local Free Church gatherings. J. D. Jones, a leading Congregational minister at Bournemouth, for instance, devoted two sermons to endorsing the book's argument.[12] *Nonconformity and Politics* did much to bring about a recoil from political activity among Nonconformist leaders.

New political circumstances contributed to this drastic reappraisal of the proper role of the Free Churches. The emergence of the Labour Party raised the spectre of acute internal controversy in Nonconformity and so discouraged the public airing of political views. Between 1907 and 1909 Nonconformists were forced to come to terms with Labour and the political theory of many of its activists, socialism. For many years Clifford and a small circle of ministers had declared themselves socialists, but, for Clifford at least, this avowal had entailed no break with Liberalism and few Nonconformists had troubled to look into the subject. But in 1906 thirty MPs constituted themselves a Labour Party, and in 1907 the government suffered two by-election defeats at the hands of a Labour candidate and an independent socialist. Labour was clearly an option for Nonconformists: probably eight of the original MPs were regular chapel-goers[13] and their chairman in 1908, Arthur Henderson, was a well-known Wesleyan layman. Ministers, in particular, were attracted by the social idealism of the movement. R. J. Campbell, Parker's successor at the City Temple, began to teach that socialism and his 'new theology' were identical;[14] the Wesleyan J. E. Rattenbury, with greater caution and greater orthodoxy, argued that socialism and Evangelicalism were compatible.[15] By 1909 there was a socialist organisation for Wesleyan ministers, the Sigma Club, with sixty-five members.[16] A considerable number of Nonconformists were prepared to shed their allegiance to the Liberal Party. The consequence was that Nonconformity was marked by unprecedented political divisions. It had hitherto been possible to dismiss the Unionist minority in the Free Churches as a strange aberration, and so to treat Nonconformity as though it were a single political entity. Now progressive Nonconformity was itself divided. Rattenbury, for instance, made a show of being on the Free Church Council executive while not being a Liberal.[17] Others were openly hostile to Labour, and specially to the socialism of which it was the vehicle. Speaking as 'an old Individualist' in 1908, J. G. Greenhough denounced socialism as a threat to the commercial virtues.[18] He was soon to be found in the ranks of the Nonconformist Anti-Socialistic Union, a small but vociferous body that in 1909 articulated the private worries of many a prosperous layman.[19] There were risks of polarisation on a whole range of issues. Denominational bodies began to avoid all declarations that could be interpreted as partisan. With Meyer replacing Law as secretary of the National Free Church Council in 1910, it followed the same path. Chapel members remained predominantly Liberal in allegiance, but the Liberal Party was deprived of one of the strengths it had enjoyed since 1874 – public endorsement by representative Nonconformist bodies. In a new political era the Free Churches were finding refuge from the danger of internal rifts in a display of neutrality.

For these two reasons – recognition of the secularising effect of politics and divisions brought about by the rise of Labour – the prevailing mood among Nonconformist leaders in the four years before the First World War was a desire to withdraw a little from the political tumult. The crescendo of the education controversy was succeeded by no other prolonged agitation. A period of calm ensued in which the Free Church Council redirected its energies into evangelism and inter-church co-operation. No longer was there a cause driving Nonconformists into politics *en masse*. Their political beliefs were far less distinctive than they had been twenty or thirty years before. The disestablishment campaign was in decay, they had ceased to be critics of empire, and Home Rule seemed a matter of technical adjustment rather than an insistent moral cause. In none of these spheres was there an obvious wrong to attack. The crusading temper that bound together religion and politics had suddenly waned. It did not entirely disappear for there were still assaults on wickedness, but they were now confined to questions of essentially personal morality. Nonconformists continued to run campaigns against gambling and sabbath-breaking and to champion the causes of temperance and social purity. But these were normally taken up by local agitations and only rarely, as in the 1911 campaign against a world-title boxing match, was there a brief upsurge of the old passion directed against a national sin. There were never again to be crusades by Nonconformists which were nationwide, sustained and impinged significantly on party politics. By 1910 the period of the Nonconformist conscience had come to an end.

Notes

Abbreviations used in the Notes

Add. MS	Additional Manuscript
Bapt.	*The Baptist*
Bapt. Mag.	*Baptist Magazine*
BL	British Library
BUL	Birmingham University Library
BW	*British Weekly*
CC	Chubb Collectanea, Chubb and Son's Lock and Safe Co. Ltd, London (by kind permission of Lord Hayter)
Cong.	*The Congregationalist*
Cong. Rev.	*Congregational Review*
CW	*Christian World*
GP	Gladstone Papers
JCP	Joseph Chamberlain Papers
Lib. Un.	*Liberal Unionist*
LS	Executive Committee Minutes of the Society for the Liberation of Religion from State Patronage and Control, Greater London Council Record Office, London
Meth. Prot.	*Methodist Protest*
MM	*Minutes of Several Conversations . . . of the People called Methodists, in the connexion established by the late John Wesley, A.M.* [Minutes of Wesleyan Methodist Conference]
NLS	National Library of Scotland, Edinburgh
NLW	National Library of Wales, Aberystwyth
Parl. Deb.	*Parliamentary Debates* [Hansard]
Prot.	*Protest*
SP	Salisbury Papers, Christ Church, Oxford

Notes: Chapter 1

1 'The Nonconformist conscience in its relation to our national life', *Baptist Hand Book* (1904), p. 113.
2 *CW*, 8 February 1906, p. 11.
3 *Cong.*, December 1884, p. 102.
4 Robert Currie, Alan Gilbert and Lee Horsley, *Churches and Churchgoers: Patterns of Church Growth in the British Isles since 1700* (Oxford, 1977).
5 K. S. Inglis, 'Patterns of religious worship in 1851', *Journal of Ecclesiastical History*, vol. 11 (1960), pp. 83–6.
6 Alan Everitt, *The Pattern of Rural Dissent: The Nineteenth Century* (Leicester, 1972), pp. 10f., 20–46.
7 J. E. B. Munson, 'A study of Nonconformity in Edwardian England as revealed by the Passive Resistance Movement against the 1902 Education Act' (D. Phil., University of Oxford, 1973), p. 7.
8 Charles Booth, *Life and Labour of the People in London: Third Series: Religious Influences*, Vol. 7 (London, 1902), p. 132.

9   Hugh McLeod, *Class and Religion in the Late Victorian City* (London, 1974), p. 312.
10   Booth, *Life and Labour*, Vol. 7, p. 123.
11   J. C. G. Binfield, 'Congregationalism's Two Sides of the Baptistery: A Paedobaptist View', *Baptist Quarterly*, vol. 26 (1975), pp. 119–33.
12   *English Independent*, 18 November 1869, p. 1,145. *CW*, 15 February 1906, p. 4.
13   *The Freeman*, 5 July 1895, p. 354.
14   McLeod, *Class and Religion*, pp. 300, 303.
15   Stephen Yeo, *Religion and Voluntary Organisations in Crisis* (London, 1976), pp. 119–24.
16   D. W. Bebbington, *A History of Queensberry Street Baptist Church, Old Basford, Nottingham* (Nottingham, 1977), pp. 14–17, 29–32.
17   J. E. B. Munson, 'The education of Baptist ministers, 1870–1900', *Baptist Quarterly*, vol. 26 (1976), p. 321.
18   Munson, 'Nonconformity in Edwardian England', p. 36.
19   Booth, *Life and Labour*, Vol. 7, p. 113.
20   Clyde Binfield, *So Down to Prayers: Studies in English Nonconformity, 1780–1920* (London, 1977), pp. 145–61, 170ff., 240. J. R. Harris, *The Life of Francis William Crossley* (London, 1900).
21   *Wesleyan Methodist Church, Chislehurst, AD 1870–AD 1920* (Chislehurst, 1920). W. T. Cranfield ['Denis Crane'], *The Life-Story of Sir Robert W. Perks, Bart, MP* (London, 1909), pp. 98f.
22   MS copy of Reply of Deacons on Resignation of the Rev. Paxton Hood, March 1880, Cutting-Book of J. H. Davidson, Manchester Public Libraries, Records of Cavendish Street Chapel, M162, Box 41.
23   *CW*, 27 May 1886, p. 433; 3 June 1886, p. 455.
24   Janet Howarth, 'The Liberal revival in Northamptonshire, 1880–1895: a case study in late nineteenth-century elections', *Historical Journal*, vol. 12 (1969), p. 106.
25   Arthur Porritt, *The Best I Remember* (London, 1922), p. 158. *CW*, 3 October 1889, p. 759.
26   J. F. Glaser, 'Nonconformity and Liberalism, 1868–1885: a study in English party history' (PhD, Harvard University, 1948), p. 430.
27   *Cong.*, January 1886, p. 8.
28   Shropshire Baptist Association Minutes, 9 and 10 November 1885.
29   John Vincent, *Pollbooks: How Victorians Voted* (Cambridge, 1967), pp. 69f.
30   A. R. Meredith, 'The social and political views of Charles Haddon Spurgeon, 1834–1892' (PhD, Michigan State University, 1973), pp. 65f.
31   J. H. Lea, 'Charles Williams of Accrington, 1827–1907', *Baptist Quarterly*, vol. 23 (1969), p. 187.
32   H. C. Colman, *Jeremiah James Colman: A Memoir* (London, 1905), p. 344.
33   *The Times*, 29 December 1890, p. 4.
34   D. W. Bebbington, 'Gladstone and the Nonconformists: a religious affinity in politics', in *Church, Society and Politics* (Studies in Church History, Vol. 12), ed. Derek Baker (Oxford, 1975), pp. 378f.; 'Gladstone and the Baptists', *Baptist Quarterly*, vol. 26 (1976), pp. 229ff.
35   C. W. McCree, *George Wilson McCree: His Life and Work* (London, 1893), p. 167.
36   W. E. Gladstone, 'The county franchise and Mr Lowe thereon' [1877], *Gleanings of Past Years, 1843–78* (London, 1879), p. 158.
37   *Cong.*, December 1882, pp. 953ff.
38   Glaser, 'Nonconformity and Liberalism', pp. 424f.
39   C. S. Horne, *Pulpit, Platform and Parliament* (London, 1913), pp. 193–6.
40   Booth, *Life and Labour*, Vol. 4, p. 86.
41   *CW*, 25 March 1897, p. 10.
42   *CW*, 4 October 1900, p. 5.
43   R. F. Horton, *Oliver Cromwell: A Study in Personal Religion* (London, 1897), p. v.

44 H. P. Hughes, *Social Christianity: Sermons Delivered in St James's Hall* (London, 1889), pp. 139–45.
45 Ross McKibbin, 'Working-class gambling in Britain, 1880–1939', *Past and Present*, vol. 82 (1979), p. 148.
46 Frances Finnegan, *Poverty and Prostitution: A Study of Victorian Prostitutes in York* (Cambridge, 1979), pp. 69f.
47 H. M. Bompas, 'Nonconformists and Home Rule', *Fortnightly Review*, new series, vol. 52 (1892), p. 7.
48 K. S. Inglis, 'English Nonconformity and social reform, 1880–1900', *Past and Present*, vol. 13 (1958). J. H. S. Kent, 'Hugh Price Hughes and the Nonconformist Conscience', in G. V. Bennett and J. D. Walsh (eds), *Essays in Modern English Church History* (London, 1966). R. J. Helmstadter, 'The Nonconformist Conscience', in Peter Marsh (ed.), *The Conscience of the Victorian State* (Hassocks, Sussex, 1979).
49 George Stephen, *Anti-Slavery Recollections in a Series of Letters Addressed to Mrs Beecher Stowe* [1854] (London, 1971), p. 248.
50 Dietrich Bonhoeffer, *Ethics* [1949] (London, 1964), p. 56.
51 George White, *Baptist Hand Book* (1904), p. 108.
52 J. G. Bowran, *The Life of Arthur Thomas Guttery, D.D.* (London, n.d.), p. 63.
53 *The Times*, 28 November 1890, p. 8.
54 Booth, *Life and Labour*, Vol. 7, p. 218.
55 Bowran, *Guttery*, p. 63.
56 *CW*, 4 June 1896, p. 443.
57 *The Nonconformist Conscience considered as a Social Evil and a Mischief-Monger by One Who Has Had It* (London, 1903), p. 191.
58 'A Nonconformist minister', *Nonconformity and Politics* (London, 1909), p. 55.

Notes: Chapter 2

1 Arthur Miall, *Life of Edward Miall, formerly Member of Parliament for Rochdale and Bradford* (London, 1884), p. 360.
2 ibid., pp. 315f.
3 ibid., pp. 318f.
4 LS, 10 October 1881, p. 411; 3 April 1882, p. 458; 2 July 1883, p. 30; 16 July 1883, p. 33.
5 LS, 3 July 1889, p. 459.
6 C. S. Miall, *Henry Richard, M.P.: A Biography* (London, 1889), pp. 268ff.
7 James Cropper, *Notes and Memories* (Kendal, 1900), p. 189.
8 *Labour Leader*, 30 June 1894, p. 5.
9 *CW*, 25 October 1894, p. 786.
10 Sidney Webb, 'The moral of the elections', *Contemporary Review*, August 1892, p. 273.
11 Joseph Chamberlain to H. J. Wilson, 27 May 1873, H. J. Wilson Papers, Box 1, Sheffield University Library.
12 W. H. Mackintosh, *Disestablishment and Liberation: The Movement for the Separation of the Anglican Church from State Control* (London, 1972), pp. 218, 227.
13 ibid., pp. 218f. Alfred Illingworth to B. S. Olding, 9 December 1892, LS, A/LIB/253.
14 *CW*, 14 February 1895, p. 115.
15 A. H. Welch, 'John Carvell Williams, the Nonconformist watchdog (1821–1907)'. (PhD, Kansas University, 1968).
16 LS, 17 December 1900, p. 153.
17 Arthur Porritt, *The Best I Remember* (London, 1922), p. 225.
18 LS, 12 September 1881, p. 398.

19   D. A. Hamer, *The Politics of Electoral Pressure: A Study in the History of Victorian Reform Agitations* (Hassocks, Sussex, 1977), pp. 147–51.
20   LS, 16 June 1886, p. 273.
21   *Liberal Year Book* (1887), p. 86.
22   *CW*, 2 May 1888, p. 6.
23   LS, 25 May 1886, p. 261; 9 December 1889, p. 489.
24   LS, 20 October 1890, p. 58.
25   Alan Simon, 'Church disestablishment as a factor in the general election of 1885', *Historical Journal*, vol. 18 (1975).
26   Hamer, *Electoral Pressure*, pp. 154–7. LS, 12 January 1885, p. 153; 26 January 1885, pp. 155f.; 5 October 1885, p. 205.
27   Hamer, *Electoral Pressure*, pp. 144ff., 150f.
28   LS, 12 September 1881, p. 399.
29   Edwin Hodder, *Life of Samuel Morley* (London, 1888), pp. 209–17.
30   *CW*, 4 January 1894, p. 1; 11 January 1894, p. 21.
31   David Lloyd George to Margaret Lloyd George, 1 January 1893 [for 1894], in K. O. Morgan (ed.), *Lloyd George: Family Letters, 1885–1936* (Cardiff, 1973), pp. 65f.
32   LS, 1 January 1894, p. 275; 4 January 1894, pp. 276f. David Lloyd George to Margaret Lloyd George, 3, 4 and 6 January 1893 [for 1894], *Lloyd George: Family Letters*, pp. 66f.
33   *The Times*, 20 January 1894, p. 12.
34   David Lloyd George to Margaret Lloyd George, 4 January 1893 [for 1894], *Lloyd George: Family Letters*, p. 66.
35   LS, 22 January 1894, p. 279.
36   LS, 17 June 1895, p. 361.
37   J. C. Williams to H. H. Asquith, 19 June 1895, MS Asquith 68, f. 98, Bodleian Library, Oxford.
38   K. O. Morgan, *Wales in British Politics, 1868–1922* (Cardiff, 1970), pp. 155–8.
39   *The Liberation Society: A Jubilee Retrospect* (London, 1894), p. 60.
40   Miall, *Miall*, p. 263. LS, 14 December 1885, p. 216; 29 July 1895, p. 368.
41   LS, 1 February 1897, p. 463. *CW*, 11 February 1897, p. 1.
42   *CW*, 16 May 1901, p. 11.
43   LS, 26 June 1893, p. 244; 25 September 1893, p. 254.
44   J. J. Dryhurst to J. C. Williams, 20 December 1894, and reply, 21 December 1894, MS Asquith 66, ff. 9, 11, Bodleian Library, Oxford.
45   LS, 19 March 1894, p. 290.
46   LS, 19 June 1899, p. 75; 18 September 1899, p. 89.
47   LS, 21 May 1883, p. 12.
48   LS, 8 June 1886, p. 269; 27 January 1890, p. 6.
49   LS, 23 March 1885, p. 170.
50   LS, 6 December 1886, p. 302; 25 April 1887, p. 332.
51   LS.
52   LS, 13 June 1887, p. 341.
53   *CW*, 2 May 1901, p. 5.
54   *CW*, 3 October 1901, p. 22. LS, 17 June 1901, p. 189; 23 September 1901, p. 203.
55   *CW*, 2 May 1901, p. 5.
56   Miall, *Miall*, pp. 29ff.
57   Minutes of the Baptist Union of Great Britain and Ireland, 1833–42, 1 May 1839, p. 181, Baptist Church House, London.
58   J. H. Lea, 'Charles Williams of Accrington, 1827–1907', *Baptist Quarterly*, vol. 23 (1969), p. 185.
59   Miall, *Miall*, pp. 281, 312.
60   *The Case for Disestablishment: A Handbook of Facts and Arguments in Support of the Claim for Religious Equality* (London, 1894), pp. 13f.
61   *CW*, 5 May 1892, p. 368.

62 *CW*, 12 May 1887, p. 373.
63 R. W. Dale to J. G. Rogers, 1 January 1876, in A. W. W. Dale. *The Life of R. W. Dale of Birmingham* (London, 1898), p. 385.
64 Dale, *Dale*, pp. 368–87.
65 G. H. Pike, *Dr Parker and his Friends* (London, 1904), pp. 118f.
66 Porritt, *Best I Remember*, p. 72. Harry Jeffs, *Press, Preachers and Politicians: Reminiscences, 1874 to 1932* (London, 1933), p. 106.
67 Pike, *Dr Parker and his Friends*, p. 119.
68 *CW*, 3 May 1889, p. 10; 9 May 1889, pp. 371, 375; 16 May 1889, p. 401. J. S. Drummond, *Charles A. Berry, D.D.: A Memoir* (London, 1899), p. 73.
69 Joseph Parker, *Paterson's Parish: A Lifetime amongst the Dissenters* (London, 1898), p. 48.
70 *The Sword and the Trowel*, May 1886, p. 246.
71 LS, 16 February 1891, p. 837; 2 March 1891, p. 86.
72 *The Sword and the Trowel*, April 1891, p. 199.
73 *CW*, 14 May 1891, p. 398.
74 LS, 12 January 1891, p. 74.
75 *The Times*, 18 March 1898, p. 5.
76 LS, 13 June 1887, p. 342.
77 LS, 3 October 1887, p. 370; 16 February 1891, p. 84.
78 LS, 27 November 1893, p. 266; 1 January 1894, pp. 274f. *CW*, 15 February 1894, p. 120; 24 March 1898, p. 3.
79 Mackintosh, *Disestablishment*, p. 297.
80 LS, 12 January 1891, p. 74. *CW*, 15 February 1894, p. 120.
81 *CW*, 2 May 1901, p. 5.
82 *CW*, 7 June 1894, p. 439; 14 June 1894, p. 455; 21 June 1894, p. 480. D. G. Fountain, *E. J. Poole-Connor (1872–1962): Contender for the Faith* (Worthing, 1966), pp. 72ff.
83 *CW*, 9 December 1897, p. 11; 16 December 1897, p. 11; 23 December 1897, p. 7; 30 December 1897, p. 2.
84 *CW*, 27 May 1897, p. 11; 24 June 1897, p. 2.
85 *CW*, 20 February 1896, p. 136.
86 'A Nonconformist minister', *Nonconformity and Politics* (London, 1909), p. 227.
87 Howard Evans, *Radical Fights of Forty Years* (London, n.d.), p. 17.
88 *BW*, 19 March 1896, p. 13.
89 Edwin Hodder, *Life of Samuel Morley* (London, 1888), p. 72.
90 LS, 13 September 1880, p. 308.
91 *CW*, 16 August 1894, p. 606.
92 *CW*, 3 October 1901, p. 22.
93 *CW*, 25 October 1900, p. 11; 1 November 1900, p. 7.
94 Evans, *Radical Fights*, pp. 90f. *CW*, 17 November 1892, p. 940.
95 Ronald Fletcher, *The Akenham Burial Case* (London, 1974).
96 *Daily News*, 6 April 1886, pp. 3, 5. *The Liberator*, April 1886, p. 54.
97 *The Liberator*, May 1886, pp. 70f.
98 *CW*, 14 March 1895, p. 204.
99 *CW*, 12 July 1900, p. 3.
100 [Thomas Hayes], *Methodism in 1879: Impressions of the Wesleyan Church and its Ministers* (London, 1879), pp. 89–110.
101 C. H. Kelly, *Memories* (London, 1910), pp. 351ff. *MM* (1875), pp. 217f.
102 *MM* (1883), p. 247; (1882), p. 234.
103 W. T. Cranfield ['Denis Crane'], *The Life-Story of Sir Robert W. Perks, Bart, MP* (London, 1909).
104 Mackintosh, *Disestablishment*, p. 316.
105 *CW*, 15 June 1893, p. 483.
106 LS, 23 January 1888, pp. 377f.
107 *CW*, 10 August 1893, p. 625.

108   *CW*, 16 December 1897, p. 7; 17 February 1898, p. 4.
109   LS, 12 September 1881, p. 403.
110   F. E. Hamer (ed.), *The Personal Papers of Lord Rendel* (London, 1931), p. 306.
111   J. C. Williams to Rendel, 15 February 1884, 29 March 1884 and 30 March 1886, Rendel Papers, MS 19455 D, ff. 558f.; MS 19454 D, f. 475, NLW.
112   *Daily News*, 5 May 1886, p. 6.
113   Rendel to Thomas Gee, 16 March 1887, Thomas Gee MSS, 8308D, f. 257.
114   Rendel to Humphreys-Owen, 31 January 1887 and 27 March 1887, Glansevern Collection, MSS 301, 312, NLW.
115   Morgan, *Wales in British Politics*, pp. 112–15.
116   Rendel to J. C. Williams, 30 March 1888 and 10 April 1888; Williams to Rendel, 5 April 1888, Rendel Papers, 2, MSS 259ff.; Rendel to Humphreys-Owen, 8 April 1889, Glansevern Collection, MS 446; Humphreys-Owen to Rendel, 10 January 1890, Rendel Papers, MS 19459C, f. 519.
117   Williams to Ellis, 3 December 1892, T. E. Ellis Collection, MS 2096, NLW.
118   J. P. D. Dunbabin, *Rural Discontent in Nineteenth-Century Britain* (London, 1974), pp. 212–30, 289, 293, 296.
119   LS, 1 December 1886, p. 296; 18 November 1889, p. 488.
120   LS, 9 January 1893, p. 214; 20 March 1893, p. 231.
121   *BW*, 11 May 1893, p. 35.
122   LS, 9 August 1893, p. 250.
123   *BW*, 23 August 1894, p. 275.
124   LS, 1 August 1902, p. 251; 15 September 1902, p. 252; 22 December 1902, p. 270.
125   *BW*, 29 January 1903, p. 422. *CW*, 5 February 1903, p. 21.
126   *CW*, 3 May 1906, p. 22.
127   *BW*, 7 March 1907, p. 583.
128   *CW*, 1 August, 1907, p. 14.
129   *CW*, 5 May 1904, p. 4.
130   'A Nonconformist minister', *Nonconformity and Politics*, pp. 226f.
131   *CW*, 6 May 1909, p. 22; 13 November 1913, p. 4.
132   *CW*, 5 May 1910, p. 22; 2 May 1912, p. 23.
133   *CW*, 25 April 1912, p. 10.

Notes: Chapter 3

1   *CW*, 7 May 1908, p. 22.
2   Kathleen Heasman, *Evangelicals in Action: An Appraisal of their Social Work in the Victorian Era* (London, 1962), p. 8.
3   Edwin Hodder, *Life of Samuel Morley* (London, 1888), p. 221.
4   Heasman, *Evangelicals in Action*, pp. 13f.
5   H. P. Hughes, *Social Christianity: Sermons Delivered in St James's Hall* (London, 1889), p. xii.
6   Beatrice Webb, *My Apprenticeship* [1926] (Harmondsworth, 1971), p. 191.
7   Paul McHugh, *Prostitution and Victorian Social Reform* (London, 1980).
8   *Prot.*, 25 July 1882, p. 81.
9   McHugh, *Prostitution and Victorian Social Reform*, pp. 188f.
10   *Prot.*, 20 June 1881, p. 65; 20 November 1880, p. 104.
11   Benjamin Scott, *A State Iniquity: Its Rise, Extension and Overthrow* (London, 1890), pp. 141, 200f.
12   *Prot.*, 20 June 1881, p. 68.
13   *Prot.*, 25 July 1882, p. 78.
14   ibid., pp. 82f.
15   McHugh, *Prostitution and Victorian Social Reform*, pp. 195f.
16   *Prot.*, 25 July 1882, p. 75.

17 *Meth. Prot.*, 15 January 1876, p. 4.
18 *Prot.*, 20 April 1880, p. 48.
19 *Prot.*, 22 April 1881, p. 31.
20 *Prot.*, 17 October 1879, p. 87.
21 *Meth. Prot.*, 15 May 1876, p. 48.
22 *Meth. Prot.*, 15 February 1876, p. 16.
23 *Meth. Prot.*, 15 May 1876, p. 7.
24 ibid., p. 5.
25 Scott, *State Iniquity*, p. 183.
26 D. P. Hughes, *The Life of Hugh Price Hughes* (London, 1905), pp. 4f., 10, 78f., 85f., 134.
27 *Meth. Prot.*, 16 November 1877, pp. 99f.
28 Arthur Porritt, *The Best I Remember* (London, 1922), pp. 60–3.
29 *Prot.*, 2 February 1883, pp. 3f.
30 *Prot.*, 30 May 1883, p. 17.
31 *MM* (1884), pp. 276f.
32 *Meth. Prot.*, 15 January 1876, p. 5.
33 *Prot.*, October 1883, p. 12.
34 [Andrew Mearns], *The Bitter Cry of Outcast London*, ed. A. S. Wohl (Leicester, 1970), p. 61.
35 *CW*, 27 September 1883, p. 659.
36 R. L. Schults, *Crusader in Babylon: W. T. Stead and the Pall Mall Gazette* (Lincoln, Nebr., 1972), p. 51.
37 *CW*, 25 October 1883, p. 731.
38 *The Freeman*, 26 October 1883, p. 710.
39 [Mearns], *Bitter Cry*, p. 71.
40 *CW*, 27 September 1883, p. 659; 25 October 1883, p. 731.
41 *CW*, 3 October 1907, p. 7.
42 *Wesleyan Methodist Magazine*, September 1885, p. 712.
43 H. P. Hughes, *The Philanthropy of God: Described and Illustrated in a Series of Sermons* (London, 1890), p. 278.
44 A. G. Gardiner, *John Benn and the Progressive Movement* (London, 1925), pp. 173f.
45 Ann Stafford, *The Age of Consent* (London, 1964).
46 *Cong.*, September 1885, pp. 705f. *CW*, 15 October 1885, p. 767.
47 E. J. Bristow, *Vice and Vigilance: Purity Movements in Britain since 1700* (Dublin, 1977), pp. 104, 111–17.
48 W. A. Coote (ed.), *A Romance of Philanthropy: Being a Record of some of the Principal Incidents connected with the Exceptionally Successful Thirty Years' Work of the National Vigilance Association* (London, 1916), pp. 7, 28, 43–7, 94–101, 71–85.
49 Bristow, *Vice and Vigilance*, p. 204.
50 Coote (ed.), *Romance of Philanthropy*, pp. 156f.
51 Bristow, *Vice and Vigilance*, pp. 193f. *BW*, 13 June 1912, p. 263.
52 Roy Jenkins, *Sir Charles Dilke: A Victorian Tragedy* (London, 1958), pp. 243ff., 368, 383.
53 *CW*, 8 October 1885, p. 746.
54 *CW*, 13 October 1887, p. 767.
55 Nicoll to Ellis, 22 October 1891; Ellis to Nicoll, 26 October 1891, T. E. Ellis Collection, MSS 1546, 2758, NLW.
56 *BW*, 21 July 1892, p. 199.
57 R. W. Perks to Lord Rosebery, 3 April 1904, Rosebery Papers, MS 10050,. f. 210, NLS.
58 Brian Harrison, *Drink and the Victorians: The Temperance Question in England, 1815–1872* (London, 1971), p. 163.
59 ibid., p. 181.

60   J. H. Rigg to Sir G. H. Chubb, 17 June 1895, CC, 1893–1900, p. 79.
61   Porritt, *Best I Remember*, p. 45.
62   *Albert Spicer, 1847–1934: A Man of his Time by One of his Family* (London, 1938), p. 62.
63   *CW*, 7 October 1897, p. 7; 27 July 1899, p. 4; 1 August 1901, p. 4.
64   *MM* (1875), pp. 210f.
65   *CW*, 8 October 1885, p. 745.
66   *Bapt. Mag.*, June 1874, p. 359.
67   *CW*, 29 September 1904, p. 21.
68   *CW*, 20 May 1886, p. 411.
69   *CW*, 3 October 1907, p. 31.
70   Harrison, *Drink and the Victorians*, p. 193.
71   Hodder, *Morley*, pp. 315f.
72   *Cong.*, April 1879, p. 274.
73   D. A. Hamer, *The Politics of Electoral Pressure: A Study in the History of Victorian Reform Agitations* (Hassocks, Sussex, 1977), pp. 165–304.
74   A. E. Dingle, *The Campaign for Prohibition in Victorian England* (London, 1980), p. 182.
75   *Bapt. Mag.*, October 1872, p. 678.
76   *CW*, 11 October 1894, p. 743. J. G. Smith, *A Non-Political Treatise of and Tribute to the late William Ewart Gladstone* (Newport, Monmouth, [1898]), p. 38.
77   *CW*, 7 June 1900, p. 6; 21 March 1901, p. 10; 6 June 1901, p. 5.
78   Harrison, *Drink and the Victorians*, p. 181.
79   *MM* (1879), p. 304.
80   Albert Peel, *These Hundred Years: A History of the Congregational Union of England and Wales, 1831–1931* (London, 1931), p. 282.
81   Henry Carter, *The English Temperance Movement: A Study in Objectives* (London, 1933), p. 214.
82   H. C. Colman, *Jeremiah James Colman: A Memoir* (London, 1905), p. 339.
83   *CW*, 1 June 1905, p. 1; 19 October 1907, p. 1.
84   *BW*, 12 July 1894, p. 184; 18 October 1894, p. 403.
85   *CW*, 8 June 1899, p. 6.
86   *CW*, 21 June 1900, p. 12.
87   *BW*, 8 June 1899, p. 140.
88   Joseph Malins, *The Life of Joseph Malins: Patriarch Templar, Citizen and Temperance Reformer* (Birmingham, 1932), p. 99.
89   Stuart Mews, 'Urban problems and rural solutions: drink and disestablishment in the First World War', in *The Church in Town and Countryside* (Studies in Church History, Vol. 16), ed. Derek Baker (Oxford, 1979), pp. 472f.
90   Dingle, *Campaign for Prohibition*, pp. 106–29.
91   *CW*, 26 May 1904, p. 3.
92   *CW*, 15 June 1893, p. 477; 11 April 1895, p. 276.
93   *CW*, 6 June 1895, p. 447. 'Presidential Manifesto to British Methodism', CC, 1893–1900, pp. 79f.
94   Dingle, *Campaign for Prohibition*, p. 89.
95   *CW*, 14 November 1895, p. 871.
96   D. M. Fahey, 'Temperance and the Liberal Party: Lord Peel's Report, 1899', *Journal of British Studies*, vol. 10 (1971), p. 138.
97   *CW*, 21 May 1908, p. 9; 30 July 1908, p. 2.
98   Ross McKibbin, 'Working-class gambling in Britain, 1880–1939', *Past and Present*, vol. 82 (1979), pp. 147ff., 158f.
99   H. P. Hughes, *Ethical Christianity* (London, 1892), p. 258.
100   *CW*, 14 June 1894, p. 457.
101   *CW*, 23 May 1889, p. 426.
102   *MM* (1889), p. 344.

103 Hughes, *Ethical Christianity*, pp. 262–6.
104 F. B. Meyer, *The Bells of Is: Or Voices of Human Need and Sorrow* (London, n.d.), p. 122.
105 F. A. Atkins in *Hugh Price Hughes as We Knew Him* (London, 1902), p. 82.
106 *CW*, 20 June 1889, p. 499.
107 Philip Magnus, *King Edward the Seventh* (London, 1964), pp. 222–31.
108 *CW*, 7 February 1901, p. 11.
109 *CW*, 18 June 1891, p. 497.
110 Frederic White, *The Life of W. T. Stead*, Vol. 2 (London, 1925), p. 15.
111 *Daily News*, 10 June 1891, p. 6.
112 *CW*, 8 March 1894, p. 165.
113 *CW*, 21 June 1892, p. 481.
114 *CW*, 14 June 1894, p. 458.
115 *CW*, 5 July 1894, p. 505.
116 Horton to Rosebery, 16 December 1897; Rosebery to Horton, 26 December 1897; Perks to Rosebery, 1 February 1898; Rosebery to Hughes, 29 December 1898, Rosebery Papers, Box 75, f. 231; Item 89, p. 163; MS 10050, ff. 191f.; Item 89, p. 192, NLS.
117 Hughes, *Ethical Christianity*, p. 267. *CW*, 17 March 1892, p. 214; 14 June 1894, p. 457; 6 June 1895, p. 447.
118 A. G. Gardiner, *Life of George Cadbury* (London, 1923), pp. 220f.
119 E. B. Perkins, *Gambling in English Life* (London, 1950), pp. 82f.
120 *CW*, 15 November 1906, p. 7; 13 February 1908, p. 7.
121 *BW*, 31 October 1907, p. 85.
122 *CW*, 29 August 1889, p. 673; 12 September 1889, p. 705.
123 *Cong. Rev.*, October 1889, pp. 381f.
124 *CW*, 19 September 1889, p. 721.
125 J. C. Carlile, *My Life's Little Day* (London, 1935), pp. 89ff.
126 *Cong. Rev.*, October 1889, p. 305.
127 *CW*, 3 October 1889, p. 758.
128 *CW*, 12 December 1889, p. 984; 19 December 1889, p. 1,000.
129 *Cong. Rev.*, January 1890, p. 94. C. F. Williams, 'An experiment in social service', *Congregational Quarterly*, vol. 2 (1924), p. 222.
130 *CW*, 21 May 1891, p. 419. Peel, *These Hundred Years*, pp. 332f.
131 *CW*, 26 November 1891, p. 962.
132 *CW*, 12 October 1893, p. 786.
133 *CW*, 11 May 1893, p. 378; 25 April 1895, p. 312; 21 October 1897, p. 3.
134 *CW*, 16 November 1893, p. 885; 30 November 1893, p. 925.
135 Gardiner, *Cadbury*, pp. 224f. *CW*, 16 May 1912, p. 21. A. S. Peake, *The Life of Sir William Hartley* (London, 1926), pp. 66–74.
136 *BW*, 21 September 1911, p. 593; 28 September 1911, p. 618.
137 *BW*, 24 August 1911, p. 507.
138 Hughes, *Social Christianity*, pp. 33f.
139 *CW*, 3 May 1906, p. 21.
140 *CW*, 18 October 1906, p. 23.
141 ibid.
142 Harold Moore, *Back to the Land* (London, 1893).
143 *CW*, 3 May 1906, p. 21; 18 October 1906, p. 23.
144 James Marchant, *J. B. Paton, MA, DD: Educational and Social Pioneer* (London, 1909), pp. 164f.
145 José Harris, *Unemployment and Politics: A Study in English Social Policy* (Oxford, 1972), p. 118.
146 J. B. Paton, 'Labour for the unemployed upon the land', in J. A. Hobson (ed.), *Co-operative Labour upon the Land* (London, 1895), p. 81.
147 White, *Stead*, Vol 2, p. 12.

148   W. H. Hunt, 'An interesting industrial experiment', *Westminster Review*, vol. 154 (1900), pp. 292f.
149   Ebenezer Howard, *To-morrow: A Peaceful Path to Real Reform* (London, 1898), p. 5.
150   D. W. Bebbington, 'The city, the countryside and the social gospel in late Victorian Nonconformity', *The Church in Town and Countryside* (Studies in Church History, Vol. 16), ed. Derek Baker (Oxford, 1979), pp. 424f.
151   William Hodgkins, *Sunday: Christian and Social Significance* (London, 1960), pp. 197ff.
152   *CW*, 13 June 1907, p. 9.
153   *BW*, 17 February 1910, p. 561.
154   *CW*, 7 May 1908, p. 7.
155   *CW*, 1 November 1906, p. 13; 10 May 1906, p. 4; 21 June 1906, p. 4; 10 January 1907, pp. 10f.; 11 February 1909, p. 11.
156   *CW*, 16 March 1911, p. 10.
157   *CW*, 20 February 1908, p. 7; 12 March 1908, p. 7.
158   *CW*, 28 November 1912, pp. 2, 9.
159   *CW*, 29 August 1912, p. 7.
160   *CW*, 20 February 1908, p. 9; 7 April 1910, p. 4; 13 October 1910, p. 4.
161   E. R. Norman, *Church and Society in England, 1770–1970: A Historical Study* (Oxford, 1976), pp. 279–313.
162   Cutting from the *Holmfirth Express*, 18 December 1886, H. J. Wilson Papers, Sheffield City Library.
163   Hughes, *Philanthropy of God*, p. 198.

Notes: Chapter 4

1   *CW*, 28 March 1895, p. 236.
2   ibid., p. 243.
3   A. L. Lowell, *The Government of England*, Vol. 2 (New York, 1908), p. 380.
4   J. L. Paton, *John Brown Paton: A Biography* (London, 1914), pp. 186f.
5   Arthur Porritt, *The Best I Remember* (London, 1922), pp. 242f.
6   James Marchant, *J. B. Paton, MA, DD: Educational and Social Pioneer* (London, 1909), pp. 268ff.
7   *Cong. Rev.*, October 1889, p. 379.
8   *The Free Church Federation Movement: Its Origins and Early Growth* (n.p., n.d.), p. [1].
9   *BW*, 25 July 1890, p. 202.
10   *CW*, 19 September 1889, p. 721; 10 October 1889, p. 787.
11   *CW*, 30 January 1890, p. 87; 27 February 1890, p. 167; 19 June 1890, p. 501.
12   Minutes of the General Body of the Three Denominations, 14 April 1891, Dr Williams's Library, London.
13   *BW*, 11 June 1891, p. 106.
14   Paton, *Paton*, pp. 491f.
15   Frederic White, *The Life of W. T. Stead*, Vol. 1 (London, 1925), pp. 314f.
16   *CW*, 12 January 1893, p. 22; 24 August 1893, p. 658.
17   *Daily News*, 14 May 1886, p. 3.
18   H. S. Lunn, *Chapters from My Life: With Special Reference To Reunion* (London, 1918), pp. 142–8, 157–71.
19   Dugald Macfadyen, *Alexander Mackennal, BA, DD: Life and Letters* (London, 1905), pp. 43, 170.
20   *CW*, 1 October 1891, p. 789; 15 October 1891, p. 830.
21   *CW*, 9 June 1892, p. 479. A. W. W. Dale, *The Life of R. W. Dale of Birmingham* (London, 1898), p. 674.

22 *CW*, 17 November 1892, p. 932.
23 *CW*, 9 June 1892, p. 479.
24 *CW*, 17 November 1892, p. 932.
25 *CW*, 14 January 1892, p. 28.
26 *BW*, 14 January 1892, p. 191; 21 January 1892, p. 207; 25 February 1892, p. 287; 28 April 1892, p. 1.
27 *CW*, 27 October 1892, p. 869.
28 *CW*, 10 November 1892, p. 910. *BW*, 17 November 1892, p. 57.
29 *CW*, 24 November 1892, p. 72.
30 *CW*, 10 November 1892, p. 912.
31 *CW*, 17 November 1892, p. 932. *BW*, 17 November 1892, p. 55.
32 *BW*, 11 June 1891, p. 99.
33 *CW*, 1 September 1898, p. 5.
34 *CW*, 20 June 1895, p. 483; 26 March 1896, p. 239; 23 December 1897, p. 6; 19 September 1901, p. 6.
35 *The Nonconformist*, 28 March 1877, p. 296. *Cong. Rev.*, November 1885, p. 862. *The Liberator*, June 1891, p. 97.
36 *CW*, 28 May 1891, p. 448. *The Liberator*, June 1891, p. 97.
37 *CW*, 26 October 1893, p. 831.
38 *CW*, 13 September 1894, p. 673.
39 *BW*, 10 January 1895, p. 187.
40 *CW*, 14 November 1895, p. 867.
41 *CW*, 1 November 1894, p. 811.
42 *BW*, 3 May 1894, p. 20.
43 *CW*, 30 May 1895, p. 423.
44 *CW*, 12 March 1896, p. 199.
45 *CW*, 28 November 1895, p. 906.
46 *CW*, 30 April 1896, p. 341.
47 *CW*, 9 July 1891, p. 568; 3 December 1891, p. 980.
48 *CW*, 21 April 1891, p. 315.
49 *CW*, 16 March 1893, p. 209.
50 *CW*, 23 February 1893, p. 141. A. G. Gardiner, *Life of George Cadbury* (London, 1923), pp. 175ff.
51 *CW*, 11 August 1892, p. 647.
52 *BW*, 24 January 1895, p. 224.
53 *BW*, 12 March 1896, p. 341. *CW*, 10 March 1898, p. 4; 16 March 1899, p. 5.
54 Gardiner, *Cadbury*, p. 177. *CW*, 23 November 1893, p. 909.
55 *CW*, 26 December 1895, p. 985.
56 *CW*, 23 January 1896, p. 63.
57 *CW*, 7 May 1896, p. 355.
58 *CW*, 12 March 1896, p. 196; 25 January 1900, p. 6.
59 *CW*, 12 March 1896, p. 196.
60 Gardiner, *Cadbury*, pp. 178f. *CW*, 1 February 1894, p. 83.
61 *CW*, 25 January 1894, p. 63.
62 Gardiner, *Cadbury*, p. 179.
63 *CW*, 22 March 1894, p. 214.
64 *CW*, 28 March 1895, p. 236.
65 *CW*, 28 March 1895, p. 236; 27 February 1896, p. 165.
66 *CW*, 9 May 1895, p. 355.
67 *CW*, 16 May 1895, p. 383.
68 *CW*, 14 January 1897, p. 4.
69 *CW*, 21 April 1892, p. 315.
70 *CW*, 19 December 1895, p. 967. Obituary by W. J. Townsend, *Minutes of the Third Annual Conference of the United Methodist Church, 1910* (London, 1910), p. 64. *CW*, 7 May 1896, p. 355.

71   *Baptist Times*, 8 April 1910, p. 221.
72   Porritt, *Best I Remember*, pp. 222ff.
73   *BW*, 7 April 1910, p. 4.
74   *CW*, 7 April 1910, p. 9.
75   *CW*, 4 April 1901, p. 6.
76   *CW*, 25 February 1897, p. 3.
77   *CW*, 13 August 1896, p. 625.
78   *CW*, 11 February 1897, p. 3.
79   J. S. Drummond, *Charles A. Berry, D.D.: A Memoir* (London, 1899), pp. 52–72.
80   Porritt, *Best I Remember*, pp. 76f.
81   Drummond, *Berry*, pp. 119–23. Lunn, *Chapters*, p. 378.
82   *Proceedings of the National Council of the Evangelical Free Churches* (London, 1896), p. 33.
83   ibid., p. 234.
84   *Home Counties Baptist Association Report* (Guildford, 1896), p. 15.
85   *Proceedings of the National Council*, p. 232.
86   Drummond, *Berry*, p. 121.
87   *CW*, 25 June 1896, p. 503; 30 May 1895, p. 423; 4 December 1895, p. 926; 17 October 1895, p. 787.
88   *CW*, 11 February 1897, p. 3.
89   *CW*, 23 March 1899, p. 11.
90   *CW*, 21 April 1892, p. 315.
91   *CW*, 10 March 1892, p. 188.
92   *CW*, 23 February 1893, p. 141; 2 March 1893, p. 167.
93   Porritt, *Best I Remember*, p. 62.
94   *BW*, 20 June 1895, p. 485.
95   *CW*, 7 October 1897, p. 17.
96   Dale, *Dale*, pp. 648ff.
97   *BW*, 3 November 1898, p. 58.
98   Gardiner, *Cadbury*, pp. 179f.
99   *CW*, 30 May 1895, p. 419.
100   *CW*, 18 July 1895, p. 561.
101   *CW*, 30 April 1896, p. 330.
102   *BW*, 13 January 1898, p. 263.
103   *CW*, 20 January 1898, p. 6.
104   *BW*, 20 January 1898, p. 280; 27 January 1898, p. 299.
105   *CW*, 3 February 1898, p. 7.
106   *CW*, 11 March 1897, p. 4.
107   *BW*, 11 March 1897, p. 373.
108   *CW*, 9 February 1899, p. 13.
109   *CW*, 23 August 1900, p. 9.
110   *BW*, 24 January 1895, p. 224; 21 February 1895, p. 283.
111   LS, 24 January 1898, p., 511.
112   *CW*, 2 May 1901, p. 5.
113   *CW*, 26 May 1898, p. 11.
114   David Lloyd George to Margaret Lloyd George, 23 August 1898, in K. O. Morgan (ed.), *Lloyd George: Family Letters, 1885–1936* (Cardiff, 1973), p. 115.
115   *Daily News*, 26 October 1898, p. 3.
116   *CW*, 26 May 1898, p. 11.
117   *Daily News*, 29 October 1898, p. 8.
118   *CW*, 17 November 1898, p. 3.
119   *CW*, 18 May 1899, p. 2; 9 November 1899, p. 14; 5 July 1900, p. 13.
120   *CW*, 7 December 1899, p. 11.
121   *CW*, 5 July 1900, p. 13.
122   *CW*, 20 July 1898, p. 11.

123 *National Conference of Free Church Councils on the Education Bill* (London, 1902), pp. 3f.
124 *BW*, 28 August 1902, p. 443.
125 *CW*, 29 May 1902, p. 3.
126 *BW*, 28 August 1902, p. 443.
127 *CW*, 19 March 1903, p. 5.
128 Porritt, *Best I Remember*, pp. 50–5.
129 *CW*, 7 June 1900, p. 9.
130 Porritt, *Best I Remember*, p. 52.
131 *CW*, 27 August 1903, p. 6.
132 *CW*, 20 August 1903, p. 4; 17 September 1903, p. 4; 15 October 1903, p. 4.
133 R. W. Perks to Lord Rosebery, 23 September 1903, Rosebery Papers, MS 10051, ff. 134f., NLS. Herbert Gladstone's Diary, 29 September 1903, Viscount Gladstone Papers, Add. MS 46484, f. 53, BL.
134 Stephen Koss, *Nonconformity in Modern British Politics* (London, 1975), pp. 59f.
135 Minutes of the National Council of the Evangelical Free Churches: General Committee, 28 September 1903.
136 Herbert Gladstone to Campbell-Bannerman, 3 November 1903, Campbell-Bannerman Papers, Add. MS 41217, ff. 4f. BL.
137 *CW*, 27 August 1903, p. 6.
138 *CW*, 13 April 1905, p. 2.
139 *BW*, 4 January 1906, p. 396.
140 *CW*, 14 December 1905, p. 22.
141 *CW*, 28 December 1905, p. 4.
142 *CW*, 25 January 1906, p. 7.
143 *CW*, 11 January 1906, p. 4.
144 Harry Jeffs, *Press, Preachers and Politicians: Reminiscences, 1874 to 1932* (London, 1933), pp. 113–16.
145 *CW*, 11 January 1906, p. 4.
146 *Church Times*, 12 January 1906, quoted by A. K. Russell, *Liberal Landslide: The General Election of 1906* (Newton Abbot, 1973), p. 184.
147 Autobiographical Sketch, Viscount Gladstone Papers, Add. MS 46118, f. 102, BL.
148 *CW*, 1 February 1906, p. 11.
149 *CW*, 15 February 1906, p. 4.
150 *CW*, 8 March 1906, p. 23.
151 *Free Church Yearbook* (1905), p. 175.
152 J. A. Newbold, *The Nonconformist Conscience a Persecuting Force* (Manchester, 1908), pp. 191, 193.
153 ibid., pp. 188f.
154 *CW*, 14 January 1909, p. 10.
155 *CW*, 18 March 1909, p. 3.
156 *CW*, 11 November 1909, p. 3; 25 November 1909, p. 15.
157 *CW*, 25 November 1909, p. 15.
158 *CW*, 1 December 1910, p. 3.
159 *CW*, 7 April 1910, p. 9.
160 Porritt, *Best I Remember*, pp. 223f.
161 *CW*, 10 March 1910, p. 13.
162 *CW*, 13 October 1910, p. 13.
163 M. J. Street, *F. B. Meyer: His Life and Work* (London, 1902), pp. 26, 154.
164 W. Y. Fullerton, *F. B. Meyer: A Biography* (London, n.d.), p. 71.
165 ibid., pp. 66f.
166 F. B. Meyer, *The Bells of Is: Or Voices of Human Need and Sorrow* (London, n.d.). pp. 90f., 28–74.
167 Fullerton, *Meyer*, p. 156.
168 Street, *Meyer*, p. 111.

169   Jeffs, *Press, Preachers and Politicians*, pp. 116f.
170   *B W*, 16 July 1908, p. 358.
171   *Free Church Year Book* (1909), pp. 28–31.
172   *CW*, 13 October 1910, p. 13.
173   *CW*, 20 May 1909, p. 11; 20 February 1913, p. 7; 16 July 1914, p. 16.
174   *CW*, 29 February 1912, p. 12.
175   *CW*, 12 March 1914, p. 11; 25 July 1912, p. 7.
176   *CW*, 15 September 1910, p. 7.
177   Stuart Mews, 'Puritanicalism, sport, and race: a symbolic crusade of 1911', in *Popular Belief and Practice* (Studies in Church History, Vol. 8), ed. G. J. Cuming and Derek Baker (Cambridge, 1972).
178   *CW*, 5 October 1911, p. 4.
179   *CW*, 21 March 1901, p. 4.
180   'A Nonconformist minister', *Nonconformity and Politics* (London, 1909), p. 106.
181   *CW*, 6 July 1911, p. 4.
182   Fullerton, *Meyer*, p. 115.

Notes: Chapter 5

1   *CW*, 10 May 1888, p. 4.
2   *Bapt. Mag.*, March 1874, p. 156.
3   *Cong.*, February 1881, pp. 163f.
4   *Cong.*, January 1884, p. 73.
5   *Cong.*, August 1885, pp. 641ff. *Bapt. Mag.*, August 1885, p. 371.
6   *CW*, 31 December 1885, p. 997.
7   *Bapt.*, 18 June 1886, p. 382; 25 June 1886, p. 403. Shropshire Baptist Association Minutes, 31 May and 1 June 1886.
8   A. W. W. Dale, *The Life of R. W. Dale of Birmingham* (London, 1898), p. 466. *Daily News*, 29 May 1886, p. 3.
9   *CW*, 27 May 1886, p. 439.
10   *Daily News*, 7 June 1886, p. 5.
11   W. S. Fowler, *A Study in Radicalism and Dissent: The Life and Times of Henry Joseph Wilson, 1833–1914* (London, 1961), p. 81.
12   A. T. Bassett, *The Life of the Rt Hon John Edward Ellis, MP* (London, 1914), pp. 74ff.
13   Illingworth to Gladstone and reply, 12 May 1886, GP, Add. MS 44497, ff. 201, 203, BL.
14   *Lib. Un.*, 1 May 1892, p. 186.
15   Parker to Gladstone, 27 November 1886, GP, Add. MS 44499, f. 203, BL.
16   *The Times*, 30 November 1886, pp. 8, 9.
17   Gladstone to Stockwell, 23 February 1887; and reply, 24 February 1887, GP, Add. MS 44500, ff. 129, 133, BL.
18   *Bapt.*, 25 February 1887, p. 212; 4 March 1887, pp. 137f.
19   Rogers to Gladstone, 4 March [1887], GP, Add. MS 44500, f. 148, BL.
20   *Bapt.*, 21 May 1886, p. 323.
21   ibid.
22   *Daily News*, 16 April 1886, p. 5.
23   Chamberlain to Thomas Gee, 26 April 1886, Thomas Gee MSS, 8305 D, NLW.
24   *Daily News*, 5 April 1886, p. 5.
25   J. G. Rogers, *An Autobiography* (London, 1903), pp. 2, 6.
26   Arthur Mursell, *Memories of My Life* (London, 1913), p. 185.
27   Arthur Porritt, *The Best I Remember* (London, 1922), pp. 42–6.
28   Rogers, *Autobiography*, pp. 122ff.
29   *CW*, 22 April 1886, p. 318.
30   *Cong.*, April 1886, p. 313.

31 *Cong.*, July 1886, p. 507.
32 Dale to Chamberlain, 30 April 1891, JCP, JC 5/20/19, BUL.
33 Porritt, *Best I Remember*, p. 44.
34 Caine to Chamberlain, [27?] May 1886, JCP, JC 5/10/2, BUL.
35 F. W. Macdonald, *As a Tale that Is Told: Recollections of Many Years* (London, 1919), pp. 169, 172f., 210.
36 Mursell, *Memories*, pp. 150, 161, 262.
37 Chamberlain to R. W. Dale, 2 May 1891, JCP, JC 5/20/74, BUL.
38 G. M. Trevelyan, *The Life of John Bright* (London, 1913), p. 446.
39 *The Times*, 30 December 1890, p. 5.
40 Newman Hall to Gladstone, 21 January 1887, GP, Add. MS 44188, f. 193, BL.
41 Dale, *Dale*, pp. 451–64.
42 M. C. Hurst, *Joseph Chamberlain and West Midland Politics, 1886–1895* (Oxford, 1962), pp. 42, 135f.
43 *Cong. Rev.*, January 1887, p. 75.
44 *CW*, 10 October 1888, p. 782. Dale, *Dale*, pp. 584ff.
45 Dale to Thomas Gee, 26 May 1890, Thomas Gee MSS, 8305 D, NLW.
46 Chamberlain to Dale, 10 December 1890, JCP, JC 5/20/70, BUL.
47 *The Times*, 2 July 1892, p. 10.
48 W. Y. Fullerton, *C. H. Spurgeon: A Biography* (London, 1920).
49 Rogers to Gladstone, 19 June 1886, GP, Add. MS 44498, f. 40, BL.
50 A. B. Cooke and John Vincent, *The Governing Passion: Cabinet Government and Party Politics in Britain, 1885–86* (Brighton, 1974), p. 109n.
51 Spurgeon to Gladstone, 27 May 1886; T. H. Stockwell to Gladstone, 6 May 1886, GP, Add. MS 44497, ff. 294, 138, BL.
52 *Lib. Un.*, 1 April 1892, p. 177.
53 *Daily News*, 2 June 1886, p. 5.
54 *Bapt.*, 2 July 1886, p. 9.
55 *Daily News*, 14 July 1886, p. 3.
56 *The Sword and The Trowel*, June 1886, p. 294.
57 Rogers to Gladstone, 19 June 1886, GP, Add. MS 44498, f. 40, BL.
58 *The Times*, 7 July 1892, p. 6.
59 *Bapt.*, 26 March 1886, p. 201.
60 *CW*, 13 May 1886, p. 394.
61 *CW*, 8 July 1886, p. 551.
62 *CW*, 23 March 1893, p. 228; 20 April 1893, p. 308; 27 April 1893, p. 328.
63 R. M. Edgar to Lord Salisbury, 24 June 1892, SP, M/92/6/24.
64 *Daily News*, 1 May 1886, p. 6.
65 *Daily News*, 17 July 1886, p. 3. *Lib. Un.*, 1 October 1891, p. 54.
66 *CW*, 2 March 1893, p. 165.
67 G. H. Pike, *Dr Parker and his Friends* (London, 1904), pp. 207, 226. *CW*, 1 July 1886, p. 528.
68 Thomas McCullagh, *Sir William McArthur, K.C.M.G.* (London, 1891), pp. 353, 213.
69 T. B. Stephenson, *William Arthur: A Brief Biography* (London, n.d.), p. 104.
70 *The Times*, 29 June 1892, p. 8; 7 July 1892, p. 6.
71 H. M. Pelling, *Social Geography of British Elections, 1885–1910* (London, 1967), p. 220.
72 ibid., p. 163.
73 *The Times*, 13 June 1889, p. 7.
74 *The Times*, 18 October 1889, p. 11.
75 *Lib. Un.*, 1 February 1890, p. 125.
76 *Cong.*, October 1885, p. 776.
77 Chubb to Salisbury, 15 June 1885, SP.
78 *The Times*, 27 July 1895, p. 8. *BW*, 6 February 1896, p. 261.

79 *BW*, 1 April 1897, p. 426.
80 *BW*, 20 September 1894, p. 337.
81 *The Times*, 14 July 1892, p. 7. *CW*, 18 January 1906, p. 7.
82 *The Times*, 1 February 1896, p. 9; 10 October 1888, p. 8.
83 *Daily News*, 18 April 1888, pp. 6, 8.
84 *The Times*, 15 November 1888, p. 6.
85 Noel Currer-Briggs, *Contemporary Observations on Security from the Chubb Collectanea, 1818–1968* (London, [1968]), pp. 19, 45.
86 Cuttings and papers, CC, 1893–1900, pp. 32, 253, 13, 14, 51; 1900–8, p.3; 1908–13, p. 58; Vol. 7, p. 108; Vol. 8, pp. 1D, 140; Vol. 9, pp. 52, 340.
87 Chubb to Salisbury, 19 July 1884, SP.
88 Chubb to Salisbury, 15 June 1885, SP.
89 *The Times*, 9 May 1889, p. 10.
90 *The Times*, 31 March 1892, p. 10.
91 R. W. E. Middleton to Salisbury, 21 September 1892, SP.
92 *The Times*, 11 November 1892, p. 6.
93 *CW*, 28 June 1894, p. 497.
94 S. K. McDonnell to Chubb, 13 November 1895; 11 December 1895; 20 December 1895, CC, 1893–1900, p. 112. *The Times*, 1 February 1896, p. 9.
95 *The Times*, 14 May 1901, p. 10.
96 *The Times*, 5 March 1903, p. 9.
97 Balfour to Chubb, 26 September 1905, CC, 1900–8, p. 194. A. A. Hood to J. S. Sandars, 23 September [1905], Balfour Papers, Add. MS 49771, quoted by P. F. Clarke, *Lancashire and the New Liberalism* (Cambridge, 1971), p. 56n.
98 *The Times*, 11 November 1892, p. 6.
99 Cutting from *Pall Mall Gazette*, 26 May 1893, CC, 1893–1900, p. 7.
100 *The Times*, 5 December 1893, p. 10.
101 Cutting from *Pall Mall Gazette*, 26 May 1893, CC, 1893–1900, p. 7.
102 *Daily News*, 9 June 1892, p. 5.
103 For example, *The Times*, 9 July 1892, p. 10.
104 *The Times*, 30 July 1892, p. 8.
105 Cuttings, CC, 1893–1900, pp. 85ff.
106 *The Times*, 2 July 1895, p. 5; 10 July 1895, p. 8; 27 July 1895, p. 8.
107 Circulars, CC, 1900–8, pp. 17, 82.
108 Cutting from *Methodist Times*, 7 April 1887, enclosed in Chubb to Salisbury, 19 May 1887, SP.
109 *The Times*, 7 April 1887, p. 6.
110 *Daily News*, 15 April 1887, p. 2.
111 *Lib. Un.*, 27 April 1887, pp. 70f. *CW*, 7 April 1887, p. 258; 21 April 1887, p. 303.
112 *The Freeman*, 29 April 1887, p. 263.
113 *Cong. Rev.*, June 1887, p. 565.
114 Newman Hall, *An Autobiography* (London, 1898), p. 283.
115 *The Times*, 12 May 1887, p. 10.
116 Sir James Marchant, *Dr. John Clifford, C.H.: Life, Letters and Reminiscences* (London, 1924), p. 80.
117 *The Times*, 30 July 1887, p. 12.
118 Rogers to Gladstone, 7 August [1887], GP, Add. MS 44501, f. 217, BL.
119 *The Times*, 20 October 1887, p. 6.
120 Rogers to Gladstone, 24 December [1887], GP, Add. MS 44502, f. 237, BL. *The Times*, 10 February 1888, p. 4.
121 *The Times*, 10 May 1888, p. 7.
122 Rogers to Gladstone, 14 April [1888]; 2 May [1888], GP, Add. MS 44503, ff. 166, 201, BL.
123 *CW*, 10 May 1888, p. 3.
124 *The Times*, 13 June 1889, p. 7; 31 July 1890, p. 4.

125   *CW*, 12 May 1887, p. 366.
126   *CW*, 11 October 1888, p. 781; 18 October 1888, p. 803.
127   *The Sword and the Trowel*, May 1887, p. 246.
128   *The Times*, 14 April 1887, p. 3.
129   Chubb to Salisbury, 19 May 1887, S P.
130   *The Times*, 23 May 1887, p. 12.
131   *The Times*, 17 May 1888, p. 6.
132   *Cong. Rev.*, April 1888, p. 380.
133   Perks to H. J. Gladstone, 7 June 1890, Viscount Gladstone Papers, Add. M S 46053, f. 127, B L.
134   H. J. Wilson Papers, 2564–1, Sheffield City Library.
135   *The Times*, 17 October 1889, p. 6.
136   *The Times*, 18 December 1890, p. 7.
137   *The Times*, 8 January 1891, p. 3.
138   For example, *The Times*, 29 December 1890, p. 4.
139   *The Times*, 20 November 1890, p. 5.
140   *CW*, 20 November 1890, pp. 925, 937. *Methodist Times*, 20 November 1890, p. 1,180.
141   *Lib. Un.*, December 1890, p. 91.
142   *The Times*, 24 November 1890, p. 6.
143   Wilson to sisters, 15 December 1890, H. J. Wilson Papers, 2574–6, Sheffield City Library.
144   Wilson to Alick Wilson, 27 November 1890, H. J. Wilson Papers, 2574–5, Sheffield City Library.
145   John Morley, *The Life of William Ewart Gladstone*, Vol. 3 (London, 1903), pp. 430, 435.
146   *Lib. Un.*, February 1891, p. 139.
147   J. L. Hammond, *Gladstone and the Irish Nation* (London, 1938), pp. 636f.
148   H. C. Colman, *Jeremiah James Colman: A Memoir* (London, 1905), pp. 324f.
149   J. F. Glaser, 'Parnell's fall and the Nonconformist Conscience', *Irish Historical Studies*, vol. 12 (1960).
150   *The Times*, 25 December 1890, p. 3.
151   *The Times*, 19 October 1893, p. 3. Hughes to Gladstone, 30 April 1892, G P, Add. M S 44514, f.. 225, B L.
152   *Cong. Rev.*, January 1891, p. 61.
153   *The Times*, 27 December 1890, p. 6.
154   *The Times*, 22 April 1891, p. 12; 16 July 1891, p. 10; 25 November 1891, p. 10; 3 February 1892, p. 6. Lady Gwendolin Cecil, *Life of Robert, Marquis of Salisbury*, Vol. 4 (London, 1932), pp. 398f.
155   J. L. Garvin, *The Life of Joseph Chamberlain*, Vol. 2 (London, 1933), p. 540.
156   *Lib. Un.*, 1 September 1892, p. 40.
157   *Lib. Un.*, 1 May 1892, p. 187.
158   *The Times*, 18 June 1892, pp. 10, 13.
159   *The Times*, 23 June 1892, p. 10.
160   *The Times*, 20 June 1892, p. 12.
161   *The Times*, 6 December 1892, p. 7. Sir Henry James to Joseph Chamberlain, 18 December 1892, J C P, J C 5/46/30, B U L.
162   *CW*, 14 December 1893, p. 961; 4 May 1893, p. 363.
163   *CW*, 16 March 1893, p. 216.
164   *BW*, 25 July 1895, p. 211; 8 August 1895, p. 242.
165   *BW*, 5 March 1896, p. 331.
166   *Methodist Times*, 21 May 1896, p. 337.
167   *Parl. Deb.*, 4th series, vol. 40, 12 May 1896, col. 1204.
168   *CW*, 21 May 1896, p. 397.
169   *BW*, 21 May 1896, p. 67. *CW*, 21 May 1896, p. 406.
170   *BW*, 28 May 1896, p. 81.

171   Lord Tweedmouth to W. E. Gladstone, 27 May 1896, GP, Add. MS 44332, f. 335, BL.
172   *CW*, 20 April 1899, pp. 10f.
173   *BW*, 8 December 1898, p. 143.
174   *BW*, 11 January 1912, p. 446.
175   *CW*, 18 April 1912, p. 2.
176   *CW*, 9 November 1911, p. 2.
177   *The Times*, 10 February 1912, p. 8.
178   *The Times*, 26 October 1912, p. 7; 7 November 1913, p. 10; 25 February 1914, p. 5.
179   *The Times*, 30 November 1910, p. 9; 15 June 1912, p. 7.
180   *The Times*, 14 February 1912, p. 7; 3 October 1912, p. 4; 18 October 1912, p. 8.
181   Sir Edward Carson to Chubb, 31 January 1914, CC, 1908–13, p. 198.
182   Cutting from *Belfast Evening Telegraph*, 24 April 1914; *A Nonconformist Appeal to Nonconformist Electors*, CC, 1908–13, pp. 217, 82.
183   *The Times*, 10 May 1888, p. 7.

Notes: Chapter 6

1   A. H. Wilkerson, *The Rev. R. J. Campbell: The Man and his Ministry* (London, 1907), p. 25.
2   *CW*, 21 December 1899, p. 2.
3   Donald Read, *Cobden and Bright: A Victorian Political Partnership* (London, 1967), pp. 112–49.
4   H. C. Colman, *Jeremiah James Colman: A Memoir* (London, 1905), p. 289.
5   Alexander Tyrrell, 'Making the millennium: the mid-nineteenth century peace movement', *Historical Journal*, vol. 20 (1978), pp. 92ff.
6   C. S. Miall, *Henry Richard, M.P.: A Biography* (London, 1889), pp. 30, 353.
7   *CW*, 25 May 1893, p. 421.
8   *Herald of Peace* (1885), p. 241, quoted by A. C. F. Beales, *The History of Peace: A Short Account of the Organised Movements for International Peace* (London, 1931), p. 184.
9   Elizabeth Isichei, *Victorian Quakers* (London, 1970), p. 225. *CW*, 21 May 1896, p. 400; 19 May 1898, p. 13.
10   *British Quarterly Review*, July 1864, p. 261.
11   Tyrrell, 'Making the millennium', p. 95.
12   W. E. Gladstone, *Midlothian Speeches, 1879* [1879] introd. M. R. D. Foot (Leicester, 1971), pp. 63, 123, 94, 53.
13   *Parl. Deb.*, 3rd series, vol. 272, col. 723.
14   *Cong.*, August 1882, p. 624.
15   *Cong.*, July 1884, pp. 590, 599.
16   *Cong.*, March 1885, p. 240.
17   Gloucester and Hereford Baptist Association Minutes, 10 March 1885.
18   *Cong.*, June 1885, p. 479.
19   *CW*, 16 April 1891, p. 315; 10 May 1906, p. 12.
20   *CW*, 25 April 1895, p. 319; 30 May 1895, p. 429.
21   *CW*, 19 December 1895, p. 962.
22   *CW*, 27 April 1911, p. 6.
23   *Bapt. Mag.*, September 1873, p. 454.
24   Memorial from the British and Foreign Anti-Slavery Society to W. E. Gladstone, 2 June 1881, Miscellaneous Correspondence of W. E. Gladstone, Glynne-Gladstone MSS, Clwyd County Record Office.
25   Suzanne Miers, *Britain and the Ending of the Slave Trade* (London, 1975), pp. 33, 95.
26   *CW*, 3 September 1896, p. 669.
27   *CW*, 4 April 1895, p. 256.

28   *CW*, 11 October 1894, p. 743.
29   *CW*, 3 March 1904, p. 2.
30   *CW*, 28 April 1904, p. 21; 5 May 1904, p. 5; 12 May 1904, p. 22.
31   *BW*, 30 November 1905, p. 2.
32   *CW*, 11 January 1906, p. 2.
33   R. M. Slade, 'English-speaking missions in the Congo Independent State (1878–1908)', *Académie royale des sciences coloniales: classe des sciences morales et politiques*, vol. 16 (1959), pp. 240–61.
34   W. R. Louis and Jean Stengers, *E. D. Morel's History of the Congo Reform Movement* (Oxford, 1968), pp. 107–27, 200.
35   *CW*, 20 June 1907, p. 11.
36   *CW*, 4 October 1906, p. 21.
37   Roland Oliver, *The Missionary Factor in East Africa* [1952] (London, 1965), pp. 86, 122, 154.
38   Thomas McCullagh, *Sir William McArthur, K.C.M.G.* (London, 1891), pp. 147–83.
39   ibid., p. 182.
40   ibid., pp. 183, 194, 358f.
41   D. P. Hughes, *The Life of Hugh Price Hughes* (London, 1905), p. 546.
42   H. P. Hughes, *The Philanthropy of God: Described and Illustrated in a Series of Sermons* (London, 1890), p. 95.
43   Hughes, *Hughes*, p. 553.
44   A. A. Koskinen, *Missionary Influence as a Political Factor in the Pacific Islands* (Helsinki, 1953), p. 207.
45   Åke Holmberg, *African Tribes and European Agencies: Colonialism and Humanitarianism in British South and East Africa, 1870–1895* (Göteborg, 1966), pp. 49–70.
46   A. W. W. Dale, *The Life of R. W. Dale of Birmingham* (London, 1898), p. 441.
47   *BW*, 16 May 1895, p. 51.
48   A. J. Dachs, 'Missionary imperialism: the case of Bechuanaland', *Journal of African History*, vol. 13 (1972), pp. 653–6.
49   *Cong.*, May 1883, pp. 423f.
50   Anthony Low, 'British public opinion and the Uganda question: October–December 1892', *Uganda Journal*, vol. 18 (1954), p. 86.
51   R. T. Shannon, *Gladstone and the Bulgarian Agitation, 1876* (London, 1963), pp. 67–78, 160–8.
52   *The Turkish Atrocities in Bulgaria: Letters of the Special Commissioner of the 'Daily News', J. A. MacGahan, Esq.*, (London, 1876), pp. 26f.
53   ibid., pp. 46f.
54   ibid., p. 27.
55   *The Nonconformist*, 3 October 1877, p. 997.
56   R. A. J. Walling (ed.), *The Diaries of John Bright* (London, 1930), p. 387.
57   Roy Douglas, 'Britain and the Armenian question, 1894–7', *Historical Journal*, vol. 19 (1976), pp. 113f.
58   *CW*, 29 August 1889, p. 672.
59   *CW*, 2 May 1895, p. 340.
60   *CW*, 10 January 1895, p. 21; 17 January 1895, p. 37; 9 May 1895, p. 360.
61   *CW*, 13 June 1895, p. 457.
62   G. W. E. Russell (ed.), *Malcolm MacColl: Memoirs and Correspondence* (London, 1914), pp. 146, 149, 151, 155.
63   *CW*, 19 December 1895, pp. 961, 967.
64   *CW*, 17 September 1896, p. 702.
65   *CW*, 13 July 1893, p. 557.
66   *CW*, 20 December 1894, p. 945.
67   *CW*, 23 May 1895, p. 397.
68   *CW*, 19 September 1895, p. 708.

69   *CW*, 19 December 1895, p. 961.
70   *CW*, 19 September 1895, p. 708.
71   *CW*, 19 March 1896, p. 224.
72   *CW*, 17 September 1896, p. 702.
73   *CW*, 8 October 1896, p. 760.
74   *CW*, 25 February 1897, p. 10. *Daily News*, 27 February 1897, p. 6.
75   *CW*, 11 March 1897, p. 4.
76   J. S. Mills, *Sir Edward Cook, K.B.E.* (London, 1921), pp. 175f.
77   William Adamson, *The Life of the Rev. Joseph Parker, D.D.: Pastor, City Temple, London* (London, 1902), p. 303.
78   *BW*, 17 September 1903, p. 543.
79   Memorial to Lords Rosebery and Kimberley enclosed with R. W. Perks to Lord Rosebery, 10 August 1894, Rosebery Papers, MS 10050, ff. 1–5, NLS.
80   *CW*, 2 January 1896, p. 4.
81   Frederic White, *The Life of W. T. Stead*, Vol. 2, (London, 1925), p. 87.
82   *CW*, 19 December 1895, p. 961.
83   *BW*, 8 April 1897, p. 444.
84   *BW*, 15 April 1897, pp. 462, 459.
85   R. L. Schults, *Crusader in Babylon: W. T. Stead and the Pall Mall Gazette* (Lincoln, Nebr., 1972), p. 91.
86   A. J. Marder, *British Naval Policy, 1880–1905; The Anatomy of British Sea Power* (London, [1941]), pp. 65–70.
87   ibid., p. 15.
88   *CW*, 4 March 1897, p. 10.
89   *CW*, 28 April 1898, p. 5.
90   *CW*, 12 May 1898, p. 13.
91   C. T. Bateman, *John Clifford, M.A., B.Sc., LL.B., D.D., O.M.: Free Church Leader and Preacher* (London, n.d.), p. 184.
92   Hughes, *Hughes*, p. 553.
93   *CW*, 17 March 1898, p. 12.
94   *CW*, 20 October 1898, p. 12.
95   *CW*, 19 January 1899, pp. 1, 10.
96   *BW*, 20 July 1899, p. 247.
97   *CW*, 1 March 1900, p. 7.
98   Richard Price, *An Imperial War and the British Working Class: Working-class Attitudes and Reactions to the Boer War, 1899–1902* (London, 1972), p. 13.
99   *CW*, 3 October 1901, p. 11.
100 Greenhough to Rosebery, 22 February 1902, Rosebery Papers, Box 106, NLS.
101 *Bapt. Mag.*, February 1900, p. 100.
102 S. K. Hocking, *My Book of Memory: A String of Reminiscences and Reflections* (London, 1923), p. 180.
103 *CW*, 26 October 1899, p. 13.
104 *CW*, 24 October 1901, p. 22.
105 Stephen Koss, 'Wesleyanism and Empire', *Historical Journal*, vol. 18 (1975), pp. 105–18.
106 *CW*, 22 February 1900, p. 12.
107 Ian Sellers, 'The pro-Boer movement in Liverpool', *Transactions of the Unitarian Historical Society*, vol. 12 (1960), p. 74n.
108 *CW*, 12 October 1899, p. 6.
109 *CW*, 5 October 1899, p. 6.
110 Price, *Imperial War*, p. 13.
111 Dugald Macfadyen, *Alexander Mackennal, BA, DD: Life and Letters* (London, 1905), p. 258.
112 *CW*, 9 November 1899, p. 8.
113 Sellers, 'Pro-Boer movement', p. 79.

114 W. B. Selbie, *The Life of Charles Silvester Horne, M.A., M.P.* (London, 1920), pp. 113f.
115 *CW*, 15 March 1900, p. 11.
116 *CW*, 18 January 1900, p. 2.
117 Sir James Marchant, *Dr. John Clifford, C.H.: Life, Letters and Reminiscences* (London, 1924), pp. 145f.
118 Price, *Imperial War*, p. 24.
119 *CW*, 15 March 1900, p. 2.
120 White, *Stead*, Vol. 2, p. 176.
121 *CW*, 8 March 1900, p. 8; 15 March 1900, p. 2. Bateman, *Clifford*, p. 192.
122 *CW*, 19 April 1900, p. 2.
123 *CW*, 18 July 1901, p. 1.
124 *CW*, 25 July 1901, p. 13.
125 *Daily News*, 14 December 1901, p. 8.
126 *BW*, 23 March 1911, p. 695. *CW*, 21 June 1911, p. 3.
127 *CW*, 14 April 1904, p. 10.
128 *CW*, 12 May 1904, p. 21.
129 *CW*, 20 June 1907, p. 7.
130 *CW*, 12 December 1907, p. 3.
131 *CW*, 28 May 1908, p. 4.
132 *CW*, 17 June 1909, p. 4.
133 Harry Jeffs, *Press, Preachers and Politicians: Reminiscences, 1874 to 1932* (London, 1933), pp. 171–8.
134 K. W. Clements, 'Baptists and the outbreak of the First World War', *Baptist Quarterly*, vol. 26 (1975), pp. 79f.
135 *CW*, 9 February 1911, p. 22. *BW*, 23 November 1911, p. 227.
136 *CW*, 9 May 1907, p. 4.
137 *CW*, 18 December 1913, pp. 4, 5.
138 *CW*, 22 January 1914, p. 7.
139 *CW*, 21 May 1914, p. 3.
140 *BW*, 4 June 1914, p. 258.
141 *CW*, 6 August 1914, p. 4.
142 ibid., p. 2.
143 *BW*, 3 September 1914, p. 554.
144 *CW*, 2 June 1904, p. 10.
145 *CW*, 12 September 1901, p. 11.
146 Clyde Binfield, 'Christ's choice of a battlefield?', *So Down to Prayers: Studies in English Nonconformity, 1780–1920* (London, 1977), p. 214.

Notes: Chapter 7

1 *National Conference of Free Church Councils on the Education Bill* (London 1902), p. 11.
2 Edward Baines in *Congregational Magazine* (1843), pp. 834–8.
3 A. W. W. Dale, *The Life of R. W. Dale of Birmingham* (London, 1898), pp. 266–74.
4 Francis Adams, *History of the Elementary Schools Contest in England* [1882], ed. Asa Briggs (Brighton, 1972).
5 Dale, *Dale*, pp. 274–83.
6 Gillian Sutherland, *Policy-Making in Elementary Education, 1870–1895* (London. 1973), p. 168.
7 Dale, *Dale*, pp. 280–8. Adams, *Elementary Schools Contest*, pp. 291–5.
8 W. S. Fowler, *A Study in Radicalism and Dissent: The Life and Times of Henry Joseph Wilson, 1833–1914* (London, 1961), pp. 39ff.
9 *Bapt. Mag.*, November 1873, p. 591.

10 Dale, *Dale*, pp. 278ff.
11 ibid., p. 558.
12 ibid., p. 288.
13 *Bapt. Mag.*, February 1873, p. 83.
14 Dale, *Dale*, p. 289.
15 *Cong.*, March 1872, p. 132.
16 L S, 12 September 1881, p. 400.
17 *C W*, 29 January 1891, p. 87.
18 *Third Report of the Royal Commission Appointed To Inquire into the Working of the Elementary Education Acts, England and Wales* (C. 5158), 1887, XXX.I, p. 86.
19 H. B. Philpott, *London at School: The Story of the School Board, 1870–1904* (London, 1904), p. 100.
20 *Daily News*, 20 April 1888, p. 3.
21 C. S. Miall, *Henry Richard M.P.: A Biography* (London, 1889), pp. 278f.
22 Dale to Richard, 25 May 1876 and 1 February 1877, Richard MSS, 5503B, N L W.
23 *Cong. Rev.*, March 1888, p. 260, *C W*, 11 October 1888, p. 782.
24 L S, 17 September 1888, p. 414. *Daily News*, 21 November 1888, p. 3.
25 Sutherland, *Policy-Making*, pp. 266f.
26 Salisbury to W. H. Smith, 27 October 1890, Lady Gwendoline Cecil, *Life of Robert, Marquis of Salisbury*, Vol. 4 (London, 1932), p. 159.
27 Sutherland, *Policy-Making*, pp. 286ff.
28 Alan Simon, 'Joseph Chamberlain and free education in the election of 1885', *History of Education*, vol. 2 (1973), p. 63.
29 *C W*, 7 May 1891, p. 382.
30 *C W*, 11 June 1891, p. 478.
31 *C W*, 12 February 1891, p. 129.
32 *C W*, 18 June 1891, p. 498.
33 *C W*, 5 February 1891, p. 107.
34 A. D. Gilbert, *Religion and Society in Industrial England: Church, Chapel and Social Change, 1740–1914* (London, 1976), pp. 28f.
35 Owen Chadwick, *The Victorian Church*, Vol. 2 (London, 1970), pp. 319.
36 ibid., p. 305.
37 Philpott, *London at School*, p. 103.
38 J. E. B. Munson, 'The London School Board election of 1894: a study in Victorian religious controversy', *British Journal of Educational Studies*, vol. 23 (1975), pp. 10–17.
39 *C W*, 26 October 1893, p. 826.
40 *C W*, 5 July 1894, p. 509.
41 *C W*, 10 May 1894, p. 349; 26 April 1894, p. 303.
42 W. B. Selbie, *The Life of Charles Silvester Horne, M.A., M.P.* (London, 1920), p. 154.
43 *C W*, 22 November 1894, p. 868.
44 *C W*, 25 January 1894, p. 58.
45 *C W*, 15 November 1894, p. 848.
46 John Telford, *The Life of James Harrison Rigg, D.D., 1821–1909* (London, 1909), p. 182.
47 ibid., p. 322.
48 *C W*, 15 February 1894, p. 121.
49 *C W*, 21 June 1894, p. 472.
50 *C W*, 25 October 1894, p. 798.
51 *C W*, 11 July 1895, p. 546.
52 *C W*, 4 June 1896, p. 446.
53 *C W*, 7 November 1895, p. 844. William Evans and William Claridge, *James Hirst Hollowell and the Movement for Civic Control in Education* (Manchester, 1911), p. 48.
54 *B W*, 19 March 1896, p. 364.
55 *C W*, 14 May 1891, p. 397.

56 Dale, *Dale*, p. 560.
57 J. S. Hurt, *Elementary Schooling and the Working Classes, 1860–1918* (London, 1979), pp. 174ff.
58 *CW*, 10 November 1892, p. 910.
59 *Final Report of the Royal Commission* (C. 5485), 1888, XXXV. I, p. 286.
60 *CW*, 12 June 1902, p. 3.
61 *Third Report*, pp. 57f.
62 J. H. Yoxall, 'The training college problem', *Contemporary Review*, vol. 79 (1901), p. 357.
63 *CW*, 26 December 1907, p. 1.
64 *CW*, 8 August 1907, p. 6.
65 *CW*, 22 July 1909, p. 1.
66 T. W. Moody, 'The Irish university question of the nineteenth century', *History*, vol. 43 (1958).
67 *Sir Robert William Perks, Bart* (London, 1936), p. 116.
68 *CW*, 17 February 1898, p. 7; 17 March 1898, p. 6.
69 *CW*, 10 August 1899, p. 1.
70 *CW*, 12 July 1900, p. 6.
71 Clifford to Asquith, 23 September 1908, MS Asquith 20, f. 25, Bodleian Library, Oxford.
72 *CW*, 2 April 1908, p. 10.
73 *CW*, 31 October 1901, p. 5.
74 Selbie, *Horne*, pp. 127ff.
75 *BW*, 10 June 1901, p. 231.
76 *National Conference of Free Church Councils on the Education Bill*, pp. 3, 6, 8, 9, 10, 14.
77 *BW*, 3 April 1902, p. 625.
78 *BW*, 10 April 1902, p. 645.
79 Selbie, *Horne*, pp. 129ff. *CW*, 9 October 1902, p. 22.
80 W. B. Selbie, *The Life of Andrew Martin Fairbairn, D.D., D.LITT., LL.D., F.B.A., ETC.* (London, 1914), pp. 272–8.
81 *CW*, 25 September 1902, p. 10.
82 *CW*, 18 September 1902, p. 4.
83 *CW*, 24 July 1902, p. 6.
84 Minutes of the National Council of the Evangelical Free Churches: organising committee, 17 May 1902.
85 Minutes of the National Council of the Evangelical Free Churches: general committee, 29 July 1902; organising committee, 20 October 1902, 22 October 1902.
86 J. Scott Lidgett, *Reminiscences* (London, 1928), p. 46.
87 *BW*, 13 November 1902, p. 99.
88 Minutes of the National Council of the Evangelical Free Churches: general committee, 1 December 1902.
89 *BW*, 2 July 1914, p. 365.
90 *CW*, 22 September 1904, p. 6.
91 *CW*, 3 November 1904, p. 3.
92 *CW*, 15 March 1906, p. 13.
93 Arthur Porritt, *The Best I Remember* (London, 1922), p. 91.
94 Harry Jeffs, *Press, Preachers and Politicians: Reminiscences, 1874 to 1932* (London, 1933), p. 109.
95 Sir James Marchant, *Dr John Clifford, C.H.: Life, Letters and Reminiscences* (London, 1924), pp. 43f.
96 *CW*, 22 August 1907, p. 5.
97 Selbie, *Horne*, p. 130.
98 Porritt, *Best I Remember*, p. 92.
99 *CW*, 18 February 1892, p. 133.

100　*National Conference of Free Church Councils on the Education Bill*, p. 7.
101　For example, ibid., p. 8.
102　*CW*, 15 April 1909, p. 12.
103　*BW*, 5 March 1903, p. 543.
104　*CW*, 31 July 1902, p. 1.
105　Perks to Rosebery, 30 July 1902, Rosebery Papers, MS 10050, f.286, NLS.
106　*BW*, 28 August 1902, p. 443.
107　*CW*, 25 September 1902, p. 4.
108　*BW*, 14 August 1902, p. 397.
109　*CW*, 22 January 1903, p. 9.
110　Porritt, *Best I Remember*, pp. 95ff.
111　*BW*, 12 February 1903, p. 475.
112　*CW*, 4 June 1903, p. 2.
113　*CW*, 7 February 1907, p. 23.
114　Augustine Birrell, *Things Past Redress* (London, 1937).
115　*BW*, 29 March 1906, p. 691.
116　Perks to Rosebery, 14 May 1906, Rosebery Papers, MS 10052, f. 164, NLS.
117　*CW*, 21 June 1906, p. 11.
118　Perks to Rosebery, 18 February 1906 and 23 March 1906, MS 10052, ff. 128f., 136ff., NLS.
119　Perks to Rosebery, 14 May 1906, Rosebery Papers, MS 10052, f. 166, NLS.
120　Perks to Rosebery, 3 June 1906 and 22 July 1906, Rosebery Papers, MS 10052, ff. 174, 185f., NLS.
121　*CW*, 8 November 1906, p. 21f.
122　*CW*, 29 November 1906, p. 4.
123　*CW*, 29 November 1906, p. 11.
124　Perks to Rosebery, 12 December 1906, Rosebery Papers, MS 10052, ff. 236–9, NLS.
125　G. K. A. Bell, *Randall Davidson: Archbishop of Canterbury*, 3rd edn (London, 1952), pp. 527–30.
126　Perks to Rosebery, 20 December 1902, Rosebery Papers, MS 10052, f. 244, NLS.
127　*BW*, 30 May 1907, p. 186.
128　*CW*, 30 May 1907, p. 3.
129　Jeffs, *Press, Preachers and Politicians*, pp. 145f.
130　*CW*, 6 June 1907, p. 3.
131　*BW*, 20 June 1907, p. 268.
132　*CW*, 29 August 1907, p. 4.
133　*CW*, 5 September 1907, p. 9.
134　*BW*, 7 November 1907, p. 122.
135　*CW*, 27 February 1908, p. 11.
136　ibid., p. 22.
137　*CW*, 5 March 1908, pp. 21f.
138　Bell, *Davidson*, pp. 531f.
139　*CW*, 18 June 1908, p. 9.
140　*CW*, 2 April 1908, p. 10.
141　Clifford to Asquith, 23 September 1908, MS Asquith 20, ff. 25ff., Bodleian Library, Oxford.
142　Selbie, *Horne*, pp. 199–202.
143　*CW*, 12 November 1908, p. 4. *BW*, 12 November 1908, p. 147.
144　Bell, *Davidson*, pp. 533–40.
145　*CW*, 2 June 1910, p. 4.
146　*BW*, 18 January 1912, p. 477.
147　Meyer to Asquith, 28 February 1912; Asquith to Meyer, 1 March 1912, MS Asquith 13, ff. 62, 64, Bodleian Library, Oxford.
148　*CW*, 7 March 1912, p. 22.
149　*CW*, 13 February 1913, p. 9; 27 February 1913, p. 15.

150 *CW*, 1 May 1913, p. 11.
151 *CW*, 21 August 1913, p. 11.
152 *CW*, 16 July 1914, p. 11.

Notes: Chapter 8

1 'A Nonconformist minister', *Nonconformity and Politics* (London, 1909), p. 3.
2 *CW*, 1 February 1906, p. 11.
3 *BW*, 24 September 1908, p. 556.
4 William Cunningham, *Christianity and Social Questions* (London, 1910), p. 217.
5 *CW*, 7 March 1907, p. 6.
6 W. E. Gladstone, 'The place of heresy and schism in the modern Christian church', *Later Gleanings: A New Series of Gleanings from Past Years* (London, 1898), p. 288.
7 *Nonconformity and Politics*, pp. 105ff., 150, 130.
8 ibid., p. 123.
9 ibid., p. 158.
10 A. W. W. Dale, *The Life of R. W. Dale of Birmingham* (London, 1898), pp. 648ff.
11 *CW*, 11 March 1909, p. 22.
12 *BW*, 25 March 1909, p. 669.
13 K. D. Brown, 'Nonconformity and the British Labour movement', *Journal of Social History*, (1975), pp. 116ff.
14 R. J. Campbell, *Christianity and the Social Order* (London, 1907), pp. ixff.
15 J. E. Rattenbury, *Six Sermons on Social Subjects* (London, [1908]).
16 Maldwyn Edwards, *S. E. Keeble: Pioneer and Prophet* (London, 1949), pp. 67f.
17 *CW*, 28 January 1909, p. 8.
18 *CW*, 7 May 1908, p. 21.
19 *CW*, 8 April 1909, p. 13.

Index

Note: Entries in italics include some biographical detail.